1990

University of St. Francis
GFN 811.3 G795

SO-BOL-439
3 0301 00086007

CAMBRIDGE STUDIES IN AMERICAN LITERATURE AND CULTURE

Walt Whitman and the American Reader

Cambridge Studies in American Literature and Culture

Editor

Albert Gelpi, Stanford University

Advisory Board

Nina Baym, University of Illinois, Champaign–Urbana
Sacvan Bercovitch, Harvard University
David Levin, University of Virginia
Joel Porte, Cornell University
Eric Sundquist, University of California, Berkeley
Mike Weaver, Oxford University

Selected books in the series

Charles Altieri, *Painterly Abstraction in Modernist American Poetry: The Contemporaneity of Modernism*
Douglas Anderson, *A House Undivided: Domesticity and Community in American Literature*
Steven Axelrod and Helen Deese (eds.), *Robert Lowell: Essays on the Poetry*
Sacvan Bercovitch and Myra Jehlen (eds.), *Ideology and Classic American Literature*
Peter Conn, *The Divided Mind: Ideology and Imagination in America, 1898–1917*
Michael Davidson, *The San Francisco Renaissance: Poetics and Community at Mid-Century*
George Dekker, *The American Historical Romance*
Stephen Fredman, *Poet's Prose: The Crisis in American Verse*, 2nd edition
Albert Gelpi (ed.), *Wallace Stevens: The Poetics of Modernism*
Richard Gray, *Writing the South: Ideas of an American Region*
Alfred Habegger, *Henry James and the "Woman Business"*
David Halliburton, *The Color of the Sky: A Study of Stephen Crane*
Susan K. Harris, *19th-Century American Women's Novels: Interpretive Strategies*
John Limon, *The Place of Fiction in the Time of Science: A Disciplinary History of American Writing*
John McWilliams, *The American Epic: Transformations of a Genre, 1770–1860*
David Miller, *Dark Eden: The Swamp in Nineteenth-Century American Culture*
Marjorie Perloff, *The Dance of the Intellect: Studies of Poetry of the Pound Tradition*
Eric Sigg, *The American T. S. Eliot: A Study of the Early Writings*

For a complete listing of books available in the series, see the pages following the Index.

Walt Whitman and the American Reader

EZRA GREENSPAN
University of South Carolina

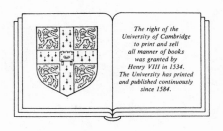

The right of the
University of Cambridge
to print and sell
all manner of books
was granted by
Henry VIII in 1534.
The University has printed
and published continuously
since 1584.

CAMBRIDGE UNIVERSITY PRESS

Cambridge
New York   Port Chester   Melbourne   Sydney

LIBRARY
College of St. Francis
JOLIET, ILLINOIS

Published by the Press Syndicate of the University of Cambridge
The Pitt Building, Trumpington Street, Cambridge CB2 1RP
40 West 20th Street, New York, NY 10011, USA
10 Stamford Road, Oakleigh, Melbourne 3166, Australia

© Cambridge University Press 1990

First published 1990

Printed in Canada

Library of Congress Cataloging-in-Publication Data
Greenspan, Ezra, 1952–
Walt Whitman and the American reader / by Ezra Greenspan.
p. cm. – (Cambridge Studies in American literature and culture)
Includes index.
ISBN 0-521-38469-9
1. Whitman, Walt, 1819–1892 – Criticism and interpretation – History. 2. Whitman, Walt, 1819–1892 – Appreciation – United States.
3. Authors and readers – United States – History – 19th century.
4. Books and reading – United States – History – 19th century.
I. Title. II. Series.
PS3237.4.U6G74   1990
811'.3 – dc20   90–1474
                                                                      CIP

British Library Cataloging in Publication Data
Greenspan, Ezra, 1952–
Walt Whitman and the American reader.
1. Poetry in English. American writers. Whitman, Walt, 1819–1892
I. Title II. Series
811.3

ISBN 0-521-38469-9 hardback

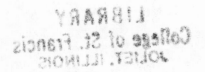
LIBRARY
College of St. Francis
JOLIET, ILLINOIS

811.3
G 795

Contents

137,945

v

Illustrations

Preface

This is a study of what Whitman and his contemporaries might have thought of as democratic culture, but of what I feel more comfortable in calling the democratization of culture. While I have attempted to document the ways such a phenomenon would necessarily affect each and every aspect of literary culture – indeed, even what we mean by literary culture – I have been primarily intent on exploring the resulting meeting grounds between readers and writers as they developed in nineteenth-century America. Originally, I had hoped to address this subject in general terms; but as my work progressed, I gradually came to the conclusion that I could make a stronger, more closely argued presentation of my ideas by setting them into the format of a case study of a single writer. After considerable thought, my choice of subject became absolutely clear; however I formulated the matter of literary culture, whatever considerations I raised – poetic, historical, biographical, literary professional, contemporaneous reception – I came to the conclusion that no other American writer served the purposes of my project as well as did Walt Whitman. And with the presumption of Whitman's centrality in American culture once made, the formulation of the book around him quickly followed.

The key to my thinking was to plot out a trail between Whitman and his society which would carry the discussion of his relations with the reading public through what were, to my mind, the central features of nineteenth-century literary culture. To do that meant to address as fully as possible the question: What does it mean to say and how does one understand the proposition that writers write, readers read, and the two sides, in Whitman's term, "interchange"? In contrast to the attention paid by much recent literary criticism to the privatized encounter between writer, reader, and text, my own attention has been drawn primarily to the historicity of these agents and of their patterns of interaction, to the ways literary culture – and in particular, the creation, production, distribution, consumption, interpretation, and critical evaluation of imaginative literature – is created out of and in response to the changing circumstances of human life lived in society. In setting up my study along these guidelines, I have sought to demonstrate the worth of such an historically posed idea of reader-writer relations both for the study of Whitman and more broadly for the study of nineteenth-century American culture.

In the first of the two sections of the book, I have set the issue of Whitman and his readers into its literary historical context, describing the specific conditions of literary culture in the United States during its spectacular growth period of 1820–50 (by no coincidence, Whitman's formative years) and analyzing the changing nature of the tripartite author-publisher-reader relationship as it emerged by midcentury. Against the frame of his literary culture, I have resketched Whitman's early biography along tightly professional lines, assembling the known facts of his many-sided activity as a printer, magazinist, editor, and publisher into a composite picture of the pre–*Leaves of Grass* Whitman as a literary professional and highlighting the lines of continuity, as well as of discontinuity, between his work as a printer-journalist in the 1840s and as a poet in the 1850s.

That opening section is preparatory to the longer second section, which analyzes Whitman's poetry, career, and reception over the course of the nineteenth century. I have been particularly concerned here to account for and examine the strongly reader-addressed quality of Whitman's poetry, which seems to me one of the most culturally significant and aesthetically cultivated features of Whitman's art. Fine work has been done on this subject by C. Carroll Hollis in the most important study of Whitman's poetics to date, *Language and Style in "Leaves of Grass"* (1983), which for my purposes has been most valuable for the way it brings to bear the large body of mostly post–World War II literary theory on the issue of Whitman and his relations with his readers. I have been especially intrigued by Hollis's attempt to link the vocative poetics of *Leaves of Grass* to the idea of speech acts and to Whitman's well-known interest in oratory and journalism, Hollis's assumption (and also mine) being that the primary influence on Whitman's style came from nonliterary sources. My own examination of Whitman's involvement with the reader, however, has been based less on my concern with his poetics per se than on my ambition to reattach the reader-addressed poetics and poetry of *Leaves of Grass* to the culture from which they derived.

Whitman was by no means a rigorously systematic thinker, but he gave to his idea of the reading act, the reader, and the readership of his poems as intense a consideration as he gave to virtually any aspect of his art during his *Leaves of Grass* career. This he did within the scope of his largest understanding of the purposes the printed word, in all its forms, was to serve in his society – America, in his eyes, a type of modern, democratic society generally. While there was nothing particularly original about a writer's of Whitman's time making bold claims for the social utility of the arts, Whitman's vaunting ambitiousness for the arts was singular; and so, too, was the programmatic way he went about fitting means to ends in his own poems by shifting responsibility for their making from poet alone to poet and reader in "partnership." In assigning the "modern intelligent reader" a primary role within the poem as addressee and coactor, Whitman was self-consciously transforming the traditional idea of reader reception into a more dynamic form of reader involvement, one which more closely approximated the ideal of culture he believed was required by an open-ended, participatory democracy. Properly understood in terms of his aspirations of building a modern American culture through cooperative acts of poetry making, the relations Whitman was cultivating between "I" and "you," as he habitually posed the matter in his poems, conveyed one of the most ambitious, presumptuous, and significant conceptions of literary communication to be found in American writing.

But not even as persistent and resourceful a writer and literary strategist as Whitman, try though he did, could dictate his own reception; indeed, with Whitman, the self-styled national poet coming before his nation of readers, one enters into a fascinatingly complex, incongruous case of literary creation and reception. No matter whether one takes the critical high road for the overview or the critical low road for detail in tracking *Leaves of Grass* across nineteenth-century America, the grounds on which Whitman constructed his meeting with the public ensured that it would be one of the classic meetings between writers and readers in American literature. Given my desire to keep the analytic focus held closely to Whitman, I have necessarily taken the low road, banging along over the ruts and holes and hanging on through the twisting turns left by the inconsistencies between Whitman's program and practice, his expectations and actualities, which sometimes led Whitman into conflict not only with his public but even at times with the bases of his own thinking. Convoluted as the patterns of relation sometimes become, I have tried just the same to analyze the interaction between Whitman and his contemporaries as closely and concisely as possible, particularly during the period of 1855–60 when Whitman's receptivity to life was freshest, his art most flexible and inventive, and his faith in a broad, national readership strongest. But wherever the discussion turns and however far it ranges, I have tried consistently to keep it directed, whether I have stated so explicitly or not, toward the issue that Whitman recognized as the central one of his society: the relation between democracy and culture.

One practice I have adopted in this book should be stated explicitly here. In order to accentuate the historicity of Whitman's writing in and for its own time, I have quoted in all but a few instances from the edition of *Leaves of Grass* most immediately germane to the time period of the discussion, rather than from the better-known edition of 1891–2. To avoid possible confusion, however, I have generally referred to the poems by the final titles given them by Whitman.

The opportunity to thank friends, colleagues, and family at the end of a long project for their help and encouragement comes as a genuine pleasure, all the more so at the end of a project of this sort which, with its complicated logistics, its unavoidable, sometimes solo, sometimes family itinerary, and its aura of uncertain circumstances, placed extreme pressures and demands upon the members of my family. To all of them and to all the other people who helped to make this project not only possible but, in the end, enjoyable, I owe my deepest thanks.

Some of those people I would like to thank here personally. My interest in Whitman goes back many years, and I owe part of it to Arnold and Leon (Chick) Soloway, who gave me a child's rare, privileged initiation into the world of Walt Whitman. In more recent years, I have been aided by a number of professional scholars in formulating the ideas and shaping the form of this book. Kenneth Dauber helped me to crystallize my thinking by exchanging ideas with me about author-reader relations in American culture at a time when my own ideas for this study were still taking shape. Arthur Golden listened patiently to my early thoughts on the content of this study, shared with me some of his own views on Whitman's personality and habits, and gave me the idea of looking into the publishing arrangements of William Prescott and other New England historians as a source of background material for my discussion of author-publisher relations. Florence Bernstein Freedman opened up to me her private files on Whitman and O'Connor and shared with me her copy of William Thayer's autobiography, when I was unable to find it in the Library of Congress. I would also like to thank her for her donation of her fine, private collection of Whitman material to the Sourasky Library of Tel Aviv University. Hana Wirth-Nesher read a draft of the first three-quarters of the manuscript and raised questions which sharpened my thinking about the appropriate form for the framework of this book. Finally, Al Gelpi read the full manuscript, criticized it intelligently, and facilitated its transformation into a book. To all of them, my thanks.

I have received generous help in my work from the staffs of the various libraries where most of the research for this book was done: Tel Aviv University, the Hebrew University of Jerusalem, the New York Public Library, Rutgers University, the Library of Congress, and the Pennsylvania State University. I would like to thank the following institutions for permission to use material from their manuscript collections: the Library of Congress, Duke University, Columbia University, Harvard University, Smith College, and the New York Public Library.

I owe thanks to the *Walt Whitman Quarterly Review* and to its editor, Ed Folsom, for permission to reuse in Chapter 10 parts of my discussion of Whitman's relations in 1860 with his publishers in New York and Boston, which originally appeared, in slightly different form, in "The Earliest French Review of Whitman," *Walt Whitman Quarterly Review* 6 (Winter 1989): 109–16.

I would also like to thank my entire family, in Israel and America, for their support in making this book possible. My brother and sister and their families received me warmly and generously opened up their homes to me during my transatlantic research trips. I owe a different sort of gratitude to my children, Yoni, Noam, and Tamar, whose lives became mixed up, through no doing of their own, with the life of some strange, distant man named Whitman; I look forward to the day when they make his acquaintance on their own. My final and most important words of appreciation are for my wife, Riki, for sharing with me in every way possible the undertaking of this project. I was once asked during the composition of this book whom I conceived as its ideal reader; after several years of work, I can now see that the nearest answer is that it was written, Riki, to "you."

I

Whitman and the Conditions for Authorship in Nineteenth-Century America

Les autres forment l'homme; je le récite et en représente un particulier bien mal formé, et lequel, si j'avais à façonner de nouveau, je ferais vraiment bien autre qu'il n'est...

Je propose une vie basse et sans lustre, c'est tout un. On attache aussi bien toute la philosophie morale à une vie populaire et privée qu'à une vie de plus riche étoffe; chaque homme porte la forme entière de l'humaine condition.

Les auteurs se communiquent au peuple par quelque marque particulière et étrangère; moi, le premier, par mon être universel, comme Michel de Montaigne, non comme grammairien, ou poète, ou jurisconsulte. Si le monde se plaint de quoi je parle trop de moi, je me plains de quoi il ne pense seulement pas à soi.

Montaigne, "Du Repentir"

Books and the Man I sing.

Pope, The Dunciad

Writing, when properly managed, (as you may be sure I think mine is) is but a different name for conversation: As no one, who knows what he is about in good company, would venture to talk all; – so no author, who understands the just boundaries of decorum and good breeding, would presume to think all: The truest respect which you can pay to the reader's understanding, is to halve this matter amicably, and leave him something to imagine, in his turn, as well as yourself.

Sterne, Tristram Shandy

...an outline is the best, –
A lively reader's fancy does the rest.

Byron, Don Juan

I find certain books vital and spermatic, not leaving the reader what he was.

Emerson, Society and Solitude

...in this country who does not read?

Whitman, Brooklyn Eagle

1

Homage to the Tenth Muse

On the evening of September 27, 1855, New York's Crystal Palace played host to nineteenth-century America's greatest gathering of literary talent and achievement. Organized by the recently formed New York Publishers' Association and timed to follow its extensive trade sale of the previous week, the "Complimentary Fruit and Floral Festival to Authors" was designed to celebrate the accomplishments of the partners in the creation of American literary culture: American writers, publishers, and their reading public. The setting chosen for the evening, the imposing glass- and iron-domed pavilion built behind Croton Reservoir for the New York World's Fair of 1853, the first hosted in the Americas, was itself a national symbol of pride, of a nation self-consciously on the rise and able to match the accomplishments of Europe.

The 650 invited guests entered upon an impressive scene. The vast expanse of the building was sectioned off for the occasion at its northern nave by a red, white, and blue partition and illuminated by octagonal gaslights. Before the nave was set a raised dais with a long table reserved for the president of the Publishers' Association, the invited speakers, and various dignitaries. The table was decorated with statues of the Graces, and a statue of Gutenberg and his press was positioned opposite the president's place. Perpendicular to the dais ran six long, parallel tables extending the full length of the enclosure, the two on the flanks reserved for authors and the interior ones primarily for members of the Publishers' Association. Galleries for spectators, filled primarily by women, rose up behind and to the sides of the speaker's dais, the northern gallery holding the orchestra and illuminated by gaslights arranged so as to depict a statue of Clio in the temple of wisdom crowned with lights spelling out "Honor to Genius." Beneath the galleries hung portraits of the pioneer publishers Mathew Carey and Daniel Appleton. A huge cornucopia garlanded with flowers and flowing fruit juices was symbolically positioned in the center of the nave.

3

But the most impressive element of the evening was the human assemblage, the visible proof to those in attendance of one of the central developments of their lives: the proliferation of American literary, journalistic, educational, and scientific talent and of the publishing industry which had grown up to publicize it. Among the dozens of well-known writers in attendance were William Cullen Bryant, Washington Irving, Fitz-Greene Halleck, Nathaniel Parker Willis, Henry Ward Beecher, John Pendleton Kennedy, Timothy Shay Arthur, Bayard Taylor, Henry Tuckerman, Cornelius Mathews, Evert and George Duyckinck, Lewis Gaylord Clark, Charles Briggs, Seba Smith, Thomas Bangs Thorpe, Rufus Griswold, Henry William Herbert, Henry Barnard, Richard Grant White, Park Benjamin, Henry Carey, Henry Schoolcraft, Frederick Law Olmsted, James and Sara ("Fanny Fern") Parton, Samuel Goodrich, Horace Bushnell, Adam Gurowski, Caroline Gilman, Maria Mcintosh, Catherine Beecher, Lydia Maria Child, Lydia Sigourney, Alice and Phoebe Cary, Caroline Kirkland, and Susan Warner. Among the more prominent of the American publishing houses represented were Harper's, Appleton's, Putnam's, Mason's, Little, Brown and Company, and Ticknor and Fields. The mayors of the three major publishing centers of New York, Philadelphia, and Boston were all present, as were the presidents of Columbia, Yale, and Girard colleges. Well publicized in advance, the dinner also attracted a large press delegation, including reporters from most of the major New York City newspapers. Letters from writers unable to attend, some read on the spot and others printed the next day in the papers, were sent by Emerson, Melville, Holmes, Longfellow, Whittier, Dana, Sumner, Everett, Prescott, Sparks, Palfrey, Whipple, Mann, Ripley, Curtis, Anthon, the Stowes, Tappan, and Agassiz. Hawthorne, who would otherwise have been invited, was American consul at Liverpool. Thoreau, uninvited and uninterested, was at Concord. Whitman was probably several miles away in Brooklyn.[1]

The evening began with a multicourse meal consisting of assorted cold meats, fruits, salads, creams, and pastries (the last shaped as geographical places – not what Whitman had had in mind several months earlier when he advised the American poet to "incarnate" his country). William Appleton, as president of the Publishers' Association, then opened the long series of speeches and toasts by greeting the guests at the entrance to "a new era in the history" of publishing and by delivering an exhortation to his colleagues on the moral responsibilities of their profession:

> I surely need not remind those who are now within reach of the sound of my voice that it very often depends upon the decision of the bookseller whether a new work shall or shall not be published. If we, brethren, can cordially unite in a determination that no book of a questionable

moral tendency, or of a useless or pernicious character in any point of
view, shall receive our imprint, we have done more for our country
than a dozen societies for the suppression of vice and immorality can
ever do. If, on the other hand, we are always ready to take some risk
in order to enable genius, guided by virtue and sanctified by religion,
to struggle into the sunshine of public favor, we shall lend still more
important aid to our country's glory and happiness.[2]

His own firm, though well known for its conservatism, was soon to
become the American publisher of Darwin's *Origin of Species*.

Appleton was followed by George Palmer Putnam, secretary of the
Publishers' Association and one of the seminal figures in the institutionalization of publishing in America. For more than a decade, Putnam had
been the most articulate voice among American publishers in calling for
the promotion of American literature. He had led a generally reluctant
industry in supporting the cause of international copyright for American
authors, had set an industry precedent by taking an author – Washington
Irving – in hand and according him the privileged treatment reserved for
"standard" authors, had publicized American achievements to a skeptical
world – working particularly hard to open the British market to American books – and had established an in-house monthly magazine (*Putnam's
Monthly*) in 1853, which quickly became, as had been his intention from
the start, the leading periodical publisher of American talent of its time.[3]
His own firm, in fact, had taken a large – and, as it turned out, losing
– risk in publishing the official catalogue of the Crystal Palace. So when
Putnam was asked to address the current state of American letters, he
could speak with authority unrivaled among American publishers.

Putnam began, amidst the atmosphere of good feelings, by emphasizing the salutary features in author-publisher relations in America, a
theme repeated through the night: "The interests of writers, publishers
and sellers of books are daily growing in magnitude and importance,
and these interests are and should be mutual and identical."[4] He then
turned to his main theme, well suited to the occasion: the extraordinary
advances made by American literary culture in all its aspects during the
past generation. He noted with pride the rapid expansion of population
and the even more rapid expansion of book and magazine circulation,
the increase in native as opposed to foreign authorship of books printed
in America, and the enlarged size of editions necessitated by the growing
demand for books and periodicals. Citing the deprecating remark of the
Scottish historian Archibald Alison that "the literature and intellectual
ability of the highest class meet but little encouragement in America,"
Putnam proceeded to recite at length the already familiar midcentury
litany of American achievements in the various fields of learning, listing

names and compiling statistics as he went. Although he did not draw out the far-reaching implications of his vision, Putnam sketched out for his audience a scene of a new era in publishing and literature:

> Think of eighteen thousand double, or thirty-six thousand single reams of paper, required yearly for a single magazine, which courses over the country, unprecedented in cheapness and attraction, at the rate of one hundred and fifty thousand per month. The wildest imaginings, at home or abroad, twenty years ago, would not have stretched so far as this. Why, Sir, the sheets from our book-presses alone, in a single year, would reach nearly twice around the globe; and if we add the periodicals and newspapers, the issues of our presses in about eighteen months would make a belt, two feet wide, printed on both sides, which would stretch from New-York to the Moon! In the *machinery* for this great manufacture, our artisans, I will venture to say, are not yet excelled, if equaled, elsewhere. The printing-presses of Hoe and of Adams are said to surpass any used in Europe. The important art of stereotyping, which there is reason to believe originated in this country, has certainly been brought to greater perfection here than it has reached abroad – and naturally so; for our wide market requires this permanent form, for nearly all we print. And by a recent beautiful invention of another of those citizens, whom we are proud to "adopt" and "develope," the types themselves are set up by steam, aided by rapid girlish fingers, touching keys like those of a piano, and sliding words of thought into "form" about four times as fast as the quickest compositor.

Putnam's remarks, as one might expect, were enthusiastically received; and so it went through the long night of self-congratulation, as speaker after speaker – author, publisher, minister, politician – offered his tribute to things American. The Reverend E. H. Chapin gave one of the best-received speeches of the night in praising the power of the printing press in "the age of steam and electricity." Henry Tappan sent a letter in which he noted: "Nothing characterizes our age more strongly than the immense number of books which are written, printed, and scattered abroad. The power of steam is invoked to move the press, and the manufactories of books stately and imposing rival the manufactories of the useful commodities. Booksellers carry on their trade in splendid palaces."[5] Emerson joined the chorus of praise in expressing his sentiment by mail that "the friendliest meeting of the authors and publishers of good books I must think one of the fairest omens for mankind."[6]

In one of the best received performances of the night, the publisher-turned-poet-for-the-occasion, James Fields, read a poem in which he praised the publishing ways of the present at the expense of those of the past:

> How slow and sure they set their types,
> How small editions ran!

Then fifty thousand never sold –
Before the sale began.
For how could they, poor plodding souls,
Be either swift or wise,
Who never learned the mighty art
Of *how* to advertise.[7]

William Cullen Bryant, who was called on to respond to a toast of American literature, ignored his own previous troubled dealings with publishers in denying the truism that "booksellers are the natural enemies of the authors": "But I deny the antagonism; and I do not agree with those who complain of booksellers becoming rich. If the bookseller be not enriched, how can he give liberal terms to authors? and when I hear of rich booksellers, I also remember that there have been well-paid authors."[8] Perhaps the most interesting observation of the night was one attributed by a reporter to Henry Ward Beecher: "He had been looking about to see if he could tell authors by their looks, but he could not find any indications by which he could distinguish authors from publishers, and they all looked remarkably like other people."[9] On that night, at least, he was probably right.

One man who would certainly have deviated from that pattern, uninvited but no longer completely unknown – the current issue of *Putnam's* was running a slightly bedazzled but generally appreciative review of *Leaves of Grass* – was Walt Whitman, poet and self-publisher.[10] *Leaves of Grass* had almost certainly been offered by his distributor, Fowler and Wells, at the publishers' giant trade sale of the previous week, its price having been halved from the original two dollars to coincide with the sale; but it is not likely that there had been much, if any, demand for it. Whitman, it is well known, had keen ambitions for the national distribution and acceptance of his first volume of poetry and was doing everything possible, even resorting to promoting it in eulogistic self-reviews, in order to advance his ambition. One therefore wonders how he reacted to the highly publicized events of September 27, what feelings and thoughts he had as the literary establishment gathered across the river to celebrate itself en masse.

He would certainly have been among the first to appreciate the scene of the occasion. Always drawn to a good spectacle, Whitman had been an early devotee of the Crystal Palace. He visited it early and often – "I went a long time (nearly a year) – days and nights – especially the latter" – and kept up his fascination with it and its exhibitions until its destruction by fire in 1858, which he noted sadly in the newspaper he was then editing.[11] It stood out, to his eyes, from other buildings in New York as "an edifice certainly unsurpassed any where for beauty and all the other requisites of a perfect edifice," "an original, esthetic, perfectly proportioned, American edifice."[12] He probably read and would certainly have shared in the view of the *American Phrenological Journal* (in which he had an article the following month), which saw the Palace as presiding over an idyllic harmony of interests:

> There will be gathered here the choicest products of the luxury of the Old World, and the most cunning devices of the ingenuity of the New. The interests of Manufacture, Commerce, and the Arts, will all find encouragement and protection within these walls, and another guarantee will be given to the permanence of peace. Here will be collected multitudes of all nations; but the great and crowning feature of the enterprise is, that it will offer amusement and recreation to the working classes, such as they can find no where else; that it will be a *Palace For The People*.[13]

Whitman's attraction to the Palace was visceral; parts of several of his 1855 poems, such as "A Song for Occupations," might but for their idiosyncrasies be read as tributes to the Palace's "Exposition of the Industry of the Nations." In making poetry of "the cylinder press . . the handpress . . the frisket and tympan . . the compositor's stick and rule," Whitman was in effect touching the precise point of intersection between the Crystal Palace, its exhibitions, and the publishers–authors dinner.

One can easily find his or her ironies in the matter, Whitman's absence – he would later think of such things rather as "exclusion" – not only from the dinner but from the author-publisher relationship, a crucial connection if he was to reach the American public; and his nonpareil devotion to the ideal of a national literature, itself an underlying reason for the dinner and its main toast, matched by his open contempt for the forms of the dinner and for the forms and conventions of the literary establishment. But to appreciate the full significance of the scenario I am drawing, one must step back and view from the proper perspective the long foreground of events leading up to the curious situation of Whitman and his poetry in 1855.

As he grew older, Whitman liked to glance backward on his life and identify it on the grand scale with the events of the nineteenth century. In one of his most carefully and "authoritatively" considered pronouncements of later years, he would remember his overarching ambition in writing *Leaves of Grass* as having been "to articulate and faithfully express in literary or poetic form, and uncompromisingly, my own physical, emotional, moral, intellectual, and aesthetic Personality, in the midst of, and tallying, the momentous spirit and facts of its immediate days, and of current America – and to exploit that Personality, identified with place and date, in a far more candid and comprehensive sense than any hitherto poem or book."[14] The officiousness of his old-age views notwithstanding, Whitman had solid justification for this claim; no American writer had ever been able to lay hold to as much of the continent as had Whitman. Of course, this is not to say that Whitman was particularly successful in convincing his contemporaries that his ideas of art and "personality" were theirs. But whatever the discrepancy between his own sense of mission and his reception by the contemporaneous reading public, a subject to be taken up in due course, I do believe that Whitman's claim for the superimposition of himself and his book on America is to be taken seriously. In the first part of this study, I will be making my own "tally" between Whitman and America, exploring the connection between Whitman's *Leaves of Grass* and the bookmaking culture of his society and the more general connection between his career and the conditions for authorship in midnineteenth-century America.

Whitman came to maturity during a period of great ferment in American history, as he and his contemporaries were keenly aware. His early years coincided with what contemporaries widely interpreted as the greatest explosion of energies – technological, demographic, economic, and cultural – since Renaissance times. Nowhere in the Western world was the impact of the released forces more powerful than on its western flank, where what had taken centuries to transpire in Europe was compressed into several generations: the conquest of a continent; the growth of cities; the establishment of modern systems of transportation, commerce, and education; the self-conscious construction of a culture. Having no model or precedent by which to evaluate such rapid historical change, men and women of Whitman's era reacted in widely various ways to the developments taking place about them. Where a slightly later figure than Whitman would react with fear and anxiety and uncomfortably symbolize the new era with its accelerating pace and unpredictable direction by the figure of the dynamo, Whitman was generally inclined to see his emerging society and world with confidence and satisfaction.

Never one to overvalue the past, Whitman was given to moments when he genuinely believed himself and his countrymen to be living in an age apart: "Think of the absence and ignorance, in all cases hitherto, of the multitudinousness, vitality, and the unprecedented stimulants of to-day and here. It almost seems as if a poetry with cosmic and dynamic features of magnitude and limitlessness suitable to the human soul, were never possible before."[15] Thrilling to the recent achievements of the magnetic telegraph, photography, steamships, and railroads, he conscientiously worked the wonders of modern technology into his poetry: "See! steamers steaming through my poems! . . . / See, the many-cylinder'd steam printing-press – See, the electric telegraph – See, the strong and quick locomotive, as it departs, panting, blowing the steam whistle" ("Starting from Paumanok"). On the occasion of his seventieth birthday, he received a strangely appropriate letter from Mark Twain, who without really knowing him identified him with the technological advances of the age:

> You have lived just the seventy years which are greatest in the world's history, and richest in benefit and advancement to its peoples. These seventy years have done much more to widen the interval between men and the other animals than was accomplished by any five centuries which preceded them.
>
> What great births you have witnessed! The steam–press, the steam-ship, the steel-ship, the railroad, the perfected cotton-gin, the telegraph, the telephone, the phonograph, the photograph, the photogravure, the electrotype, the gaslight, the electric light, the sewing machine . . . Yes, you have indeed seen much; but tarry yet awhile, for the greatest is yet to come.[16]

From among the tens of inventions Twain listed in his letter, the most fitting technological symbol for Whitman – indeed, for nineteenth-century literary culture in general – was one with which Whitman had an insider's familiarity and a lifetime of acquaintance: the modernized printing press. We of the twentieth century so take for granted the means of production of our literary culture that we do not easily grasp how much closer a literary culture, such as that of the nineteenth century, was to the machines which made possible its production and distribution, nor do we readily understand how considerably the presence of the new technology affected the culture which issued through it.

Compared to previous times, the nineteenth century was the age of the printing press; and to judge from its newspapers and magazines, it knew it. In the largest sense, the early nineteenth century in Europe and America was witnessing an outright revolution in printing and its related industries, as the knowledge and methods of the Industrial Revolution were applied to the written word. The printing press, not significantly improved since the time of Gutenberg, underwent rapid, extensive mod-ification over the course of the century. Iron replaced wood; manual power gave way briefly to horsepower, then to steam power. The tra-ditional principle of flatbed impressions was gradually superseded by the concept of rotating cylinders, which, as they increased in number, pro-duced a geometrical expansion of printing capacity over that of the an-tiquated presses. As a result of the many and various improvements in their technology and design, presses grew rapidly during the century in size, capacity, and sophistication. To give an example of how dramati-cally press technology was changing, the largest of the new presses put into service in the midnineteenth century, the Hoe 10-cylinder rotary press used by some of the biggest newspaper publishers in the United States and England, was itself as large as was a building capable of housing a printing office of the cottage-industry era.

At the same time, corresponding developments were transforming other printing-related industries. The utilization of stereotyping and electroplating became the commonly accepted practice of American publishers by midcentury, providing them with a cheaper and more efficient alternative to printing from type. Both authors and publishers, not to mention the reading public, benefited from the resultant ability to print additional editions of works with a minimum of additional expense, making possible wider markets, larger sales, larger profits, and expanded reputations. Likewise, the production of paper, long a slow and costly procedure performed by hand, became mechanized by the turn of the century, with the output of paper increasing exponentially. Meanwhile, the search for materials more plentiful and reliable than rags for the production of paper continued through the century, culminating in the use of wood pulp and helping to make the productive potentiality of the giant presses a reality.

It was for contemporaries a dazzling display of technological and industrial advances, and one of the most impressive of its characteristics was the rapidity with which it developed. A grown person at midcentury might have seen much of this development transpire within his or her lifetime – a striking case in point being Whitman. When he first went out in 1831 as an apprentice to a local printer in the village of Brooklyn, he was trained at the shop's simple wooden handpress, which was all that a local newspaper of the time would have needed (it was all Whitman needed when he established his own country newspaper on Long Island seven years later). During the next several years of his apprenticeship, he trained at the more sophisticated Rust press used in the shop of a rival Brooklyn newspaper. By the time he returned to the area in 1841 after the lapse of a half dozen years to work in the bustling printing shop of Park Benjamin's *New World,* he entered the new world of press technology, working at the new Napier cylinder presses needed to print the paper and later its popular series of "Books for the People" – the people in this case warranting editions of ten to twenty thousand copies.

Five years later, when he was in control of the Brooklyn *Eagle,* he proudly introduced to his readers in the accepted manner of the day the paper's new Napier press – "about as pretty and clean-working a piece of machinery as a man might wish to look on, (with all the 'latest improvements')" – which was to give him access to the reading community of Brooklyn and Long Island.[17] A decade later, he was able to announce with pride the imminent acquisition by his most recent newspaper of a double-cylinder steam press capable of turning out five thousand printed sheets per hour and of improving the size and the range of the paper's circulation.[18] By that time, he had already begun to treat the new cylindrical presses poetically in *Leaves of Grass;* and in later editions, he would bring his readers right up to the edge of printing technology: "You shall mark in amazement the Hoe press whirling its cylinders, shedding the printed leaves steady and fast" ("Song of the Exposition").

What was transpiring all about him, in short, was a revolution sweeping not only through printing technology and book and periodical production but also through all the factors involved in the creation, manufacture, marketing, and consumption of printed works, radically transforming the professions of printer, publisher, bookseller, and author alike and setting the relations between them on a new basis. That new basis, characterized by a gradual reorientation toward commercialization, professionalization, and democratization, was to influence the course of nineteenth-century America's developing literary culture, whose greatest poetic offspring was also its most vociferous champion: Walt Whitman.

2

The Evolution of American Literary Culture, 1820–1850

Whitman liked to speak of "my book and me," but though they make one of the tightest, most intriguing couplings in nineteenth-century literary history, there is also an important sense in which Whitman and his book can be located in, can even be said to derive from, the frame story of America and its books during the midnineteenth century. Right through the early decades of the century, that was a story largely of limited markets, small editions of fancy, expensive volumes, more or less amateur authorship, and foreign (mostly English) domination of the authorship and manufacture of books for the American market. The publishing industry, as an industry, was not yet in existence. Limited in capital and regional in outlook, publishers had not yet found their separate identities, were often only printers or booksellers but in another guise, a Franklin in Philadelphia, a Rivington or Duyckinck in New York, a Thomas in Worcester, or a country printer issuing occasional works for a regional market. Or just as likely, they were merely the designated agents of the author, who took upon himself the expenses and risk of publication and hired the publisher on a commission basis as his distributor. There was as yet no national market for books – the term is an anachronism – and there would not be until the midnineteenth century, when America became more fully a nation not only politically but culturally.

Nor can the profession of authorship be said to have existed; writing was still the avocation of amateurs whose primary vocation was most often in law, religion, or government. Payment was sporadic and often voluntary; outlets for publication were few; authorial anonymity was still the rule. Not until the passage of the United States Constitution in 1787, whose Article I, Section 8 authorized Congress "to promote the progress of science and useful arts, by securing for limited times to authors and inventors the exclusive right to their respective writings and discoveries," and the subsequent passage of the first federal copyright

13

law in 1790 was there even a legal basis for literary professionalism. Even then, the new law denied to books the property right theory underlying the circulation of other articles of commerce.[1]

Authorship was at best a risky venture, an unlikely choice of career for young men of talent and ambition. Not a single American writer before the time of Irving and Cooper was capable of making a living by writing alone. Charles Brockden Brown, one of the most dedicated writers of his generation, was expressing a despair not exclusively his own when he wrote in 1799, "If an author be defined to be a creature who devotes regular and daily portions of his time to writing that which shall some time be published, I question whether one such shall be found among us."[2] The young Joel Barlow was advised to choose the pulpit over the pen by his ex-tutor at Yale, who warned him that "neither our country nor our Country men are sufficiently refined enriched and improved to give a sufficient support to works of Genius, merely and had you the genius of a Pope or a Milton nay as much superior as you wish might starve upon the pittance that a few Persons capable of relishing your productions would give."[3] Philip Freneau, a more genuinely gifted poet who had lived in disregard of such advice, had his own bitter advice to give in old age to prospective American poets of the generation to follow:

> Though skilled in latin and in greek,
> And earning fifty cents a week,
> Such knowledge, and the income, too,
> Should teach you better what to do:
> The meanest drudges, kept in pay,
> Can pocket fifty cents a day.
>
> Why stay in such a *tasteless land,*
> Where ALL must on a *level* stand,
> (Excepting people, *at their ease,*
> Who choose the *level* where they please:)
> See IRVING gone to Britain's court
> To people of *another sort,*
> He will return, with wealth and fame,
> While *Yankees* hardly know *your* name.
> . . . .
> Dear Bard, I pray you, take the hint,
> In England what you write and print,
> Republished here in shop, or stall,
> Will perfectly enchant us all:
> It will assume a different face,
> And post your name at every place,
> From splendid domes of first degree,
> Where *ladies* meet, to sip their tea;

From marble halls, where lawyers plead,
Or Congress-men talk loud, indeed,
To huts, where evening clubs appear,
And 'squires resort – to guzzle Beer.[4]

Freneau's angry lines make clear the fact that the problems confronting a prospective American poet were not only economic but sociocultural, as well. The idea of a "gentlemanly" writer addressing a "gentle" readership was already rapidly becoming an anachronism in eighteenth-century England, where Henry Fielding was able to open *Tom Jones* (1749) with the declaration, "An author ought to consider himself, not as a gentleman who gives a private or eleemosynary treat, but rather as one who keeps a public ordinary, at which all persons are welcome for their money." If Fielding was already signaling important audience changes in midcentury England, then how much more inappropriate should have been the tradition of literary gentility in Freneau's more democratic, postrevolutionary America; nevertheless, it lingered on there in cultural circles well into the nineteenth century, producing open incongruities, such as that in Freneau's poem between writers trained in the classics and used to keeping company with the Muses forced to seek common ground with, not to mention patronage from, a crowd of Yankee beer guzzlers. Or, to shift the analogy in the case of Barlow, it left a writer to ponder the question: how were the well-bred producers and consumers of literature to be expected to gather proudly around the plebian meal of a hasty pudding? A century later on the other side of the cultural revolution, Americans would be able to buy cans of fruit cocktail imprinted with the face of their self-styled national poet.

The problematic nature of committing oneself to the profession of letters continued well into the first third of the nineteenth century. The letters, for example, of the young Poe and Longfellow to their fathers requesting permission to pursue literary careers are defensive to the point of whining; then again, few young men of their class and time would probably have known how to handle the matter any better. Still, a change in the professional climate was becoming discernible by the time these men reached maturity in the 1820s. The enormous success of Scott and Byron in Britain had had its American parallel in the careers of Irving and Cooper, with whom twentieth-century literary historians generally date the inception of literary professionalism in America. Their own contemporaries, in fact, were able to take note of and commented on the first stirrings in the new literary culture. One of the most perceptive observations was made from afar by a commentator writing in the 1820 *Edinburgh Review,* the same periodical which only earlier that year published what would redound through the nineteenth century as the most notorious aspersion against American claims to intellect, Sydney Smith's

"In the four quarters of the globe, who reads an American book?"[5] Although Smith's quip was to draw the defensive attention of American magazines and newspapers for decades, it was his colleague on the *Edinburgh* who offered the best rejoinder in the course of giving a favorable review to Irving's recently published *Sketch Book*. Writing with obvious surprise at seeing his own expectations overturned, he was forced to admit that the tripartite author-publisher-reader relationship might be said to exist even in America: "It is the work of an American, entirely bred and trained in that country – originally published within its territory – and, as we understand, very extensively circulated, and very much admired among its natives."[6]

He could not, of course, have foreseen the speed or the direction of developments in America during the dynamic decades to come, as America rushed into a new era in its literary and cultural history. Each of the trio of factors he mentioned with regard to the phenomenon of Irving was to undergo a thoroughgoing transformation in the decades preceding the Civil War, enough to have left a Rip Van Winkle of 1820 awakening at midcentury in amazement to signs of a modern literary culture: the growth of a class of writers primarily devoted to letters; the emergence of a publishing industry to manufacture, promote, and distribute the work of those authors and to subsidize periodical outlets in which to feature their work; and the growth of a nationwide audience of readers.

The careers of Irving and Cooper offer a convenient synopsis of the early stage of literary professionalism in America. Rightly understood as transitional figures, both Irving and Cooper were born to good families, families of a class which in previous years might have been expected, had that been their sons' orientation, to provide candidates for amateur authorship. Both men began their careers with many of the expectations and views of their background; they started out by assuming the traditional social pose of authorial anonymity, published their own works at their own expense, and priced them high for what they assumed would be a small, select audience. Irving, quickly defensive about his calling, was given to deflating himself as "a mere belles lettres writer" and his work as "merely literary," and he intensely disliked and tried to distance himself from the "petty, puffing arts" of most publishers. Cooper, likewise, began his literary career in strictly amateur fashion; his first book, as the story goes, was written in response to a simple dare by his wife to outdo the work of a contemporary English novelist. While composing that first novel, the normally self-assured Cooper wrote an uncharacteristically uncertain letter – marked "Most-Strictly confidential" – to his publisher in which he ingenuously asked a beginner's questions about the proper size of novels, printing expenses, and probable sales.[7]

Both men, however, quickly learned how to take advantage of the favorable conditions for writers in the 1820s. With a growing taste for fiction, an expanding readership, and the lingering high price of books (two dollars or more for a two-volume novel), large profits could be made by the enterprising; and the immature condition of the publishing industry allowed a resourceful writer to steer those profits into his own pocket. By financing and overseeing the manufacture of their own works and limiting publishers to the role of distributor, Irving and Cooper were able to earn an unprecedented 30–45 percent profit on each work sold – this against the traditional royalty of 10–15 percent that publishers would pay writers once the publishing industry became rationalized and volume, not price, became its primary criterion.[8] To the post–Civil War publisher Henry Holt, commenting at a time when author-publisher relations had stabilized, royalties in excess of 15 percent were "immoral."[9]

Irving rapidly mastered the art of doubling his literary income by selling his works to publishers on both sides of the Atlantic, demanding – and usually receiving – hefty fees from John Murray in England and Henry Carey in America. After having established his reputation and marketability with the *Sketch Book* in 1819–20, Irving was able to set a high price, generally between one thousand to two thousand pounds, on the manuscripts he sold to Murray. Meanwhile in America, where he was entitled to hold the copyright in his own name, he leased printing rights to his works at lucrative rates for limited terms, then at the expiration of the original period contracted for a second period so as to maximize what he called "the regular produce of my copyright property."[10] The letters he wrote to his publishers reveal Irving to be an informed bargainer, skillful in negotiating favorable terms and compensation, while at the same time a loyal adherent to a code of loyalty to his "gentlemanlike" publishers. A reciprocal gesture, such as Murray's (the old Tory's) tactful placing of a picture of his valuable American author in a place of honor next to that of Byron, his most cherished author, was sure to please Irving inordinately.[11]

His literary income during these years was exceptionally high, nine thousand dollars a year, he claimed, before he entered government service in 1829.[12] What made such munificent payment possible was the fortuitous but temporary convergence in the 1820s of the vogue for his books and the high price he could charge for them. Even though his profit margin began to shrink in the 1830s with changing, less favorable market conditions for authors, he still remained confident that his works would continue to prosper; as he wrote to his brother in 1835: "there has been a great change in the bookselling trade of late years. The inundation of cheap publications, penny magazines, etc., has brought down the market. The market here [in America], in the meantime, has immensely extended, so that, between the two, I fancy, I shall be as well off as before."[13] He also managed, for a time, to increase his income by agreeing to write occasionally for the *Knickerbocker Magazine* at beyond the magazine's normally highest rate of compensation – putting into practice the advice he had given a friend years earlier of using the bur-geoning field of periodicals as an outlet for otherwise "fugitive" pieces collecting in his portfolio.[14]

Gradually, his reputation and income declined during the 1830s and early 1840s, reaching a low point in 1842, when he sailed for Spain as American envoy with his old works out of print and the Careys unwilling to meet his terms for their reissue. His reputation languished throughout the period of his diplomatic service, but after his return to New York, he contracted with George Putnam in 1848 for a new duodecimo edition of his complete works, a stunningly successful venture for both parties. The venture was to earn him an average income of nine thousand dollars in royalties for each of the remaining years of his life and to bring him before the widest reading audience he would ever reach (three hundred fifty thousand volumes having been sold by 1857, according to his sec-retary-nephew).[15]

Cooper, meanwhile, was experiencing a generally similar pattern of successes and failures, fame and notoriety, during the three decades of his career. If anything, he pursued his career and exploited the oppor-tunities of nascent literary professionalism more single-mindedly than did Irving. His head always full of ideas for books, he wrote at a pace prolific even by Victorian standards, turning out one or more often two books a year, year in and year out. His attitude, all the while, was for the time refreshingly businesslike: "Though an author, I am a man of business," he wrote his publisher with typical candor in justification of his hard-driving dealings.[16] Writing as a profession, ironically, became the economic support of his high-living family's claim to status. Cooper wrote at a pace calculated, among other things, to pay off his family debts; and the drive to do so often led him to conduct himself with his publishers as one hardheaded man of affairs among his like: "In dealing with my publishers," he openly admitted to Colburn and Bentley, "I can only consider a work as an article of traffick, and must be content to take as much as I can get, and no more."[17]

What he could get in the early years was what writers of previous generations could only have fantasized about. Like Irving, he maximized his income by publishing simultaneously in England and America; in addition, he also worked the Continental market whenever he could. In the spring of 1827, for instance, he was simultaneously overseeing the publication of five authorized editions of *The Prairie* – three in English, one in French, and one in German.[18] During his glory years of the 1820s and early 1830s, he regularly earned five thousand dollars a book from the Careys in Philadelphia, while from Colburn and Bentley, the primary dealers in American writings in the London trade, he received on the average of three hundred to six hundred pounds for each work of fiction and perhaps half as much for each work of nonfiction. He was able to boast to correspondents in 1831, the most lucrative year of his career, that in that year alone he expected to earn twenty thousand dollars from his writing.[19] Later in the decade, he experienced a similar decline in income to that of Irving and for similar reasons, as his popularity waned and his profit margin per book thinned in the new era of cheap publications and increased literary competition. Because he had allowed most of his American copyrights to pass out of his hands, he was unable to share in Irving's final fortune of seeing the successful reissue of his complete works; the reissuing of his complete works in the decade after his death would be a major success for his publishers, Stringer and Townsend, but only a marginal benefit for his family.

I do not mean by this to claim that the exclusive or even the primary measure of Irving's and Cooper's success as literary professionals is to be made in pounds and dollars. The argument that William Dean Howells tried to make later in the century for "the man of letters" as being "the man of business" was a profoundly unsimple and problematic one for a writer of his century.[20] Cooper, for one, could complacently accept as his due large payments from publishers for the very works in which he excoriated the commercialism of his society. An interesting example of this tangle of interests is a novella that Cooper serialized in 1843 in *Graham's,* which provides a pointedly ironic commentary on the complexity of the concept of literary professionalism in a capitalistic, democratic society and highlights the cultural as well as economic basis of the issues involved.[21]

Cooper, oblivious to what would become one of the great publishing options available to the Victorian novelist, had previously made it his policy not to serialize his fictions, mistakenly considering serialization a poorly paying substitute for book publication. But he made an exception in the case of *Autobiography of a Pocket-Handkerchief,* a rare Cooper fiction not published in book form and not issued outside of the United States. The plot of the story is simply told; it traces the life history of a fancy *mouchoir de poche* from the fields of France and the factory of a ruined aristocratic family to the possession of the last heiress of the house, impoverished by the Bourbon revolution of 1830; then follows its passage, via deceptive neighbors and shady tradesmen, through increasingly indelicate hands across the Atlantic to New York (land of long noses, according to Cooper in the story) and families of grasping nouveaux riches, before it is finally reunited with its original – and, the story makes clear, legitimate – aristocratic owner. Cooper, it is clear, was evening old scores with Whig newspaper editors and expressing his broad disgust with the crass materialism and commercialism of American society. On the other hand, Cooper – that "magnificent moral hermaphrodite," to call him by the term by which Balzac called Natty Bumppo – was too much the American democrat simply to have knocked down democratic America in order to build up aristocratic France. He therefore contrived to locate not only the plot but the moral center of the story in the character of the impoverished noblewoman, who is filled with the social virtues of her class and who eventually leaves France and, without a bit of mercenary motivation, marries happily into the American upper middle class.

Cooper, of course, was already notorious in America for airing his dirty linen in public. He had been taking his journalistic critics to court and holding his countrymen to account for years in print, but this was altogether a more fascinating affair. It put Cooper in the uncomfortable position of being a writer who, to paraphrase William Charvat, worked within the emerging system of democratic patronage while adamantly refusing to be of it.[22] For printing rights to his story, Cooper received from George Graham, then making himself known as the most generous magazine publisher of the time, the highest going rate of payment and the satisfaction of having his work appear in the most popular magazine of the decade.[23] The irony of this situation is so striking that one cannot but wonder: Was Cooper aware of the parallel between the commercialization of the handkerchief he satirized in the story and the commercialization of the story of that handkerchief by its sale to Graham, ex-cabinet-maker-turned-publisher? And was he aware that he was publishing his story in a magazine – its full title was *Graham's Lady's and Gentleman's Magazine* – which was precisely the kind of publication most likely to be found on the parlor tables of the arrivistes families he mocked in the story? And how, for their part, did Cooper's middle-class American readers respond to their unattractive portraiture in the novella?[24]

I take this as a representative instance of the tangle of contradictions which might arise out of the nascent system of literary professionalism, of old ideas ill suited to meet new social, economic, and cultural realities. The example of Cooper is of particular interest, for Cooper did more than any of his contemporaries to fill out the idea as well as to establish the economic viability of literary professionalism in his time – no matter whether he did so consciously or voluntarily. How Cooper took upon himself what he considered "the arduous task" of Americanizing the inherited genre of the novel with his Chingachgooks and Natty Bumppos, Effinghams and lowlifes, Templetons and Glimmerglasses, has been an old theme among literary historians, many of whom nevertheless receive Cooper with the same reluctance with which Gide spoke of Victor

Hugo as a national treasure ("hélas"). But literary criticism, with its reoriented focus on reader reception, may now be widening its appreciation of Cooper as it begins to recognize Cooper's formative role in creating an American audience for his and others' works. A recent critic has argued the point most strongly, as follows: "Quite simply, Cooper created the community of readers whose taste would dominate the market for fiction in America (and for American fiction abroad) throughout the nineteenth century. Most of the fiction we recognize as most characteristic and valuable in this period was designed for Cooper's audience and is unthinkable outside the horizon of expectations Cooper had established."[25] This may be putting the matter rather sweepingly and without taking into full account the considerable complexity involved in proving such an assertion – the case of *Autobiography of a Pocket-Handkerchief* shows how difficult such a proof might be – but it does project Cooper's influence on American writing in an important new direction.

For all his complaints about nonrecognition – "Authors are not much considered in America, and I less than common," he once tried to convince a representative of Tauchnitz – Cooper was effectually leading America into its initial period of literary professionalism, with the concept and terms of authorship undergoing significant transformation.[26] The careers of Irving and Cooper, though exceptional in the degree of their successes, were otherwise far from unique. One can see the obvious signs of changing times and conditions simply by glancing through a copy of *Graham's* from the early 1840s; the title page breaks with the longstanding tradition of authorial anonymity by listing – in effect, advertising – such "Principal Contributors" as Bryant, Cooper, Dana, Longfellow, Lowell, Paulding, Poe, and Willis, "names" known to the reading public and therefore of value to Graham, who, in turn, paid his writers in kind. Writers who would previously have had to be satisfied with one or two dollars a page payment, if payment at all, for magazine work, might receive five or more times as much from Graham, who in effect raised the standard for the entire periodical market in the 1840s.[27] This is not to say that writers could be said to be well paid, or even that they could make a sufficient living by their pens. Expectations had unquestionably risen substantially beyond realities. Even the most successful writers continued to fight for the additional security of government positions, and there were some writers who suffered from what the newspapers typically called, "actual want." For every Longfellow, there was a Poe; for every Willis, a McDonald Clarke (the "mad poet of Broadway" about whom Whitman wrote an elegy in the early 1840s).

Still, there could be no question that America was entering a new period in its cultural and intellectual history, both for the writers and readers of literature. "Authorship," noted the London publisher Nicolas

Trubner in 1859, "has assumed the dignity of a profession in the United States; and, notwithstanding the cynical complaints of a few disappointed aspirants for literary fame and fortune, the well-written American book not unfrequently brings its author both fame and profit."[28] The situation which Trubner was already asserting as fact in 1859 evolved slowly in the 1820s and 1830s, then at an accelerated rate during the 1840s and 1850s, keeping pace with the great national expansion and prosperity of the era. The extent of the transformation of the country, and something of the consequences it entailed for writers, can be quickly gleaned from a summary overview of the country's vital statistics during this forty-year period.[29] The population of the country was doubling every twenty years (exceeding thirty million by the time of the Civil War), while the rate of growth of urban centers was even faster. New York grew from a relatively small city of 60,000 in 1800 to a bustling, thriving urban center of 515,000 in 1850 (one of the largest cities in the Western world); Boston, from 24,000 to 136,000; Philadelphia, from 69,000 to 340,000; Baltimore, from 26,000 to 169,000. Cincinnati, a hamlet of 750 people in 1800, was a city of 115,000 in 1850 and an important book emporium; similarly, Whitman's Brooklyn grew during the same period from a village into a city of 115,000.[30] Chicago, not even listed in the 1850 census, was a city of 100,000 by the outbreak of the Civil War and would soon thereafter become an important bookselling and publishing center. Meanwhile, the territorial size of the country was growing apace, nearly doubling during the 1840s as a result of the Mexican War, the West (however defined) filling up and out more rapidly than any other section of the country.

The extraordinary rate of population growth and urbanization had an important effect on the literary culture of the country. "We are a nation of readers, thirty millions strong," asserted a writer for the politically and culturally nationalistic *Democratic Review* in 1847, "but where are our books, and who are our writers?"[31] The nation of readers to which he referred was a populace which loudly boasted itself the largest readership in the nineteenth-century world. The adult white literacy rate, according to the 1850 Census, was over 90 percent (and higher yet in the Middle Atlantic and New England states, the prime book-buying markets), an exceptionally high rate even if one assumes that the literacy standards used by the Census officials were minimal. Moreover, the desire for reading material, American and foreign alike, was enormous.

As to the second half of the writer's query, statistics of the American book publishing industry give a general answer. Whereas America had been a giant dumping ground for British remainders and reprints during the first quarter of the century, a situation which had led Sydney Smith to wonder in 1818, "But why should the Americans write books, when a six weeks' passage brings them, in their own tongues, our sense, science, and genius, in bales and hogsheads," matters changed dramatically during the following decades.[32] Samuel Goodrich, a small-time publisher and the author of the immensely popular Peter Parley books, which collectively sold in the millions of copies before the Civil War, produced the most nearly reliable contemporary documentation of the trends in American bookmaking: an enormous expansion in the dollar value of books from 2.5 million in 1820 to an estimated 16 million in 1856, coupled with a tendency away from foreign reprints (which were more profitable to publishers because unprotected in the absence of an international copyright) to publication of native works.[33] George Putnam, while serving as the head of Wiley and Putnam's London office, had written an important little book (*American Facts*, 1845) of national self-presentation before the English in which he stressed, among other achievements, the successes of American literary culture and the fact that the traffic in books and reprints between England and America was then becoming a two-way avenue. A decade later, the London publisher Sampson Low prefaced his company's catalogue of American books of interest to the English with the observation, "America is gradually repaying us for what she has hitherto drawn from our Literature," and drew the conclusion that an international copyright was not only necessary but equitable as now being an agreement struck between equals.[34] One magazine writer went so far in 1857 as to claim, "The Americans have become the greatest book producers in the world. More volumes are sold in this country in one year than in Great Britain, with much the same population, in five."[35]

Midcentury writers also had a major secondary – for some it was a primary – resource in the newspaper and magazine market, whose expansion during this period was interconnected with that of the book market. The Census of 1840 reported 138 daily newspapers, 141 weekly newspapers, and 227 periodicals circulating in America, already more than anywhere else in the world; but the greatest surge was still to come. By 1869, there were more than 4,000 newspapers and periodicals in the United States whose total sales approached a billion copies. The advent of the penny press, of popular monthly magazines, and of family and literary weeklies revealed the tremendous sales potential of the American market. Whereas the six-penny New York *Courier and Enquirer* claimed the largest circulation among American newspapers in 1833 with 4,500 copies a day, within a decade a new generation of penny papers, including Horace Greeley's New York *Tribune,* James Gordon Bennett's New York *Herald,* Moses Beach's New York *Sun,* and a short while later Henry Raymond's New York *Times,* popularized in form and content and printed on the new "lightning presses," was circulating in the tens of thousands and bringing its editors to national prominence. One writer boasted in the New York *Tribune* in 1854, "A considerable time elapsed after the invention of the art [of printing] before the *annual production of all the Printing Offices in the world* equaled in amount the present *daily* production of *The Tribune* Office."[36] For Whitman, who edited a number of the smaller penny papers of Manhattan and Brooklyn during the years of this journalistic heyday, newspapers were rapidly becoming the required reading of the general populace:

> What was once deemed a luxury, and a somewhat superfluous one at that, is now a matter of necessity no more to be dispensed with than one's breakfast. The man who doesn't read the papers has become obsolete. Newspapers have become the mirror of the world, without looking into which, no one can accomplish anything. The great daily journals have a department for all. The business man glances anxiously at his own corner of the sheet to mark the quotations of stock or the fluctuations of trade; the litterateur turns to his own particular columns for reviews or announcements of new books; the people who are anxious about absent friends, to their appropriate department; the unemployed, to the columns of wants; and everybody to the telegraphic head, which is glanced at as anxiously each morning by millions of readers as if it held the fate of each.[37]

A comparable transformation was overtaking the American magazine. The turn-of-the-century lament of Noah Webster that "the expectation of failure is connected with the very name of a Magazine" would have been incomprehensible to a generation nurtured on the mass-circulation magazines and story papers of the forties and fifties, the brash, often hyperbolic, sales talk by editors and publishers of circulation in the tens or hundreds of thousands, and the emergence of a highly visible new breed of magazine writer and editor.[38] Speaking in the boosterish manner of the time, Charles Briggs declared that the tendency of the age was "magazineward."[39] The average midcentury circulation of periodicals, given by the 1850 census as being 7,500, would have made the success of any periodical of the preceding generation; but by this time magazines at the upper end of the circulation gamut, such as *Godey's, Graham's,* and *Harper's,* were selling ten or more times as many copies and reaching the largest journalistic market in the world. While there was a conspicuous increase in the diversity of periodicals during these years, it was these popular monthlies which best illustrated the successful formula of the new journalism, as it gradually superseded the more formal, arid style of the older quarterly reviews. Their outlook, mirroring the composition of their audience, was generally national; their contents, a blend of fiction and verse, biographical and historical essays, travel sketches, and illustrations, were designed for the entertainment and edification of their readers; and their monthly periodicity and affordable prices (usually three dollars a year), combined with their solicitous, friendly tone, put them on a familiar basis with their broad-based, middle-class readership.

This situation was an inviting one for writers, who were quick, on the whole, to take advantage of the new channels opening up between themselves and the expanding reading public. Many of the literary figures held in highest respect today – Emerson, Fuller, Hawthorne, Lowell, Poe, Bryant, and Whitman – worked diligently and idealistically at one time or another as editors of newspapers or magazines, and there were few writers of the day, good or bad, who failed to write for the periodical market. Not even those writers generally thought remote from the popular sentiment, such as Thoreau, who acceded to the request of Greeley and other editors to "swap 'wood-notes wild' for dollars," or Melville, who, though embittered with his popular and critical reception, came to depend on the magazines to keep himself going during the downswing of his career in the fifties, could look away from the opportunities offered by the periodicals. For Poe, writing for the magazines was his primary means of support in the absence of a readership for his books, and he even came to pour his literary ambitions into the chimera of starting his own magazine. For Longfellow, a paradigm of professional resourcefulness, the magazines were an important secondary publishing option for bringing out individual poems before collecting them for book publication. In the years following the Civil War, Longfellow would receive up to three thousand dollars from *Harper's* and the New York *Ledger* for publication rights to single poems.

These writers were not alone. Robert Bonner, the publisher of the *Ledger,* capitalized on his philosophy of "A Good Article is worth a Good Price" and his reputation as the leading magazine paymaster of the middle decades of the century to induce some of the leading figures of the nation (the Smith Professor of Modern Languages at Harvard, the most famous minister of the day, a respected diplomat and ex-editor of the stodgy *North American Review,* the presidents of America's leading colleges) to join his stable of regulars in writing for his popular family weekly – people who not so many years before would have thought it inconceivable that they would write for Bonner or for anyone else on his popular, commercial terms.[40] But in the changing times and conditions of the emerging literary culture of midcentury, as shifting circumstances narrowed the gap between "popular" and "respectable," writers with various kinds of "designs" on readers – to use the phrase in Jane Tompkins' multivalent sense – were eager to exploit the new literary organs in order to come into relation with the reading public.[41]

The broadening of America's literary culture gave rise to a new class of professional writers, magazinists, and editors, among whom there developed a sense of shared, professional concerns. With the extreme

, 37, 945

College of St. Francis Library
Joliet, Illinois

self-consciousness which characterized all the parties of the literary culture of the period from printers and publishers to editors and writers, writers soon made the conditions of authorship a public issue. One can see this phenomenon at first in the journalistic writings of Nathaniel Parker Willis, Park Benjamin, and Lewis Gaylord Clark in the 1830s, then more broadly in the following decades, contemporaneously with the expansion of the book and periodical markets, as writers began to use the public forum offered by the new generation of publications – the New York *Tribune,* the *Democratic Review,* the *New World, Brother Jonathan,* the *American Whig Review,* the *Literary World,* and *Putnam's* – to address the crucial professional concerns of the day. In article after article, some redounding through the network of noncopyrighting journals, writers discussed and debated the merits of cultural nationalism, international copyright, authorial compensation, author-publisher relations, democratic patronage, conditions of the literary marketplace, printing technology, and like issues of common concern.[42] By the late 1830s and early 1840s, the issue of international copyright, which many writers and some publishers saw as a necessary precondition to the emergence of a truly indigenous American literature, had even been taken to the halls of Congress.

These articles issued in a loose, unsystematic way, much as did the periodicals themselves; and in the absence of a genuine institutional structure or center in American culture, any attempt to read them synthetically for theme is necessarily difficult. Just the same, I would like to highlight the rush of ideas, however confused or conflicting it was, during this exciting, self-consciously pathbreaking period in American cultural history by juxtaposing the views of two informed, if opposed, writers on the state of affairs in American literary culture. Their assessments appeared within a month of each other during the height of the cheap publication war of the early 1840s, in which cutthroat competition among book and newspaper publishers for the favor of the new, expanded reading public was driving book prices – and, some claimed, literary and bookmaking standards – to unprecedentedly low levels. For the conservative commentator writing in the high-toned, Whig-oriented *North American Review,* literature in the English- and French-speaking world was rapidly assuming the character of "trade," a situation to his (and presumably to his readers') distaste:

> The author's profession is becoming as mechanical as that of the printer and the bookseller, being created by the same causes, and subject to the same laws. The nature of the supply seems likely to be as strictly proportioned to the demand, as in any other commercial operation. The public appetite will not be sated with the food, which the caprice of writers and the irregular distribution of natural genius may create.

College of St. Francis Library

It must be gratified with its peculiar delicacies, its favorite cakes; and the means of satisfying it, in one way or another, are sure to be discovered. The publisher, in the name of his customers, calls for a particular kind of authorship, just as he would bespeak a dinner at a *restaurant;* and, in preparing the required article, the cooks at the desk show as much versatility and readiness as their brethren in the kitchen. The great increase of the reading public, consequent on the diffusion of education and the cheapness of paper and print, is the great cause of this extraordinary cultivation of the art of book-making. The writer's profession becomes a lucrative one, when he ministers to the pleasures of so large a circle, who are willing to pay for the amusement and gratification, which he affords them. He no longer looks for his reward to the judgment of the judicious few, or the united voice of different countries and ages. He finds a more immediate recompense in the accounts of his bookseller and the applause of the multitude. And he is able to direct his course with a view to the attainment of this reward, and to disregard the higher motive . . . In a word, the democratic principle is now exerting as visible an influence in literature as in politics . . . A literature created for the people, if not by them, must always be characterized by greater energy and simplicity, by more excitement and a broader license, and by less polish and refinement, than one which is destined for a learned and aristocratic class . . . New sources of interest and amusement will be opened, and new fields of literary execution entered, by men, who attach more importance to the number of their admirers, than to the basis on which the admiration rests. They will look to the quantity, and not the quality, of the praise obtained, and will measure their reputation by their substantial profits. Their productions will bear the popular stamp, – will represent the feelings and tastes, and be suited to the prejudices of the multitude to whom they are addressed.[43]

The new arrangement, in short, would upset relations between readers, writers, and publishers by putting them on the debased standard of "the democratic principle" of quantity over quality.

But for the anonymous writer speaking the opinion of the free-trading, progressive *Democratic Review,* the "democratic revolution" then overtaking the book trade was a welcome development for American readers, writers, and publishers – and for patriots generally:

The fact is, that our publishers are just beginning to open their eyes to the truth that their real interest is not to raise their prices to the *maximum* that a book will tolerably stand, but to bring them down to the *minimum* which will yield a very small surplus on each volume above the mechanical cost of a decent typography . . . As a general rule every reduction of price, down to a certain limit, is accompanied by an enlargement of the number of persons within whose ability the thing in question is brought, in a ratio much greater than that of the reduction. An arithmetical progression of the one will be accompanied by a geometrical progression of the other. If a certain number of persons can afford to give a dollar for any such purpose – the book, for instance – far more than twice as many can afford to give a half-dollar; probably at least four times, perhaps six or eight times as many. If the price be still further reduced to a quarter-dollar, the circle of ability will continue to widen with still larger and larger sweep, and the multiplication of the number of profit will be found to proceed faster than the division of their individual amount . . . Under the operation of this system, we shall no longer have the public for whom good books are furnished, by the combined labor of author and publisher, limited to a little aristocracy of readers of one or two thousand enjoying the privilege of possession, with another set of "the inferior sort" waiting humbly for their more distant chance of possible perusal by loan from friends or hire from libraries. Editions will be numbered by thousands, where they before were counted by tens or hundreds.[44]

The benefits of a literature based on inexpensive pricing and volume, he went on, would be shared not only by readers and publishers but also by American writers, whose work until then had always been less attractive to American publishers than were the "free" because uncopyrighted works of foreign writers. The new literary culture of scale would reduce the comparative price differential between foreign and domestic works by lowering book prices generally, while simultaneously enlarging the natural advantage of native writers in writing for an audience of countrymen. The result would be a significant advance in the lot of American writers and in the cause of national letters.

Both writers intelligently discerned the changing character of America's new "system" of literary culture, which gave increasing consideration to volume, profit, and popularity at the expense of profit margin, classical standards of taste, and restricted readership. While they agreed that such conditions would provide a strong stimulus to authorship, they reached opposing conclusions as to the value of such authorship or of the literature to issue from it. The writer of the *North American Review* believed that a literature "for the people" – he could not even imagine a literature "by" the people – would inevitably be a throwaway literature of "trash." Or as a self-declared "conservative in literature" complained in the *American Whig Review* in 1847, "authors less and less address themselves to a judicious few, and more and more to an unreflecting many."[45] The writer for the *Democratic Review*, by contrast, had no reservations about popular taste and welcomed the new era, as did the *Review* itself, which later that year enthusiastically supported the idea of "Poetry for the People."[46]

The opening up of opportunities for writers which I have been discussing occurred simultaneously with the development of the publishing industry; the growth of one would have been inconceivable without the growth of the other. The increasing professionalization of writers nicely complemented parallel developments then overtaking and transforming the publishing industry. Writers who staked their livelihood and reputation on their work depended on the ability of publishers to read public taste and to present and promote their work accordingly, while publishers able and willing to invest large amounts of capital and manpower in the manufacture and distribution of books required a pool of full-time, productive writers skillful in and committed to cultivating an audience for their works. This is not to say that relations between writers and publishers were purely mutualistic. The historian Prescott spoke the opinion of many writers when he labeled the publishing industry, "the slippery 'trade.' "[47] His fate of having publishers collapse from beneath him was the rule rather than the exception during the nineteenth century. Many writers criticized the methods, and some even challenged the honesty, of their publishers, while publishers, for their part, were just as quick to defend their integrity and to question the loyalty or profitability of their authors.

Far more significant than the occasional quarrels and controversies between writers and publishers was the fact that midcentury relations between them were gradually working toward a new position of equilibrium, one far removed from that common in the early days of Cooper and Irving. Back then, many writers, especially those with means, preferred to finance the publication of their own works and to delegate to publishers responsibility only for the distribution of their work. The primary risk and incentive, in such cases, remained with the author, not with the publisher, an arrangement which few publishers then had the ambition or the capital to reverse. One who did, Henry Carey, attempted to persuade his new client, Cooper, whom he considered a meddler in matters better left to professional publishers, that "one occupation is enough for one man . . . authors rarely make money by being at once authors and booksellers."[48] But Cooper was not easily dissuaded from his customary practices, nor were other writers who continued to base their expectations on a limited circle of readers willing to pay high prices for their reading pleasure. In the absence of a strong, independent publishing industry and the conditions for popular, commercial literature, the old system of author-initiated publication remained intact, surviving in some places right through the 1830s. That arrangement was particularly popular in New England, where the tradition of regional publishing and authorial initiative was strong. The New England historians Prescott, Bancroft, Sparks, and Motley, for instance, were among those who continued to subsidize their own works, paying the expenses of stereotyping their works and leasing the plates to publishers on specified terms. Like Cooper and Irving, they were the beneficiaries of an expanding audience for history as well as for fiction they themselves had not foreseen, and they worked the arrangement in most cases to their considerable profit.

Some creative writers, such as Longfellow and Emerson, also engaged in various forms of self-financed publication via control of their own plates. Later in their careers, however, they sold their literary property to Ticknor and Fields, the expanding publishing house of most of the leading creative New England writers of midcentury, in return for life annuities for their old works and royalty payments for their new ones, much as Irving had signed over his copyrights to George Putnam in return for royalties. Even as Prescott and Motley continued to publish with the Harpers on their accustomed author-initiated terms, the Harpers were solidifying their policy of putting their authors on either a half-profits or a royalties system of compensation, the latter gradually becoming the norm of authorial payment in the industry. Such cases as I have been describing were indicative of the changing norms of the mid-century literature market, as that market expanded in territory and population with the nation.

Gradually, with opportunities opening up for writers, the reading population swelling, and the spreading network of steamboats and railroads providing improved access to the far-flung public, publishers found a niche for themselves as necessary intermediaries in the large-scale business of manufacturing and supplying reading matter of various sorts for a broad-based national audience. No longer relegated to the secondary status of booksellers, printers, or authorial agents, they were gradually able to work themselves into the important centrist position in the tri-partite author-publisher-reader relationship which has characterized modern literary culture ever since the nineteenth century.

In the euphoria of the Crystal Palace gathering, William Cullen Bryant had stated, "I wonder why we have not biographies of great booksellers [i.e., publishers]; such works would be histories of the literature of the times their subjects lived in."[49] Among America's nineteenth-century publishing firms, none reveals more fully the growth of the publishing industry and its role in shaping the literary culture of the time than does that of Harper and Brothers.[50] Its beginnings were typically modest. The oldest of the four founding brothers, James, left the family farm in 1810 at age fifteen to work as an apprentice to a New York printer, his path soon followed by brother John. Where in an earlier generation they could realistically have had no higher prospect after finishing their apprentice-ship than eventually to found a small city or country printing establish-ment of their own, their actual fortune was to ride high on the waves of American literary and commercial expansionism to size and prosperity on an unprecedentedly grand scale.

They first went into business in 1817 as J. and J. Harper, Printers. The speed and quality of their work were among the best in New York, and their mastery of the new technology of stereotyping gained them a local reputation as operators of one of New York's finest printing offices. But in the jumble of bookmaking and bookselling roles then current, they also occasionally ventured across the line into the general territory of publishing by bringing out small editions of English reprints and texts for the trade. By the mid–1820s, they thought of themselves as publishers first and printers second, with their burgeoning printing facilities primarily at the service of their own book list. Their growth in both capacities was swift; by the 1830s, the reorganized firm of Harper and Brothers, with all four brothers involved as partners, was emerging as the leading book publisher and manufacturer of the United States and as one of the great publishing houses of the world.

The story of its expansion during the decades preceding the Civil War is the story in brief of the transformation of the publishing industry nationally. The chief factors responsible for the rise of the Harpers repeated themselves throughout the industry: the concentration of the industry in a small number of urban centers, linked by an improved system of rail and river transportation and with New York at its acknowledged center; the shift to a publishing strategy favoring high volume and low prices; the utilization of the most advanced forms of printing technology; the reliance on a nationwide system of distribution; the development of in-house magazines as an adjunct to the main business of the house; and the adoption of hardheaded business techniques in the administration of the house and in the promotion of its works.

The Harpers set an example for the rest of the industry in various respects. Their catalogue, growing rapidly in breadth and depth, indicated the various paths available to resourceful publishers. While some houses began to specialize in one kind of literature, the Harpers offered the model of a large, flexible firm catering to the various interests of a growing, increasingly heterogeneous reading public. They were among the earliest publishers to recognize the enormous sales potential opened up by the drive for universal education and became major suppliers of textbooks and schoolbooks; their success in this market was one of the few things which sustained them while other publishers were failing during the hard times of the late 1830s and early 1840s. They published many of the leading American writers of the time, including Dana, Melville, Simms, Prescott, and Bryant, as well as numerous women novelists and travel writers, two of the most popular "departments" of contemporary literature. They were the most ambitious early American publisher of "libraries," inexpensively priced series of books (theological, educational, classical, general, fictional, family) aimed at specific segments of the public. They offered standard works in geography, lexicography, religion, history, and education.

The greatest source of profitability to the Harpers, however, and the one which brought them their widespread notoriety, was the unsolicited reprinting of uncopyrighted foreign works, especially fiction. The leading literary pirates of the century, the Harpers took advantage of the public's insatiable appetite for fiction by reprinting, usually in the early years without permission or compensation, the works of the most popular foreign novelists: Scott, Bulwer, James, and Dickens. This policy inevitably brought them into conflict with the other great publishing house and pirate of the 1820s and 1830s, the Careys of Philadelphia, who similarly exercised free-sailing rights through the English reprint trade. While the escapades between the two companies in attempting to outwit each other became the talk of the trade, the two sides were eventually able to work out a "gentlemanly" set of compromises, which became part of the unwritten, loosely binding rules the industry referred to as "courtesy of the trade."

By that time, the Harpers were quickly outpacing the Careys as the leaders in American publishing, just as New York was superseding Philadelphia as the leading American publishing center. Its geographical position gave New York a decided advantage over Philadelphia in its dealings both with Europe and with most of the major book markets of America (exclusive of the South, which was, in any case, of steadily decreasing importance as a book market in the years leading up to the Civil War). With its rail and telegraphic ties pushing further and further into the interior and water connections in all directions, its fast-growing population, and its commercial supremacy, New York quickly became, as it has since remained, the center of the book and periodical industries of the country. The Harpers were only one, if the most opportunistic, of the numerous publishing firms to exploit New York's most favored position in their attempt to fashion a nationwide network for the distribution of their works. Whereas in earlier times, the size of the country, the inaccessibility of the interior, and the limited market had imposed formidable limits on the distribution of books in the United States, a situation in which publishing could be carried out only on a regional basis, the Harpers were developing in the midcentury years a complicated national gridwork of connections. Moses Beach, who had had professional dealings with them as the publisher of the New York *Sun,* described their operations with grudging admiration in 1845:

They are now the most extensive publishers in this country, and their names in the history of publishing will be associated with Galliane, Constable, Murray and Longman. They have in different parts of America, from twelve to fifteen hundred booksellers acting as their agents, besides a large number of travelling clergymen and other itinerants. So extensive is their business connexion that should they dispose of but one or two copies to each agency, they would be sure to pay the expenses of publication, and no matter what work they may publish, (and they have published several of the worst and most stupid books ever issued) they are sure to dispose of an average more than two copies to each house with which they deal. They have a correspondence established not only with every considerable place in this country, but with cities abroad, where books are published, informing them of every work worthy of publication. They have besides in this city, and other parts of the United States, many literary men in their employment, to pronounce their opinion of manuscripts submitted for publication, to revise those that are imperfect, and to write notices and puffs for the more important newspapers and magazines which they have either directly or indirectly subsidized to their interest.[51]

Their ambitions for themselves as publishers on a national scale required a commensurate commitment to their book manufacturing capacity, which had been from the start one of the strengths of the firm. Harper's was the first American firm to stereotype its books on a routine basis, as it was among the leaders in adopting the latest press technology. Steam replaced horsepower by the early 1830s, and the handpresses used in the early days were gradually replaced by dozens of Adams and Napier steam presses, housed in a giant manufacturing facility which contained equipment for the printing, binding, and storage of books, as well as office space for the administration of the business. The Cliff Street plant, like those of the Appletons of New York and the Lippincotts of Philadelphia a decade later, became one of the leading tourist sites of the city, which itself was becoming one of the leading book emporia of the world. A visible sign of concentration, scale, and capital, the Cliff Street factory could easily have stood to visitors walking through it as impressive testimony to an industry coming of age. One visitor who saw it in exactly these terms was Whitman, who as editor of the Brooklyn *Eagle* regularly singled out in his reviews the literary and typographical excellence of the Harpers' books and who was in the habit of strolling by the factory on his "jaunts" through the city. On at least one occasion, he took the grand tour through the facility, his impression still glowing as he passed it on to his readers:

> We had an opportunity yesterday of going through the great Cliff street publishing house in New York; and we don't see how James

Harper [elected the Nativist mayor of New York in 1844] ever made himself willing to stand as a candidate for the Mayorality of Gotham! The only *office* we should care about, indeed, would be his printing office – a place employing hundreds of hands, and sending abroad myriads of books, to the uttermost parts of the western world.

If the reader was never in the Cliff street establishment, he can have little idea of the immense business done there – and in view of that immense business, we write the latter part of the first sentence of our article. Surely, when a man has his hands full already, it is not well to grasp after more and larger honors. And yet *not* larger; for we don't know a more noble, useful, and beneficial position than that of a great publisher – sending forth day after day the rays of intellectual improvement, and literary excellence.[52]

With their book list expanding rapidly, their books reaching a larger and larger audience, and their reputation solidified as one of the leading publishers in the world, the Harpers stood on top of the American publishing industry at midcentury, itself thriving as never before. Even in the economically depressed times of the early 1840s, when the entire industry was hard pressed, one of the brothers could boast to Thoreau – Thoreau of all people – that they were making fifty thousand dollars a year, and much greater prosperity for them was soon to come.[53] In 1850, they embarked in a new direction by establishing *Harper's Monthly Magazine,* brought out under the general supervision of Fletcher Harper but edited by several of the leading literary journalists of the time. The idea of an in-house journal was hardly original with the Harpers – they had the example of the English publisher Bentley before their eyes – but their ambition for their new periodical was unparalleled. Issued with the intent of "bringing within the reach of the great mass of the American people, an immense amount of useful and entertaining reading matter," *Harper's* was reaching fifty thousand subscribers within its first half year, and with its publishers each succeeding year proudly calling out the mounting circulation figures, was soon well on its way to fulfilling their goal of "a popular circulation unequaled by that of any similar periodical ever published in the world."[54] Despite their claims of serving the general public with the magazine, the Harpers were clearly also serving themselves, using the magazine as a convenient forum for printing serials which could later be profitably reprinted by the house as books, for giving additional publishing opportunities to Harpers authors as well as for enticing other writers into the house, and for publicizing the merits of the works and achievements of the house. The profitability of the magazine and its many-sided utility to the house inspired numerous other American publishers to go a similar route; in the years to follow, other major publishing houses, such as those of Putnam, Ticknor and Fields,

Scribner, and Lippincott, would bring out general magazines of their own.

The spectacular achievements the Harpers made in their book and magazine publishing operations could not have been accomplished without sound business policies and a well-coordinated strategy of promoting their works. Where book promotion in an earlier era in America had been lax due to the persisting stigma of trade among writers and publishers and to the decentralized, regional nature of the profession, the Harpers were early in adopting a frankly commercial attitude and the corresponding methods to the management of their business. Despite their firm adherence to Methodism and their public proclamation that they would publish no book which was not "interesting, instructive, and moral," the Harpers were widely perceived as essentially crude, unsentimental entrepreneurs who followed the profit motive, in most cases, to wherever it led.[55] That often meant, particularly in the early years of the firm's existence, to the foreign reprint trade, which supplied a disproportionately larger portion of their books and magazines as compared, say, to those of a more idealistic publisher, such as George Putnam. But gradually they, too, saw the expediency and desirability of cultivating native writers and reoriented their books and magazines more toward the patriotic preference of the American market.

The Harpers were one of the small but growing numbers of exceptions by the 1850s to the criticism directed by a leading authority against publishers for "issuing" rather than "publishing" their works:

> In this age of books, when every author, *properly introduced,* is assured a large circle of readers, and an ever-widening sphere of influence, it may not be amiss for those interested in the trade – whether through the investment of money or mind – to ponder well the distinction between the *issuing* and the *publication* of a book . . . Comparatively few . . . of the issues of our day, or even of former years, can, with strict correctness, be said to have been published, in the true sense of the word. The publication of a book – seemingly so immaterial to its success, if viewed from the mental and mechanical accessories to its production – is, as we shall attempt to show, the hinge upon which depends the realization of the author's hopes, both as regards reputation and pecuniary remuneration. The book needs a publisher as much as it needs an author; and the selection of that publisher is sometimes more important than the theme or the style of the work itself.

His conclusion: "By far the greater part of books are lost, not because they are rejected, but because they are never introduced."[56] The ability of the Harpers to publish their works in this fuller sense improved considerably in the 1840s and 1850s, but they could not have done so had not the requisite network of national distribution and of advertising media been in place. The book contract they signed in 1844 to publish a new edition of the already popular Morse *School Geography* indicated something of the ambitiousness they (or their writers through them) were entertaining, its terms stipulating that the Harpers "do all in their power to promote its sale by causing the book to be advertised extensively in all parts of the United States and taking vigorous measure to have the book presented to school teachers and trustees throughout the land."[57] Precisely how extensive their promotion of books was at that time, when the standard means of book promotion consisted of distribution of review copies and the placement of "puffs," it would be difficult to say, since many of the firm's internal records were lost in the Harper fire of 1853. A memorandum book dating from 1856, however, indicates that the Harpers were already advertising their books in popular magazines, commercial trade sheets, and even Christian parlor magazines, as well as in newspapers throughout the country.[58]

By the middle of the nineteenth century, the Harpers and the publishing industry nationally were reaching an incipient stage of maturity. The industry was growing and prospering with the country generally and would continue to do so until the Panic of 1857 caused a sharp, if temporary, reversal of its rapid expansion. The 1850s saw the issuance of the first important trade journals, the publication of important bibliographical guides to American literature, and the movement toward greater centralization and institutionalization of the industry via trade sales and publishers' associations. Business was brisk, the sense of collegiality was strong, and the mood among publishers, as among all the partners in the production and consumption of books, was one of bounding self-confidence and optimism.

One of the most buoyant expressions of this widespread faith was made by Evert Duyckinck, the founding editor of one of the new, influential organs of the midcentury literary culture, who claimed that the *Literary World* would be, as its subtitle designated, "a Gazette for Authors, Publishers, and Readers – the editor being of opinion that the interests of all, in the end, unite."[59] In the general celebration of the success of this partnership at the Crystal Palace dinner, there were many among the crowd of writers, publishers, and spectators, twisting their necks to identify famous names previously known to them only through the refraction of print, who would unhesitatingly have given their assent to Duyckinck's sentiment. The relations between two of the participants at the dinner, both seated at the table of honor on the speakers' dais, might have been taken as an extreme exemplification of this supposed peaceable kingdom of writers and their publishers. Back in 1835, when Washington Irving was putting the profits he had made from his writings to the construction of Sunnyside, his fine country home built on land overlooking the Hudson River, he instructed the brother who served as his literary agent to exercise restraint in his financial demands on publisher Henry Carey, whom Irving knew then to be "a little pushed for the means of building another wing to [his] country seat."[60] Such solicitude may have been one of the more endearing features of Irving's personality, but in this case it also contributed to one of the more amusing, indeed aberrant, scenes in nineteenth-century author-publisher relations.

Many contemporary writers would have appreciated, even applauded Duyckinck's sentiment; and those who shared his fervent cultural nationalism might have seen in it the culmination of their long-desired goal of a domestic culture produced, handled, and consumed by Americans.[61] But the strident rhetoric so characteristic of public expressions at this time was one thing; the cold reality of dealing with publishers and readers and of making a living in the process, quite another. To read the private as opposed to the public sentiments of the writers held in the highest regard today, or even those of – a very different group – the popular women writers of the day, is to become aware of frequent expressions of tension, ambivalence, frustration, even outright hostility in their relations with publishers and the reading public. The path that led an American writer in one door to his or her publisher and out the opposite door to the reading public was immensely more difficult to negotiate than Duyckinck and other cultural nationalists had foreseen. One might consider the sad fate of Melville as an example of how wrong Duyckinck could be – Melville's early faith in his ability to speak freely and frankly to the American public ("the Declaration of Independence makes a difference," he assured Duyckinck) counterposed against his painful experience that his right to speak freely was matched by the publisher's freedom to reject his work, the critic's to denigrate it, and the reading public's not to buy it.[62]

While it may have been equally an overreaction to Duyckinck's roseate views to see, as Melville sometimes did in embittered anger over the loss of his popularity, a law of contraries operating between himself and his publishers and readers, the reality of the situation for writers actually supported neither of these extreme positions. The new literary culture with its commercial, democratic priorities offered enticing prospects of fame and fortune for writers, but it also more silently exacted its due. For Thoreau, to be popular required a writer "to go down perpendicularly," a price which he was generally unwilling to pay.[63] The changing fortunes of a writer such as Melville with the public could be measured in the opposing tendencies he felt between writing books "calculated for popularity" and those he considered "eminently adapted for unpopularity," as he variously remarked about two of his works, the latter type predominating in time over the former. Hawthorne revealed some of the resentment he felt about the state of the literary market in 1855 and one of the reasons for his continued stay in England when he complained to his publisher, "America is now wholly given over to a d——d mob of scribbling women, and I should have no chance of success while the public taste is occupied with their trash."[64] His displeasure, it is clear, derived not only from his regard for quality but also from jealousy, his inability to equal their feat of selling editions, according to his potent exaggeration, "by the 100,000."

Waiting in the wings for the moment to "go in for [his] chances" was Walt Whitman. Whitman, as I will be showing, had spent the years of his early manhood absorbing more of the content and spirit of the evolving literary culture of midcentury than had any of his major contemporaries, gradually learning how to integrate its terms liberally with his own insights and ambitions in preparing the foundations of his new poetry. It was from the resultant platform of cultural nationalism and poetry for the people, raised high, that he would deliver his poetry in 1855. Although in his later years Whitman was to caution America against the danger of literary and cultural philistinism, paraphrasing Margaret Fuller's warning so freely as to make it virtually his own, "It does not follow that because the United States print and read more books, magazines, and newspapers than all the rest of the world, that they really have, therefore, a literature," his heart was on the other side of the argument, on the side which saw no necessary contradiction between periodicals and literature, and between democracy and culture.[65] Their synthesis, in fact, was to be a vital component of the literary credo with which Whitman would address the American public in 1855.

3

Going Forth into Literary America

In "There Was a Child Went Forth," a poem which has frequently been read (and probably overread) autobiographically for its content, Whitman gives what may be taken as a cogent rationale more generally for biographical inquiry: "There was a child went forth every day, / And the first object he looked upon and received with wonder or pity or love or dread, that object he became, / And that object became part of him for the day or a certain part of the day. . . . or for many years or stretching cycles of years." The apposite question for Whitman biographers has naturally been: What objects, what experiences, what impressions became part of the boy Whitman and set him on his way to the writing of *Leaves of Grass*? To pose the question in this fashion is perhaps to invite dramatic response, but with a writer of such grandiose gestures toward the public and unusual demands upon the reader as Whitman, such a strategy may be both necessary and appropriate. The problem, one soon finds, is that precious little is retrievable from Whitman's early years, and of what does remain nothing stands out as manifestly significant.

But if one act is to be singled out as having had a formative influence on his future development, it would unquestionably be the twelve-year-old boy's setting forth one day in 1831 into the employ of the Long Island *Patriot* and the instruction of its veteran printer, William Hartshorne. The decision to send him to learn the printing trade was presumably his father's, a self-educated man of strong opinions and Democratic principles (as would be his son) who subscribed to the *Patriot,* the Democratic organ of King's County, although it is also likely that Whitman had already developed the curiosity to be initiated into what insiders commonly called "the art and mystery" of printing. Whatever its source, that decision was to lead Whitman in the years to follow through a chain of widening connections to and through printing to journalism and on to a life and career of professional authorship.

That chain of events was not at all unusual during the first half of the century, even if Whitman's personal evolution was; at a time when apprenticeship to a craft commonly took precedence over higher education for most young men, printing was still a popular and logical starting point for a working-class or middle-class youth intent on a career as a writer, editor, or publisher. Whitman, who was to have some experience of all three, was traveling the same respected route as many of the leading literary and publishing figures of the century, a short list of whom would include Nathaniel Willis, Bayard Taylor, William Dean Howells, Mark Twain, Rufus Griswold, Thurlow Weed, Horace Greeley, Robert Bonner, Henry Oscar Houghton, and Erasmus Beadle. The bare facts of his early life, in fact, suggest those of one of his future culture heroes, the most famous printer-publisher of his day, James Harper: born of mixed Dutch-English yeoman parentage, bred on a Long Island farm, and apprenticed in his teens to established printers before making his way on his own.

During the years of his apprenticeship, a period in which the printing office replaced the schoolroom as the site of his education, Whitman gradually learned and mastered the art of printing. He spent approximately one year working in the small basement printing shop of the *Patriot,* learning to set type and to work at the primitive wooden-framed handpress on which the newspaper was printed. Brooklyn at the time was undergoing a transformation from a village to a city, but the instruction Whitman received under Hartshorne was essentially a throwback, as he considered Hartshorne himself, to the ways of the past, when printing was still a time-honored craft and not the large-scale, technologically advanced industry it was already becoming across the river. Whitman would remember Hartshorne ("a special friend of mine") fondly for life, but in fact his stay at the *Patriot* lasted only one year. By the election summer of 1832, he was working for another Brooklyn printer, Erastus Worthington, and then in the fall began what would turn out to be a longer-term association with Alden Spooner, the distinguished printer-publisher of Brooklyn's leading newspaper, the Long Island *Star.* There he remained, as far as is known, for several additional years, until he completed his apprenticeship and was able to go out in 1835 on a more mature basis as a journeyman printer.

There were other activities as well for the adolescent Whitman during this period besides the hard work of the printing office. For one thing, Whitman was indulging what would become a lifelong passion for the theater, crossing the river – for him, virtually a rite of passage – alone or with friends to enjoy the spectacles staged at the Broadway and other Manhattan theaters. Other evenings he spent reading, using his access to circulation libraries to indulge his taste for romance. He later remembered himself as having been "a most omnivorous novel-reader, these and later years, devour'd everything I could get."[1] And he was already writing during these years. He first appeared in print, if his memory is to be trusted, as early as his stint with the *Patriot,* in which he recalled placing occasional "sentimental bits." A few years later he took a further step by publishing "a piece or two" in what he characterized as the "then celebrated and fashionable" New York *Mirror,* one of the George Morris–Nathaniel Willis literary papers.[2]

These were exciting, growing years for Whitman, years of exploration and maturation; and the most formative of the influences shaping his character and aspirations, it seems to me, was the one he knew most immediately, that of the printing office. Whatever his initial feelings about his apprenticeship, he soon took a deeper interest than did most printer's "devils" in the work. He was fortunate in this regard to have inherited the size and strength of his father, which no doubt made the physical demands of press work relatively lighter for him than for the average adolescent apprentice. But I also believe that Whitman took a quick satisfaction, a pleasure in his work, bordering on the aesthetic. Whether he took special pleasure in setting in type the work of Bryant and of other writers he admired, one can only speculate; but there is no mistaking the relish he took in what he later recalled as his "first instructions in type-setting – the initiation into the trade and mystery of our printing-craft":

> What compositor, running his eye over these lines, but will easily realize the whole modus of that initiation? – the half eager, half bashful beginning – the awkward holding of the stick – the type-box, or perhaps two or three old cases, put under his feet for the novice to stand on, to raise him high enough – the thumb in the stick – the compositor's rule – the upper case almost out of reach – the lower case spread out handier before him – learning the boxes – the pleasing mystery of the different letters, and their divisions – the great "e" box – the box for spaces right by the boy's breast – the "a" box, "i" box, "o" box, and all the rest – the box for quads away off in the right hand corner – the slow and laborious formation, type by type, of the first line – its unlucky bursting by the too nervous pressure of the thumb – the first experience in "pi," and the distributing thereof – all this, I say, what jour. typo cannot go back in his own experience and easily realize?[3]

Whitman, for one, would carry this memory with him not only through the three decades separating his apprenticeship in Hartshorne's printing office from the time of this reminiscence but also afterward through the three remaining decades of his life. Although he was to work only sporadically as a practicing printer during the first half of his life and never again thereafter except for a veteran's playful reencounter with a craft long abandoned, the stamp of the profession, the peculiar literalness with which he saw print and paper, was to be on his thinking, reading, and writing throughout his life.

After completing his apprenticeship with the Long Island *Star* in 1835, he left the Spooners and Brooklyn to try his hand as a journeyman printer in New York, where printing jobs were more numerous. Specifics about where he worked have not survived, but it is known that, with the bad fortune which seemed to follow his family, he had not been employed in Manhattan long when two severe fires later that year swept through New York City, the first in August, originating in a bookbindery and destroying many of the printing and publishing establishments of the city, and the second and even more damaging, December's "Great Fire of 1835," which decimated an additional nineteen blocks of the mercantile area near the Battery.[4]

A sixteen-year-old journeyman would have been particularly vulnerable to the closing of doors on New York printers in the period of economic retrenchment which followed, and it is reasonable to assume that he went through a period of anxiety and uncertainty before reluctantly returning in May of 1836 to his ancestral Long Island, to which his family, itself forced back by his father's economic failure, had retreated two years before. Unable to find work in his profession at a time when business conditions were tight and only to get tighter as the nation approached the Panic of the following year, Whitman unwillingly was forced, as would be his equally hard-pressed contemporary, Herman Melville, several years later, to offer himself as a country-school teacher. The melancholy and self-sorrow he attributed to his fictional Archie Dean, a young man forced out of New York by the fire of 1835 and forced to teach in a district school, were presumably in part a projection of his own feelings during the several years he spent teaching around at country schools; but Whitman, at least, had the pleasure of returning to the locale of his earliest memories.[5]

His mind, meanwhile, was busily searching for a renewed opportunity for employment in printing, but business conditions in New York remained depressed, and opportunities elsewhere, if anything, were even scarcer. So in 1838, he gathered his resources and resolve and founded his own weekly newspaper, the *Long Islander,* in Huntington, a venture he was later to recall with nostalgic pleasure:

> I had been teaching country school for two or three years in various parts of Suffolk and Queens counties, but liked printing; had been at it while a lad, learn'd the trade of compositor, and was encouraged to start a paper in the region where I was born. I went to New York, bought a press and types, hired some little help, but did most of the work myself, including the presswork. Everything seem'd turning out

well; (only my own restlessness prevented me gradually establishing a permanent property there.) I bought a good horse, and every week went all round the country serving my papers, devoting one day and night to it. I never had happier jaunts.[6]

With his brother George serving as his printer's devil, Whitman got his first taste of printing, editing, and publishing his own paper, which could only have fed his future appetite for journalism.

This situation continued for a year, until he tired of the monotony of the work and sold the paper. His motivation was, no doubt, as he himself later claimed, simply restlessness, the paper with its limited circulation and investment probably having neither earned nor cost him very much money, but his desire to return to the center of printing and publishing activity remaining unappeased. So in May 1839, he tried again to find employment in New York, discovered that doors were still shut, and retreated a second time to Long Island and a new round of country-school teaching assignments. He was also trying his hand at writing, had probably been doing so intermittently for some time, and made a temporary connection as a writer and printer with James Brenton, the editor and publisher of the Long Island *Democrat*. Even after he had left Brenton to resume school teaching, he continued to write periodically for the *Democrat,* which published in 1840–1 his "Sun-Down Papers from the Desk of a School-Master," a series of short, personal essays similar to the "Fragments from a Writing Desk" that Melville had submitted for a brief period the previous year to the local Democratic newspaper of his upstate New York community.

These post-adolescent, juvenile essays are neither particularly interesting nor original – the most salient thing about them, as about the verse of the same period, is their utter conventionality, their teary-eyed tribute to capitalized abstractions – but there are occasional musings and accents which an alert reader can readily identify as foreshadowing the writing of the future author of *Leaves of Grass*. The most self-revealing of these passages indicate that the young man whom his Long Island friends and co-workers, as well as his family, saw in these years as indolent and unmotivated was harboring ambitions and dreams far beyond anything then being attributed to him:

> In good truth, I think the world suffers from this much-bepraised modesty. Who should be a better judge of a man's talents than the man himself? I see no reason why we should let our lights shine under bushels. Yes: I *would* write a book! And who shall say that it might not be a very pretty book? Who knows but that I might do something very respectable?[7]

That Whitman had as yet little idea of what form this "wonderful and ponderous book" might take – the book he was contemplating was apparently a work of moral philosophy rather than of poetry – matters less actually than the fact that his ambitions were then running high, had probably always been running high, and that his mind was hazily posing questions to which fifteen years of experience, growth, and reflection would give definitive answer.

Finally, in the spring of 1841, breaking with schoolteaching and turning his back on Long Island, he made his successful return to New York City. That particular trip across the East River, he might then have hoped but could not have known, was to be of a different, portentous sort from his many crossings of years past; this time he was not merely making his successful return to the big city printing office of his earlier years but also his entrance into a new era in American printing and publishing. Although the book publishing sector had not yet recovered from the effects of the Panic of 1837, journalism in New York City was thriving and expanding as never before in its history. The penny newspaper revolution was in full swing, accompanied by and linked to a vastly expanded readership, a new generation of printing technology, changing editorial policies, and – of most immediate relevance to Whitman – a need for compositors. Circulating side by side with the new, successful penny newspapers were popular literary weeklies, curious hybrid publications neither newspaper nor magazine, which, hawked on the streets by newsboys or mailed to subscribers around the country, competed with both the periodical and the book publishers to capture the large and growing market for fiction and foreign reprints.

It was with the most resourceful of the literary weekly editors, Park Benjamin, whose driving force had made a success of the *New World,* that Whitman found work as a compositor upon his arrival in New York. The bustling atmosphere and rapid-fire cylinder presses of the *New World* printing shop were unlike anything that Whitman had encountered in the small, backward printing offices in which he had previously worked, nor had he encountered anything like the cheap publishing war just then beginning to intensify, the first of its kind in America. Displaying a masthead showing Columbus' setting foot on American soil with Addison's couplet set below, "No pent-up Utica contracts our powers: / For the whole boundless continent is ours," the *New World* explicitly set out to conquer the American literary market. As early as the opening number issued in 1839, the editors informed the public, "'Our country – our whole country' will be our guiding principle; and to the whole country we confidently look for a liberal support and a boundless circulation."[8]

The paper during Whitman's service in 1841 was unquestionably thriving, with a circulation of nearly twenty-five thousand (which Benjamin confidently boasted of soon doubling) and a market encompassing most parts of the country. It offered a mixture of prose, verse, and general intelligence; but its primary selling point was unquestionably its serials, usually taken from the most popular English novelists and speedily printed from proof sheets or early copies acquired by Benjamin's London agent. The *New World* also published that year several complete works in special "leviathan" editions, later called "extras," at prices incomparably below the standard prices set by book publishers. By the spring of 1842, Benjamin took the logical next step of occasionally issuing books in sheets or in paper covers separately from the *New World* for twelve and a half cents (an American shilling) or twenty-five cents – this, in contrast to the standard one dollar or more charged by book publishers. His goal, he announced, was

> the commencement of an entire revolution in the book publishing business, by which, indeed, thousands and tens of thousands of copies of new and popular works, inaccessible to the people at large, will be disseminated, as on the wings of the wind, to the remotest hamlet and cabin of our wide-spread continent. Only think of Bulwer's novel [*Zanoni*] copies of which cost *one dollar* at the bookstores, being published and sold at *twelve and a half cents!* and forwarded to all parts of the country at *newspaper postage.*[9]

By the end of the year, Benjamin was congratulating himself and his readers publicly on their shared success: "The day of costly literature has passed away for ever. Ours is the era of cheap books – an era, which owes its birth to the proprietors of the very journal which you now hold in your hands."[10]

The smooth-talking rhetoric and tender solicitude toward the public were in actuality a veneer for what was basically Benjamin's policy of rapacity, of all-out piracy on foreign authors and cutthroat competition with American rivals. A measure of his ethical standards was his behavior toward Charles Dickens, every pirate's favorite booty, who had visited America in 1842 for, among other reasons, the purpose of pleading for an international copyright to protect himself and other writers against just such unscrupulous foreign publishers as Benjamin. Infuriated by his lack of success and revolted by the voracity and vulgarity he saw in America, Dickens retaliated by having the hero of his next novel, Martin Chuzzlewit, disembark his packet, the *Screw,* in New York harbor to the sights and sounds of dirty newsboys hawking the local papers – the New York *Sewer, Stabber, Family Spy, Rowdy Journal* – to a filth-loving, gossip-mongering public. Benjamin, without the slightest hesitation, responded in kind by immediately pirating *Martin Chuzzlewit,* just as he had previously pirated Dickens' unfavorable account of his American tour, *American Notes,* for readers of the *New World* (or for what Dickens might have thought the real-life readers of the real-life *Sewer*). But Dickens was not alone in his victimization; a quick look around would have showed him that he was in the good company of his countrymen Bulwer, James, Marryat, and others. Likewise, the *New World,* for its part, was not alone in its piracy but was forced to divide the spoils with *Brother Jonathan,* a rival, look-alike literary weekly, and with book publishers such as the Harpers and Careys. By the middle of 1842, an outright price war over foreign reprints had broken out, matching the two rival weeklies individually against each other and collectively against the book publishers, who reacted in fury to the intrusion of newspapers into their territory by dropping their prices to ruinous levels.[11]

Once committed, Benjamin had no choice but to persevere to the limit. He increased the rate of his book publication during the second half of 1842 and of necessity added to his series of "Books for the People" a broader variety of works than the old staple of foreign fiction. Among the new works was a temperance novel he commissioned in order to take advantage of the growing national sentiment for prohibition and grandiosely advertised as a book which "will create a sensation, both for the ability with which it is written, as well as the interest of the subject, and will be universally read and admired. It was written expressly for the *New World,* by one of the best Novelists in this country, with a view to aid the great work of Reform, and rescue Young Men from the demon of Intemperance."[12] The "popular American Author" whose merits he consciously exaggerated was Whitman, whom he knew both as a printer and as a writer, having employed him in his shop and published several of his poems and stories in the *New World* in late 1841. He had also seen a string of Whitman's stories appear in the *Democratic Review,* which Benjamin (like many) thought the outstanding periodical in the United States.

Franklin Evans appeared as a shilling octavo pamphlet in the "Books for the People" series on November 23, 1842, next in order after Dickens' *American Notes.* Whitman, in old age, would tell Traubel that he wrote his novella under the inspiration of liquor and solely for the seventy-five dollars Benjamin offered him, but that claim was pure obfuscation.[13] The Whitman who wrote *Franklin Evans* was incapable of such cynicism; the mawkish story of the young man from the country tempted by the lures of city life was too close to his own psychic experience to have been the work of a hardened professional out purely for the money. Rather, the "temptation" to which he confessed himself as having succumbed in writing the tale was less the offer of money, though doubtless welcome, than the prospect of popular recognition. Indeed, it was Whitman who far more nearly approached the declared idealism of the *New World*'s "Books for the People" series than did Benjamin; he introduced

Franklin Evans with his hope that his book was "not written for the critics, but for *The People*" and concluded with the promise that "if my story meets with that favor which writers are perhaps too fond of relying upon, my readers may hear from me again, in [a] method similar to that which has already made us acquainted."[14] Sales of the tale were probably in the upper part of the ten thousand to twenty thousand copy range of other titles in the *New World* series, which, ironically, would have made it the best selling of Whitman's works in the nineteenth century and the one which most nearly put him, according to Gay Wilson Allen, "on the right road to the kind of expression by which he could establish contact with the masses."[15] Encouraged by its reception, within a month or two he was at work again, true to his word, on a new temperance novel, only part of which has survived.

The year 1842 was an important one in Whitman's professional education and early career; besides the authorship of *Franklin Evans,* he came before the American public a number of times and in a variety of forms. Even before leaving the *New World* pressroom in late 1841, Whitman had begun to place his stories in the *Democratic Review* ("the leading magazine published this side of the Atlantic"), with whose political and cultural nationalism and party ideals he was in fervent agreement, and he continued to write for the review right up to his authorship of *Franklin Evans.* The *Democratic*'s crusading editor, John O'Sullivan, published the leading American writers of the time, so that during 1841–2 Whitman's name regularly appeared beside those of Hawthorne, Longfellow, Bryant, Whittier, and Lowell in belles lettres; Greenough on architecture; Catlin on the Indians; and Downing on landscape gardening. He was also pursuing his poetry, placing several pieces with Benjamin's *New World* during his last months in the pressroom in late 1841, and then, after his break with Benjamin, several more in early 1842 with the arch-rival *Brother Jonathan.* He also published in the latter a vigorous defense of Dickens, newly landed in America and the talk of the entire country, whom he defended against aspersions as – in a significant Whitman phrase – "a democratic writer."[16]

Simultaneously with the freelance writing he was doing for the *Democratic Review* and *Brother Jonathan,* Whitman also began contributing freelance articles to the New York *Aurora,* a new twopenny daily newspaper distinguished from its competitors primarily by its political independence and its eye to New York society. The right man at the right place, Whitman moved into the editorial chair in March in place of its first editor, dismissed for libel. He thus became, at age twenty-two, the junior member of a distinguished New York editorial corps which included Horace Greeley, William Cullen Bryant, Moses Beach, James Gordon Bennett, and Mordechai Noah, with most of whom he would in the following years be on terms of acquaintance or friendship. The importuning but undefined ambitions he had been harboring for the past several years, which he had been compelled to suppress during the years of teaching school or working at the type case setting other people's thoughts into print, now took a specific direction as he assumed editorial control of a Manhattan daily. His enthusiasm and commitment must have been quickly apparent to the readers of the *Aurora,* who could hardly have missed them in Whitman's tête-à-tête editorializing style or in the vigorous manner in which he conducted the paper generally. Overseeing the various operations of a daily newspaper, he assured them, was an "arduous employment":

> The consciousness that several thousand people will look for their *Aurora* as regularly as for their breakfasts, and that they expect to find in it an intellectual repast – something *piquant,* and something solid, and something sentimental, and something humorous – and all dished up in "our own peculiar way" – this consciousness, we say, implies no small responsibility upon a man. Yet it is delightful. Heavy as it weighs, we have no indisposition to "take the responsibility."[17]

Clearly, during the several months of his editorship, Whitman worked faithfully to carry out his responsibility. He committed the paper to the Americanist side in the then raging nativist controversy; spotlighted the sights and attractions of New York ("the heart, the brain, the focus, the main spring, the pinnacle, the extremity, the no more beyond, of the New World"); covered the theater, opera, and other goings-on around town; commented freely about personalities and issues; and, with the self-advertising spirit of 1840s journalism, boosted the merits of cheap journalism generally and of the *Aurora* in particular.

Whitman's *Aurora* was like most of its competitors in carrying the strong impress of its editor's personality – with Whitman, only more so. Readers who could have discerned the lineaments of Greeley's personality behind the tone and policy of the *Tribune* or of Bennett's behind those of the *Herald,* had they been interested, might have been treated to revealing glimpses not only of the *Aurora* editor's ideas but also of the editor himself, who obviously took pleasure in parading himself before his readers' eyes. The editor of the neighboring Brooklyn *Eagle* was quick to notice this trait, praising the "marked change for the better" he spotted since the beginning of Whitman's tenure but criticizing "a dash of egotism" he observed in Whitman's editorial conduct.[18] That dash of egotism, in fact, was one of the most salient characteristics of Whitman's editorial style, beginning at the time of his service with the *Aurora* and continuing through a full decade of journalistic activity. Though surrounded by leading figures in the arts, politics, finance, and journalism, as well as by larger, more influential editors and newspapers, Whitman was curiously preoccupied with himself and with the merits of his own newspaper. Whether easing himself into the familiar editorial "we," taking his readers alongside himself on jaunts through the city, sharing with them his ambition to make the *Aurora* "*the* paper of the city," or bringing them into the editorial office to see the inner workings of a daily newspaper, Whitman right from the first made it his practice to personalize himself and his relations with his readers to a degree exceptional even in a day of editor-dominated journalism.

Lacking a lead editorial for the paper, Whitman knew how to reverse the situation by making the lack of material the subject for the day's editorial. Or lacking ideas or inspiration, he could always fall back on himself or his activity that day for material. One of the more interesting editorials he wrote for the *Aurora*, for example, began with a self-portrait and a description of his daily stroll down Broadway:

> Then finding it impossible to do anything either in the way of "heavy business," or humor, we took our cane, (a heavy, dark beautifully polished, hook ended one,) and our hat, (a plain, neat fashionable one, from Banta's, 130 Chatham street, which we got gratis, on the strength of giving him this puff,) and sauntered forth to have a stroll down Broadway to the Battery. Strangely enough, nobody stared at us with admiration – nobody said "there goes *the* Whitman, of Aurora!" – nobody ran after us to take a better, and second better look – no ladies turned their beautiful necks and smiled at us – no apple women became pale with awe – no news boys stopped, and trembled, and took off their hats, and cried "behold the man what uses up the Great Bamboozle [Park Benjamin, with whom Whitman was then feuding]!" – no person wheeled out of our path deferentially – but on we went, swinging our stick, (the before mentioned dark and polished one,) in our right hand – and with our left hand tastily thrust in its appropriate pocket, in our frock coat, (a gray one.)

Several paragraphs of observation and chitchat follow, before he concludes in a spirit similar to the one with which he begins:

> Then we came up, and out, and along Broadway, to whence we started. And for the next two or three hours, we possess no recollection of having done anything in particular. And at half past 8, P.M. (fifteen minutes before this present writing) the chilling consciousness came over us that we hadn't written anything for a leader. And so we concocted the foregoing (what were you about, at half past 8, last night, dear reader?)
>
> And all we have to add is, that if you read it over a second time you will find more meaning in it, than you might at first imagine.[19]

There was more meaning in this than he himself then knew. The seem-ingly informal method – at that time it probably was informal – of foregrounding his self-portraiture so boldly as to push his self, as it were, out of the frame of the sketch toward the reader was to evolve into one of the methods which distinguished his poetry of the next decade.

The earliest surviving daguerreotype of Whitman almost certainly dates from this period, and it corresponds quite closely to this and other verbal self-portraits Whitman drew in the pages of the *Aurora*. It shows Whitman as a conspicuously well-dressed and well-groomed, dreamy-eyed young man flaunting a polished cane and a stylish hat, a dandy clearly preoccupied with his own image.[20] Whitman had followed the coming of the new art to America several years earlier with unusual interest: "We recollect that, when this art was introduced in New York, (by the late professor Gouraud, we believe,) we saw many of the first specimens."[21] If he was among the first American writers to take an interest in photography, he was also certainly one of the first to have his portrait captured by the new process, sitting for the camera several years before it became the rage of the cities, the democratic equivalent to having one's portrait done in oils. This early acquaintance with the camera was more than a simple coincidence, since Whitman seems virtually from the first to have been possessed of an uncanny, intuitive understanding of the image-creating possibilities of the new art. In the decades to follow, he would become – or, more accurately, would make himself – the most frequently and flamboyantly photographed of American poets and the most astute manipulator among them of the art of photography for the purposes of poetry. He was fully aware of this fact; as he was to comment wryly to Horace Traubel in 1888, "I have been photographed, photo-graphed, photographed, until the cameras themselves are tired of me."[22]

All this, of course, was still far beyond the vision of the twenty-two-year-old editor, whose enjoyment of his current position was virtually palpable. Within weeks of his editorship, he was able to share congrat-ulations with his readers in reporting a gain in the paper's circulation, and throughout his tenure he worked diligently to promote the interests of the paper. A man of strong tastes, Whitman knew how to utilize his position with the paper in ways which allowed him to cultivate his favorite pleasures; as "Whitman of the *Aurora*" he could command free tickets to operas, plays, and lectures, which he frequently did. His po-sition also gave him a forum from which to speak out on issues important to him, some of which are particularly interesting in view of his future career. He came out in favor of international copyright, advocated a national drama, gave his opinion about the importance of cheap jour-nalism to society ("Among newspapers, the penny press is the same as common schools among seminaries of education"), and consistently stressed the value of Americanism in politics and culture. But for all his idealism and dedication, his connection with the *Aurora* did not last even the three months of his predecessor; he quarreled with his publishers over the loss of the paper's political independence and resigned in late April.[23]

He was still at the time selling his stories to the *Democratic Review* and trying to form a connection with a Boston magazine, but selling occasional stories to the periodicals would not have satisfied his ambition any more than it would have met his financial needs.[24] By June, he had returned to full-time journalism with Dillon and Hooper, publishers of *Brother Jonathan,* as writer or editor (his accounts conflict) for their daily newspaper, the *Evening Tattler,* and shortly thereafter became editor of their *Sunday Times.*[25] Complete files of each, as of most of Whitman's early papers, are lacking; but from the few surviving issues one can infer that Whitman was continuing his previous pattern of personal journalism, describing himself and his activities, following the social, cultural and political life of the times, and publishing an occasional poem.

His extensive journalistic activity of 1842 was having a certain effect. His stories were attracting notice and some were even being reprinted. The publishers of the *Evening Tattler* issued a prospectus for a weekly edition of their paper in which they used Whitman's name alongside those of Bryant and Hawthorne in order to attract potential subscribers.[26] The November 9 issue of the New York *Herald* listed Whitman (misnaming him "Wm. Whitman") among the fifty-two leading newspaper writers of New York, a compliment Whitman would have particularly appreciated since it was given in the context of statements about the rising glory of journalism in harmony with his own ideological convictions. At the same time, the *New World* was touting his forthcoming *Franklin Evans* as having been written by a "Popular American Author," and the story was to be reviewed widely upon its appearance by the leading papers of New York and Brooklyn.

Taken all in all, 1842 was an active, fruitful year for Whitman, only recently removed from the printing office. A published poet and story writer, author of a popular novelette, occasional essayist, and moderately influential newspaper editor, he had quickly established himself as a competent literary professional, one of the growing number of writers who made their living by writing for the new middle-class magazines and newspapers. Though less facile with the pen than Nathaniel Willis, less aggressive in marketing himself than Park Benjamin, and less successful in using personal acquaintances to advance himself professionally than Rufus Griswold, Whitman managed to earn himself a modest reputation among his peers and contemporaries. If he was forced at times into a hand-to-mouth existence and to scramble from job to job, he was only doing what more talented and experienced magazinists, such as Poe, were also doing in adapting themselves to the helter-skelter, as yet unsystematized ways of the new literary culture, in which positions were often tenuous and ventures frequently failed. Such was to be the pattern of Whitman's activity throughout his journalistic career.

During the rest of the decade, his professional life tracked a similar course to, if without quite the success of, the one he followed in 1842. His own notebook jotting gives a sense of the volatility of his career during these years:

> Edited *Tattler* in summer of '42
> Edited *Statesman* in Spring of '43
> Edited *Democrat* in Summer of 44
> Wrote for *Dem Review, American Review,* and *Columbian Magazines* during 45 and 6 – as previously.
> About the latter part of February '46, commenced editing the Brooklyn *Eagle* – continued till last of January '48.
> Left Brooklyn for New Orleans, Feb. 11th '48.[27]

But these and other notes he left of the period are at best only fragmentary; they give little of the substance or flavor of his activities during these years and leave gaps in their continuity. And since files of most of the newspapers with which he was connected are no longer extant, some of the holes are unfillable. It is known, however, that Whitman worked – as editor, correspondent, or penny-a-liner – on a number of other newspapers before beginning his two-year editorship of the Brooklyn *Eagle* in 1846.[28] He edited the short-lived daily, the New York *Statesman,* in the spring of 1843, and then worked briefly as a reporter for Beach's New York *Sun,* one of the most popular penny dailies in Manhattan. In early 1844, he resumed selling stories to the magazines, primarily for the newly founded *Columbian Lady's and Gentleman's Magazine,* a monthly which obviously imitated the pretensions and tastes but never approached the popularity of *Graham's* and *Godey's.* The editor of the *Columbian,* John Inman, informed his readers that he, as editor, would be conducting the magazine in the belief that "there was much more talent in the country than had yet won or even sought for itself a place on the muster-roll of popular applause, and seeking as one of his principal objects the discovery of this talent, with a view to its production before the public, he has had the satisfaction of bringing forward several writers of admirable cleverness, as yet unknown to fame, but certain of acquiring a distinguished reputation."[29] Inman's editorial philosophy would have perfectly suited the aspirations of Whitman in 1844, who was among the magazine's most frequent contributors during its first year of publication.

But in the summer of that year, the political animal in Whitman awakened to the challenge to manage a new, partisan daily newspaper, the New York *Democrat*, through the tumultuous presidential and gubernatorial campaigns of 1844. After the paper was abandoned following the successful conclusion of the campaigns, Whitman went to work for a time as a writer for Nathaniel Willis and George Morris' *Mirror*, where he made the acquaintance of Poe, also there between editorial stints. In early 1845, he resumed his magazine writing. He published stories in both the *Democratic Review* and the *American Review*, its Whig counterpart; but the primary recipient of his contributions was the newly founded *Aristidean* of Thomas Dunn English. A well-printed critical monthly with pretensions to excellence, the *Aristidean* lasted barely a year, during which time Whitman was one of its most frequent and respected fiction contributors.

In August of that year, he made an important personal and career move, leaving New York after four years of service to the metropolitan printing shops, newspapers, and magazines to return to Brooklyn. Part of his motivation for the move, no doubt, was sentimental, his desire to end the absence from his family, which had recently returned to Brooklyn after a decade's residence on Long Island; but it is just as likely that Whitman had also tired of the insecurity, frustrations, and ill pay of his professional life in New York and was looking for a fresh start in changed surroundings. Several years before, he had concluded a poem with the injunction, directed as much to himself as to others,

> No turning back! O, youth, a weary road
> Spreads out before you! Hidden grief lurks there,
> And burning fires of vice lie smoldering there,
> And disappointment's clutching fangs wait there;
> But far ahead, up in the height of heaven,
> Glitters a star. O, let thy constant gaze
> Be fixed upon that star; step not away,
> But gazing on the brightness of the guide,
> Press forward to the end and falter not![30]

A person who had experienced as many professional disappointments as had Whitman would have had numerous occasions to fortify himself with this advice, but returning to Brooklyn in 1845 was not a turning back exactly but merely one of the redirections he was forced periodically to make in charting the still unclear course of his career. In Brooklyn, at least, he could take comfort in familiarity in making a fresh start, and he quickly took advantage of his connections by becoming a contributor to the Brooklyn *Evening Star*, still controlled by the Spooners with whom he had served his apprenticeship during the midthirties.

Many of the articles he wrote for the *Star* dealt with matters of education; but even in those which did not, Whitman played the role of civic instructor to the citizenry of Brooklyn, the same kind of advisory function he had frequently taken when in control of his own papers (and, for that matter, in his periodical poetry and fiction). Drawing on his experience as a teacher, writer, editor, and opera and theater goer, he was free with his opinions on a wide variety of issues. In article after article, he put his readers through a course of instruction on manners, pedagogy, civics, and popularized culture. Much of what he had to say was conventional, so conventional that he sounded at times as though he were handing down to the young a prude's version of the ten commandments – "Loaf not!" "Swear not!" "Smoke not!" "rough and tumble not!" The tone and manner of some of his pieces, however, were strikingly idiosyncratic, and the intensity of conviction in the power of communication one finds in them was wholly Whitman's, as in this piece of typically Whitmanesque advice for the young:

> Boy, or young man, whose eyes hover over these lines! how much of your leisure time do you give to *loafing*? What vulgar habits of smoking cigars, chewing tobacco, or making frequent use of blasphemous or obscene language have you begun to form? What associations and appetites are you idly falling into, that future years will ripen in wickedness or shame? Consider these questions as addressed, not to everybody in general, but to *you*, in particular – and answer them honestly to your own heart. The one who speaks to you through this printed page, never has spoken, and probably never will speak, to you in any other way; but it would be a deep and abiding joy for him to know that he had awakened wholesome reflection in your mind, even if it lasts for only a passing five minutes.[31]

Several weeks later, Whitman returned to his idea of effective communication, repeating with emphasis: "The great mistake of advice addressed in print to youth, is, that the reader takes the application in too general a way. We have, therefore, to repeat what we observed in a former article, – our wish that the boy or young man now perusing these lines should think they are meant for *him*, in particular – as far as they can apply."[32]

Whitman continued to supply the *Star* with his articles on a more or less regular basis for half a year, but in all likelihood his political views made his position with the Whig paper delicate. When the editor of the rival Brooklyn *Eagle* died in late February, Whitman eagerly accepted the editorship of the paper and assumed his new position within days. There thus began what he would later recall as "one of the pleasantest sits of my life – a good owner, good pay, and easy work and hours" with the official Democratic newspaper of Kings County and one of the party's most important organs in the region.[33] The credentials Whitman could offer his new publisher, Isaac Van Anden, were impressive – years of editorships of newspapers in New York, unquestioned loyalty and energetic service to the Democratic party, a reputation as a gifted writer – but so, too, was the situation he entered. The *Eagle,* founded in 1841, was a thriving paper, growing with Brooklyn and enjoying the patronage and prestige of the state party, which in 1844 had played an instrumental role in placing James Polk in the White House.

The two years of Whitman's editorship of the *Eagle* coincided with a dynamic, tumultuous period both locally and nationally; but Whitman unhesitatingly accepted his new responsibility with much the same enthusiasm and idealism he had brought into previous editorships, if slightly tempered now by greater maturity. He set forth his editorial credo with his usual forthrightness as the leading article of June 1, the force of his personality overstraining the convention of the editorial "we" as he made his formal pact with the community and announced his hopes for the paper:

> We really feel a desire to talk on many subjects, to *all* the people of Brooklyn; and it *ain't* their ninepences we want so much either. There is a curious kind of sympathy (haven't you ever thought of it before?) that arises in the mind of a newspaper conductor with the public he serves. He gets to *love* them. Daily communion creates a sort of brotherhood and sisterhood between the two parties... And we want as many readers of the *Brooklyn Eagle* – even unto the half of Long Island – as possible, that we may increase the number of such friends. For are not those who daily listen to us, friends?

The responsibilities of a "true editor" and of a well-run newspaper to their community of readers, he went on, were a matter of paramount importance:

> With all and any drawbacks, however, much good can always be done, with such potent influence as a well circulated newspaper. To wield that influence, is a great responsibility. There are numerous noble reforms that have yet to be pressed upon the world. People are to be schooled, in opposition perhaps to their long established ways of thought. – In politics, too, the field of improvement is wide enough yet; the harvest is large, and waiting to be reaped – and each paper, however humble, may do good in the ranks.[34]

Whitman, naturally, showed no hesitation about his own qualifications as a "true editor"; and in truth, given the limitations inherent in editing a daily newspaper six days a week (as well as a weekly edition for the country) in which the editorials, much of the copy, selection of extracts from other papers and magazines for reprinting in the *Eagle,* review columns, and proofreading were the responsibility of the editor, he succeeded in turning out a consistently presentable newspaper. Not normally one to overextend himself in matters of routine, Whitman seems to have been reasonably industrious in fulfilling his responsibilities with the *Eagle*, something he could not have done had he found his job to be one merely of drudgery.

Perched mornings high above Fulton Street in the editorial "sanctum," Whitman enjoyed his favored position in looking down on the busy ferry slip, crowded streets, and commercial life of the city below. Ever the local booster, Whitman regularly reported to his readers on the local doings of Brooklyn's churches, schools, shops, streets, cultural facilities, and public buildings. Readers of the *Eagle* could expect to be kept apprised daily of the latest cultural doings, construction and transportation projects, crimes, and general gossip in their community, as well as in what Whitman half-deprecatingly, half-enviously called the "Gomorrah" across the river. But if it was Whitman's intention to make the *Eagle* a source of information and entertainment to his readers, it was also a high priority with him to make it a source of instruction and edification. In addition to keeping them up to date on the latest occurrences in the community and in the nation, he attempted to polish their manners, improve their taste, educate their minds, and correct their views on everything from politics to culture. He used his editorials frequently to offer advice, suggestions, and opinions to his readers on a wide variety of matters: he advised workingmen to hang prints on their walls and women to cultivate flowers, instructed ferry passengers on the safest way to board and exit and ferry conductors on the safest way to operate the ferries, exhorted everyone (but especially workingmen) to oppose the expansion of slavery into the territories, encouraged the patronage of home literature, lectured concert goers on correct behavior at concerts, urged all Democrats each election time to vote, and called on the civic authorities to clean the streets, light the lamps, and preserve the city's beauty with parks.

All this might have sounded gratuitous to readers had they perceived the remarks as in any way condescending. But one of Whitman's strengths as an editor was his ability to identify instinctively with his readers; the sincerity of his sense of service to readers of the *Eagle* must have been virtually palpable. Newspaper work, he several times told his readers, was for him no ordinary professional function but a kind of "communion": "We feel a hearty sympathy with each woman, man, and child, who communes with us, and we with them, every day; for what is giving up one's attention to another's thoughts, even in print, but communion?"[35] It would have been difficult to doubt the sincerity of an editor who spoke as openly and as often as did Whitman of the pleasure he took in his work: "That the labors of an editor are hard enough, is an undoubted fact. But for our part, we *like them*. There are many pleasures and gratifications in the position of an editor."[36]

One of those pleasures, dating back to his days at the *Aurora*, was his habit of guiding his readers into the office of the paper and of sharing with them its policies and achievements. He was an adept in the art of inclusion in journalism long before he learned to make it an integral part of his poetry. His office was their office, readers of the paper could easily infer. But he also tried to make the paper of service in a more general, national way. By now a seasoned veteran of journalistic and political skirmishes, Whitman guided the *Eagle* to stands on the important issues of the day. On such major political issues as the Oregon boundary dispute, the Mexican War, tariff, slavery in the territories, states' rights, and immigration; Whitman naturally set the paper on partisan Democratic lines. As internal dissension began to split the party into opposing factions, however, Whitman's radical views increasingly carried him away from the conservative party establishment which controlled the publication of the paper.

At the same time, Whitman was using the paper to express his personal views on matters more specifically related to American culture than to the American polity. Although the *Eagle* was still first and foremost a partisan paper, it became under Whitman a more literary-oriented publication than it had been under his predecessor or than it would be under his successor. This change in its character was entirely Whitman's doing, an expression of the faith that Whitman held in common with many cultural nationalists of the forties that, in the words of a writer for the *Democratic Review*, "the spirit of Literature and the spirit of Democracy are one."[37] In order to promote this idea, he introduced a literary miscellany of one or two columns on the front page of the *Eagle* (something he had hoped but did not have time to do in the *Aurora*), ran periodic reviews on a wide range of books and periodicals, provided frequent coverage of the stage, opera, museums and galleries, and lecture halls in Brooklyn and New York, and commented broadly on the state of the arts in the United States. Rightly understood in correlation with his declared special relations with the readers of the *Eagle*, the literary-cultural ideas and opinions he expressed in these columns offer the single best surviving source of information generally on Whitman as a journalist-literary professional in the late 1840s and in particular on his maturing views about the relation between democracy and culture, shortly before he began his gradual transformation from journalist to poet.

The literary miscellany he featured each day was clipped from the pages of the exchange newspapers and magazines he regularly "perused" in the *Eagle*'s offices. His taste for this column, in line with the pattern of his own reading and thinking, was broadly eclectic. He would "favor" his readers sometimes with reprinted short pieces by such leading writers as Hawthorne, Poe, Bryant, Longfellow (frequently), Whittier, and Irving, or more often with those by the popular sentimental and moralistic writers of the day (including himself), praising the one indiscriminately with the other. "We think our *First Page* will be found to repay the attention even of the most fastidious taste. – Reader! always look at it" – blandishments of this sort would regularly appear above the day's lead editorial, advertising works from the best and worst writers alike. He similarly made his periodic book review columns into a catchall miscellany, encompassing a wide range of works from pietistic to poetic, popular to esoteric. His remarks, obviously made in conformity with the belief he stated that "the principle of 'satisfying all tastes' . . . is the true principle for a newspaper," were normally brief, descriptive, and hortatory, only occasionally evaluative, and rarely, when that, negative.[38] In the same columns or as separate items, he also favorably reviewed the popular magazines, singling out for particular attention and praise Caroline Kirkland's undistinguished *Union Magazine* (to which he sent a contribution not long after he left the *Eagle*).

Putting sentimental poets on the same level with Carlyle, Milton, and Goethe may not say much for the state of Whitman's critical judgment; but his confusion was, in part, also the confusion of his contemporaries. The miscellaneous grouping of disparate works in review columns was a common feature of midnineteenth-century journalistic criticism, critical taste having been scrambled by the proliferation of published works and the expansion of readership of recent years. Even a more discriminating critic than Whitman, such as Poe, could make what today seem egregious lapses of taste in reviewing contemporary writing. Whitman, moreover, also had a self-conscious justification for the pseudocatholicity of his taste; "All books have their office," he said in his review of Melville's *Omoo*, an office which for him could be self-reform as legitimately as aesthetic appreciation. Forty years later, he was still expressing this view when he warned future readers about the reading of his own works: "No one will get at my verses who insists upon viewing them as a literary performance, or attempt at such performance, or as aiming mainly toward art or aestheticism."[39]

This is not to say that his reviews and editorials were uniformly bland or his intentions unvaryingly popularizing. Whitman's personality was too strong ever to be restrained completely or diverted solely into attempts to educate the "intelligent masses" or to "polish the 'Common People.'" Like every newspaper he controlled, the *Eagle* invariably took on some of the coloring of Whitman's personality, and it is interesting today precisely where the shading of his thoughts and personality most fully comes through. One of the more interesting pieces he wrote for the *Eagle* was a review of Goethe's autobiography, written with an eloquence a measure above the normally undistinguished style of his journalism, in which he anticipated the character of his own poetry in praising Goethe for writing "Life" rather than "Literature":

> What a gain it would be, if we could forego some of the heavy tomes, the fruit of an age of toil and scientific study, for the simple easy *truthful* narrative of the existence and experience of a man of genius, – how his mind unfolded in his earliest years – the impressions things made upon him – how and where and when the religious sentiment dawned in him – what he thought of God before he was inoculated with books' ideas – the development of his soul – when he first loved – the way circumstance imbued his nature, and did him good, or worked him ill, – with all the long train of occurrences, adventures, mental processes, exercises within, and trials without, which go to make up the man – for *character* is the man, after all. Such a work, fully and faithfully performed, would be a rare treasure![40]

Although he was still seasoning his journalism with the "dash of egotism" with which he had been charged several years earlier by his predecessor at the *Eagle,* he was clearly not thinking about himself as the author or subject of such a work when he made these remarks in 1846.

Nor was he thinking specifically about himself when he wrote the following editorial, distinguished more for its enthusiasm than for the originality of its thought:

> At this hour in some part of the earth, it may be that the delicate scraping of a pen over paper, like the nibbling of little mice, is at work which shall show its results sooner or later in the convulsion of the social or political world. Amid penury and destitution, unknown and unnoticed, a man may be toiling on the completion of a book destined to gain acclamations, reiterated again and again, from admiring America and astonished Europe! Such is the way, and such the magic of the pen.[41]

To have seen his own writing of recent years, some of which he was reprinting on the front page of the *Eagle,* in stark isolation would have done little to encourage Whitman to see himself in this role. But there is really no reason to believe that he did. As editor of the *Eagle,* he was too caught up in his attempt to put the paper at the service of "literary Democracy" to have been concerned overly with his own writing. Journalistically, he was often capable during his *Eagle* years of looking broadly and impersonally outside of himself.

"What a world there is, after all, in *books!*" he exclaimed one day in the paper in reading through the catalogue of Harper and Brothers, "O how those little rustling leaves – those dumb letters – enwrap a creation in their scope!" His admiration, he went on to say, was not limited to writers but extended to the producers of books: "We say that *all* books do good, and have their office. And there is not a nobler sphere of occupation than that which ushers them into the world. Then may heaven bless the manufacturers of books! say we. Not, of course, that we mean any less regard to the *writers* of books; but it really is often forgotten that there are printers and publishers too."[42] Still nearly a decade away from his own emergence as a writer and his own dealings with book publishers, he gave his high valuation of books and book culture: "At the present age, mind is moulded nearly altogether from books – and they who make books and usher them before the public, have human minds in their power, as the potter the shape of the vessel to be formed from the clay he moulds."[43]

The faith he frequently expressed in the power of books to work for the communal good he was also attributing in his *Eagle* articles to the other arts with which he was familiar. One of his favorite functions during his two years with the *Eagle* was to take advantage of his position and to make the rounds, which he seems almost to have done on a daily basis, of the various cultural centers and facilities to be found in Brooklyn and Manhattan. Freed by early afternoon from his editorial duties, he spent many of his afternoons and evenings during his *Eagle* years, as had been and would continue to be his custom as long as he resided in proximity to Manhattan, in attendance at plays, concerts, lectures, exhibitions, and art and daguerreotype galleries, the impressions of which he enjoyed sharing the next day with his readers. Worked up by what he saw, he was full of zeal for the potentiality the various arts might have for an informed and educated citizenry open and prepared to receive them.

To effect this, to make the *Eagle* an instrument of cultural nationalism for the local population, was clearly one of his chief editorial priorities. He urged publishers to publish and readers to patronize the works of American authors: "Let those who read, (and in this country who does not read?) no more condescend to patronize an inferior foreign author, when they have so many respectable writers at home. Shall Hawthorne get a paltry *seventy-five dollars* for a two volume work – shall real American genius shiver with neglect – while the public run after this foreign trash?"[44] He came out in favor of international copyright for native authors. He called for a genuine American drama, one to replace the second-rate English plays usually appearing in the New York theaters, and for an honest drama criticism freed from the reigning system of paid puffery. He popularized as best he could the arts of painting, photography, and music and spoke of their "value" to his readers. He was particularly insistent with regard to music, to which he was himself unusually receptive: "To spread a capacity and fondness for music among the masses were to refine and polish them in the truest sense."[45] A subscription to Whitman's *Eagle,* in short, provided his readers with an inexpensive ticket to a long-running course in culture, a course shaped to the needs of the newly emergent democratic public.

Whitman, true to form, was at the opera on the election night in November 1847 when the Democratic voters of Kings County, whom he had been urging for weeks to overlook their differences over the Wilmot Proviso and other issues, ignored calls for party unity and helped to vote a slate of Whigs into municipal office. Badly misinterpreting as a temporary aberration what was in actuality an early sign of the coming fissure in the party and in the nation, Whitman told his readers the next day that their party had lost because it needed more, not less, radicalism. That view, as he stated it more forcefully in the weeks to come, distanced him from his publisher and party establishment, and finally in January it cost him his job.

His departure from the *Eagle* in early 1848 has generally been seen as constituting a turning point in Whitman's career, but that seems to me a questionable view. He was as much a working journalist after his firing as before it, and his first impulse would surely have been to look for another editorship. The idea that his exit from the *Eagle* office led him on his first steps toward the writing of *Leaves of Grass* is dramatically fetching, good for spicing biographical accounts of his career, but it is not very likely. *Leaves of Grass* was still the better part of a decade before him. To take this view, furthermore, is to look away from the very real connectedness between his conception of his journalistic role in the 1840s and of his poetic role in the 1850s and to ignore the common conditions which underlay them both. Whether Whitman was already composing his thoughts into verse by the end of his tenure at the *Eagle* is an open question, although my own opinion is that he was not. But I do think it is clear that some of the most important of the ideas and ideals which would underlie his poetry were already present in his journalism; without the fervent cultural nationalism, faith in the persuasive power of the written word, and sensitivity to the terms of a broad-based mass culture he was writing into his *Eagle* journalism, there could have been no *Leaves of Grass* – at least, no *Leaves of Grass* as it appeared in 1855.

But at age twenty-nine, he was still not and did not yet think of himself as being primarily a poet. More likely, he thought of himself as a younger version of the distinguished journalist-poet with whom he had become friendly during his editorship, William Cullen Bryant: "Off and on, then, as time passed, we met and chatted together. I thought him very sociable in his way, and a man to become attached to. We were both walkers, and when I worked on *The Eagle* newspaper, in Brooklyn, he several times came over, middle of afternoons, and we took rambles miles long, till dark, in company."[46] Bryant had years before virtually given up his early dedication to poetry when he entered the world of New York journalism, and by the time of their acquaintance he was devoting himself primarily to the affairs of his influential Democratic paper, the New York *Evening Post*. As they strolled across Brooklyn and out into the countryside, talking about politics and travels, Whitman, always a hero worshipper, might well have compared his own unsubstantiated aspirations with Bryant's solid achievements. What he could not have foreseen, however, was the fact that he was soon to be embarking on a career path which would run parallel to Bryant's, but in the opposite direction.[47]

4

"I am a writer, for the press and otherwise"

Whitman's career during the first years after his departure from the *Eagle* ran the more or less haphazard course of years past of movement between various editorships, or when these were lacking, between freelancing stints. After 1851, he gradually, although never entirely, retreated from professional journalism and from the public sphere generally.

Within days of his break with the *Eagle,* Whitman was already exploring the possibility of returning to journalism. Just as he had started a Democratic sheet in the presidential election year of 1844, so he now considered a similar move in early 1848 in order to bring his ideas and beliefs before the public. The New York *Tribune* of January 28, 1848, reported him as the designated editor of a new newspaper planned by the disaffected radical Democrats of Brooklyn, with whom Whitman was on close terms; but before these plans could be put into effect, Whitman was off on an alternative gambit.[1] Between acts of a play he was attending the evening of February 9 at the Broadway Theater, he made the acquaintance of a New Orleans newspaper publisher, J. E. McClure, come North to staff his projected newspaper. McClure offered Whitman a job within minutes; and Whitman, for his part, unemployed, unattached, and undoubtedly predisposed to see with his own eyes the charming, exotic Southern city which had been vividly described in a series of articles to the *Eagle* by his Brooklyn artist friend Theodore Gould, as quickly accepted.[2]

The New Orleans episode, whose importance was romanticized by early Whitman biographers and has been emphasized by most of his modern biographers in order to explain the radical discontinuities they see between Whitman as a forties journalist and as a fifties poet, was actually only an exhilarating three-month interlude in Whitman's still directionless career. New Orleans in spring undeniably enchanted him – the South was always to draw out the latent sensuousness in his nature – and sailing down the open waterways of the West certainly filled out his imagination. But taken all in all, the trip probably did little more for Whitman than, as Gay Wilson Allen has concluded, to have "given him a sense of space, natural resources, and potential strength in the fast-growing nation."[3] Whitman took in the open spaces and novel experiences as eagerly as he took in everything, but it seems to me extremely unlikely that the young man who returned to his family in Brooklyn that May more than ever the successor to his aging father as its chief provider and to the same journalistic and political circles in which he had been active before his trip came back a radically transformed man, or one committed to a new plan for his life. Nor does his writing during these months, the place which would most likely register any sudden change of sensibility, reveal major changes, only a slightly greater freedom from conventionalism and an increased openness to experience.

Upon his return to Brooklyn, he was soon deeply involved in radical Democratic politics. Free now to follow his political ideals, he became an active member of the new Free Soil party, which disaffected anti-slavery leaders (including his editor friends, Alden Spooner and William Cullen Bryant) from the two major parties came together to form as a third-party alternative. He attended the national convention of the party in August as a delegate from Brooklyn, and early the next month, with the backing of local Free Soilers, he began the publication of the Brooklyn *Freeman,* a weekly, two-page party paper. On the front page of the opening issue, he declared his desire to bring out his paper within a couple of weeks as a daily, but that was as far as he got, since the *Freeman* office and all its equipment, uninsured, were destroyed the following night by fire. By the time he resumed publication in autumn, the election was lost.

Undaunted, Whitman energetically revived the paper in November and even managed, true to his original hope, to transform it into a daily early the next year. With his paper issuing every day neatly printed on a Napier press and with the publicity attending his early support of Senator Thomas Hart Benton of Missouri for president, Whitman was once again launched into the stream of current affairs with his customary exuberance. Now approaching his thirtieth birthday, he was as dreamily ambitious as ever, airily remarking one day in the paper on his prospects of a four-thousand-dollar annual salary and of a well-established newspaper business, a dream which has more the sound of Walter than of Walt Whitman.[4] But political reality, as it often had before, again defied his vision; he failed to foresee the possibility of a reconciliation between the warring factions of the Democratic party, and when it came in September 1849, he resigned from the *Freeman* in principled objection.

Unphased by a new round of unemployment, Whitman returned temporarily to freelancing that fall. He contracted with a progressive New

York weekly, the *Sunday Dispatch,* to provide it with a series of personal travel sketches and miscellaneous observations, a favorite genre with Whitman throughout the decade. Putting his favorite trip, the trans-Long Island jaunt to Greenport, into print, he wrote his "Letters from a Travelling Bachelor" in late 1849 during the interval of a season between editorial positions resigned and accepted. Although written with his usual journalistic speed and imprecision, these sketches have a degree of vivacity, freshness, and freedom from conventionality not at all common in his more usually pedestrian, at times even slovenly, journalistic pieces of earlier years. These quickly drawn, animated sketches of Long Island folk and folkways, of fishing on the bay, midnight parties and cruises, local customs and characters; or back home, of the passing sights glimpsed in the streets and buildings and on the rivers of the city, sparkle with energy and light.

Perhaps the most impressive description among the sketches was the one he gave from different angles in two separate letters of the scene on New York's waterways, always a favorite sight with him and the incitement to some of his best pieces of prose and poetic reportage. In a November letter, he described the view as seen while strolling on the walkway above the Croton Reservoir, one of the city's finest. His pleasure at the unrestricted scope across time and place broke out into excited bursts of rhythmic prose:

> A hundred years hence, I often imagine, what an appearance that walk will present, on a fine summer afternoon! You and I, reader, and quite all the people who are now alive, won't be much thought of then; but the world will be just as jolly, and the sun will shine as bright, and the rivers off there – the Hudson on one side and the East on the other – will slap along their green waves, precisely as now; and other eyes will look upon them about the same as we do.[5]

He returned to this setting the next month, when he devoted his letter to describing the ferries he had been riding for years between the two most important ports of his life, Manhattan and Brooklyn. Following up his observation that numerous travel books about the passage between the Old World and the New had been published but that "we know of no work – at least we feel sure none has yet been issued by the Harpers, Appletons, or any of our great publishers – describing a voyage across the Fulton Ferry," he took pen in hand and led his readers on a personally guided crossing of the river:

> Who has crossed the East River and not looked with admiration on the beautiful view afforded from the middle of the stream? The forests of the New York shipping, lining the shores as far as one can see them – the tall spire of Trinity looming far up over all the other objects –

various other spires – the tops of the trees on the Battery and in the Parks – these we have left behind us. In front stands Brooklyn – Brooklyn the beautiful! The Heights stretch along in front, lined now with dwellings for nearly the whole extent; but with space still left for a Public Promenade, if it be applied to that purpose *soon* . . .

On the other side our eyes behold a still more varied scene. Governor's Island, in shape like a well proportioned wart, looks green even at this season of the year; and those straight, regularly planted poplars are in perfect accordance with the military character of the place. Far to the distance is Staten Island, and the Jersey shore. The Battery Point is hidden by the masts of the shipping.

A moving panorama is upon all parts of the waters. Sail craft and steamboats are in every direction. Observe, too, the dexterity with which our pilot plies between the crowd that cross his way.[6]

One can already begin to trace in these passages the lineaments of the future "Crossing Brooklyn Ferry": the scene on the river with the viewer positioned in midstream, the poet's expansive vision projecting across geography and through time and his direct address to the reader, even rudimentary attempts at parallelism and cataloguing – even if there is as yet no systematic or self-conscious use of the poetic technique Whitman would develop of mobilizing the scene, the spectator, and the reader as one. The last and the most engaging sketches he published in the 1840s, the "Letters from a Travelling Bachelor" reveal Whitman at the turn of the decade drawing on genuine sources of power but still unaware of where they might lead him.

On the eve of the new decade, Whitman once again returned to full-time journalism. Five years had passed since he last edited a Manhattan paper, but he eagerly accepted when offered the editorship of the New York *Daily News,* a new penny paper being started up with high hopes and heavy expenditures by a New York publisher.[7] The position was a promising one, the pay good, and the policy of the paper independent and high-toned, much as it had been at the *Aurora.* But his tenure with the *Daily News* proved as brief as had that with the *Aurora;* the paper failed to establish its own position between those staked out by other metropolitan dailies, and by late February 1850, the paper was suspended and Whitman one more time without a job.

For Whitman, it was to be his last editorial or full-time journalistic position until 1857, by which time he would have written and published the first two editions and planned a third of *Leaves of Grass.* In 1850, however, he was still thinking like a journalist, his immediate goal to get back into journalism as quickly as possible. At first that meant free-lancing; he published a number of articles and poems in various Manhattan and Brooklyn newspapers for which he had previously written and with which he retained connections, including Bryant's *Evening Post,* Greeley's *Tribune,* and Spooner's *Evening Star.* He also tried a different kind of strategy to keep himself going professionally, abridging a novel by the popular Danish poet-novelist Bernhard Severin Ingemann and offering it for serial publication to the owners of the New York *Sun,* the Beaches, for whom he had worked briefly as a reporter in 1843. Despite his modest terms – "I desire but a moderate price" – and his belief that the novel could be profitably published in book form after its serialization in the paper, the Beaches rejected his offer.[8] Several months later, still eagerly looking to get back into the journalistic mainstream, Whitman contacted their ex-editor, Carlos Stuart, whom he knew to be starting a new daily in New York, about the possibility of employment:

> I take the liberty of writing, to ask whether you have any sort of "opening" in your new enterprise, for services that I could render? I am out of regular employment, and fond of the press – and, if you would be disposed to "try it on," I should like to have an interview with you, for the purpose of seeing whether we could agree to something. My ideas of salary are *very* moderate.[9]

He also offered him the Ingemann novel for serialization, but on both matters Stuart declined his proposals.

Although he was soon supplying occasional contributions to Gamaliel Bailey's abolitionist Washington *National Era,* which the next year would burst into fame with its serialization of *Uncle Tom's Cabin,* his journalistic career was plainly taking him nowhere. In 1851, he wrote only a scattered handful of articles for the newspapers and returned, once again, if he had in fact ever left it, to the shop on the bottom floor of his house out of which for several years he had been printing job orders and selling books and stationery (including works published by the firm of Fowlers and Wells, an arrangement to be reversed in 1855). In June, he embarked on a more ambitious project; he began the publication of the *Salesman and Traveller's Directory for Long Island,* a weekly advertising sheet providing transportation timetables, practical information, and literary sketches for travelers en route between Brooklyn and Long Island.[10] A pedestrian format at best, the *Directory* lasted for only a handful of issues before Whitman tired or despaired of it and gave it up. By late June, Whitman was summering in Greenport and sending back his "Letters from Paumanok" to the *Evening Post,* after which he again returned to his shop.

He could not possibly have known it at this time, but he was now gradually coming to the end of his career as a journalist–literary professional along the lines of Park Benjamin, Nathaniel Willis, William Cullen Bryant, or Horace Greeley, the men by whom he could have sought parallels to his own career. For a full decade he had been devoting himself energetically and idealistically to the full range of literary professional roles of his time – as a printer, reporter, editor, freelancer, periodical poet and story writer, bookseller, and publisher – but to little apparent avail. Although he had entered more deeply into the spirit of his literary culture and experienced it from more angles than had any of his major contemporaries, by late 1851 he was virtually finished as a conventionally defined journalist or writer. He had wound down to writing for the press only sporadically ever since the demise of the *Daily News* in early 1850, and after the failure of his several gambits in 1851, his contributions to the press were to become even more infrequent. Between the summer of 1851 and the publication of *Leaves of Grass* four years later, he would place only a scattering of articles and poems with the press, mostly in the papers which remained friendly to his work. The printing-shop– bookstore to which he had retired periodically when between full-time jobs probably supported him and his family through the fall of 1851, but at some time shortly thereafter (and certainly not later than May 1852, when he sold the house in which the shop was located) he gave that up.

It was not that Whitman had lost faith in journalism. He was as "fond of the press" then and as faithful to its mission as he had ever been. What had changed, or was changing, was Whitman himself. Whitman was reported as having told his newspaper friend, Talcott Williams, that his unexpected salvation in the early 1850s had come from his failure with the newspapers: "The best thing that happened to me was that all my articles were rejected. If anybody had accepted any articles, even one, I should have been lost. I should have begun to write like that for I needed the money cruelly, but as they rejected all and I could not sell anything, I wrote to satisfy myself."[11] The facts sound dubious, rather like one of Whitman's late-in-life, after-the-fact rationalizations; but the spirit of the facts is basically accurate. Whitman had too irregular and creative a personality ever to have found his truest self, by which I mean his poetic self, in the restrictive forms of conventional newspaper and magazine journalism. Many of the ideas and presuppositions about the populari- zation of culture he absorbed during his journalistic years would survive into the next period, would pass easily into the conceptualization of *Leaves of Grass*; but they could not take actual shape until Whitman created his own artistic forms, responsive to his personality and to his insights into modern culture and society.

The most conspicuous change in his life at this time was that at some point in 1852 he began devoting his working time primarily to house building, riding the current wave of speculation and investment in Brook- lyn, fast growing into a major urban center, much as his father, by now disabled, had done in Whitman's boyhood. The sharp break in career, however, was more apparent than real. He did not allow house building at this time any more than he had ever allowed any other workaday activity to distract his attention from his deepest interests; and in any case, he may well have found in this work a source of genuine aesthetic pleasure, much as he had in his years as a printer. The notebooks he was beginning to carry around with him and to fill up with his thoughts and observations were now carrying references, among other things, to the working professions. In one of them, for instance, even before he was reborn as the carpenter-poet of 1855, he jotted down the idea for a possible "Poem of Architecture? The Carpenter's and Mason's Poem."[12] When once launched as a poet – the written reminder, "Make *the Works*," overhung his writing desk – he would never cease referring to his writing in architectonic terms.

He might still have been worshipping the idols of the workingman – Jackson, Leggett, and Wright – but one thing about the young Whitman of the early 1850s is certain: He himself was no ordinary workingman. One gets a rare look at him behind the carpenter's apron he was wearing in 1852 in a letter he sent that summer to Senator John F. Hale of New Hampshire, whom he urged to accept the presidential nomination of the Free Soil party. This letter, the sole surviving letter of substance from this period, reveals much about Whitman's continuing political loyalty, even without a paper at his service in a presidential election year, to what he considered the party of the genuine "American Democracy." More importantly, it also provides a direct insight into the ferment of his psyche as he began to recreate himself as "Walt" Whitman, American poet. The strong-minded young man who came forward to instruct Hale showed himself to be an enthusiast writing on behalf of the people, as he had done for years in and through his newspapers, but writing now with the charged rhetoric which would characterize the Preface to *Leaves of Grass* and *The Eighteenth Presidency*!:

> Look to the young men – appeal specially to them. Enter into this condition of affairs, with spirit, too. Take two or three occasions within the coming month to make personal addresses directly to the people, giving condensed embodiments of the principal ideas which distinguish our liberal faith from the drag-parties and their platforms. Boldly promulge these, with that temper of rounded and good-natured moderation which is peculiar to you; but abate not one jot of your fullest radicalism. After these two or three speeches, which should be well-considered and not too long, possess your soul in patience, and take as little personal action in the election as may be. Depend upon it, there is no way so good as the face-to-face of candidates and people – in the old heroic

Roman fashion. I would suggest that one of these addresses be delivered in New York, and one in Cincinnati – with a third either in Baltimore or Washington.

As for himself, as though anticipating Hale's skepticism toward his unknown and unsolicited campaign manager, Whitman assured him of his ability to speak with authority on these matters: "But I know the people. I know well, (for I am practically in New York,) the real heart of this mighty city – the tens of thousands of young men, the mechanics, the writers, etc. etc."[13]

He did not bother to characterize his profession to Hale as mechanic, writer, or anything else (whereas three years later, writing supportively to Senator William Seward shortly after bringing out the first *Leaves of Grass*, he defined himself as "a writer, for the press and otherwise"); one's curiosity can only wish that he had. Outwardly, he was now presenting the appearance of the sturdy, young mechanic he described to Hale as the soul of the nation, the housebuilder as American democrat. He had taken recently to dressing like a workingman in flannels, open-throated work shirt, and high boots, in self-conscious contrast to the fashionable clothes he affected in the 1840s; the hat that he was now cocking indoors and out as he pleased was not the fancy one he had described in the *Aurora* but the wide-brimmed "wide-awake" which had caught his fancy of late. After years of apparent indecision, he was now wearing his face fully bearded, an embellishment he would affect the rest of his life. With his facial and head hair conspicuously flecked with gray and his body filled out to the full extent of its impressive frame, he presented – and knew he presented – an imposing figure of a man, one with at least an inchoate sense of what "changes of garments" can do and mean for a man.

He was no more the typical workingman now than he had been the dandy in the past. He was already playing with the magical fluidity of character which he would soon learn to transpose deftly from his life to his poetry. His brother George, his temperamental opposite, remembered him during this period as going "strictly his own way": "There was a great boom in Brooklyn in the early fifties, and he had his chance then, but you know he made nothing of that chance. Some of us reckoned that he had by this neglect wasted his best opportunity, for no other equally good chance ever after appeared."[14] Whitman would himself later make a similar claim about having deliberately forsaken his best economic opportunity in the early fifties, but by then he was already pursuing a different conception of opportunity.

He was out, as he purportedly told Talcott Williams, to satisfy himself. It had always been his style to do this in one way or another, but by the early 1850s he was doing this with greater flair and disregard of convention. Whatever satisfaction he drew from work in the out-of-doors and among workingmen, the chief source of his satisfaction, as always, remained the jaunts across the river to Manhattan, which in the early 1850s often ended in the theaters, opera halls, and art galleries he was attending with growing enthusiasm. He was even keeping company, the first known company in the Whitman record, with a number of energetic young artists at work in Manhattan and Brooklyn.

The New York art world he was patronizing was thriving in the early 1850s, with art galleries and academies and daguerreotype parlors opening up to exhibit and distribute the work of native and foreign artists to a public eager for art. Whitman enthused with other cultural nationalists in the achievements of the "American school" and hoped to see its successes replicated in Brooklyn, where he was on friendly terms with the painters Jesse Talbot and Walter Libbey, the daguerreotypist Gabriel Harrison, and the sculptor Henry Kirke Browne. He would often make the rounds of their studios to study their methods and to exchange ideas with them about art. For Libbey and Harrison, he even sat for his portrait, the latter to be used as his photographic signature to the 1855 *Leaves of Grass*. At Browne's studio, where he sat among the young artists, some fresh from Paris and Rome, and listened to excited talk about the latest ideas and movements in the arts, he passed – to his great delight – as "Beranger." A young French landscape artist of his acquaintance, whom he had made known to William Cullen Bryant, he also introduced to his favorite sister, Hannah, the rare instance in which his artistic and family lives intersected (the result, however, was a marriage which brought all three of them unrelenting regret and discord). Looking back on these days of camaraderie with young men of creative energy and vision, Whitman would remember them fondly as "big, strong days – our young days – days of preparation: the gathering of the forces."[15]

It is impossible, however, to imagine Whitman's playing a forward role in the discussions at the ateliers of his comrades any more than his coming forth freely with his ideas and opinions in the spirited debates later that decade among the bohemian wits at Pfaff's beer cellar. Garrulity was to come to Whitman only in old age, and even true sociability, with him, had its tight confines. It was more in character for him to listen carefully to what others had to say, then later, withdrawing into his accustomed solitude, to test what he had heard by his own thoughts and translate what was usable into his own terms. The real workshop, he intuitively understood, for all his love of the glitter of the outward show, was in the privacy of the self, where the irreducible agent he would soon take to calling the "Me myself" was housed.

There can be no doubt that the "Me myself" was emerging by the early 1850s. The vague, undirected ambitions of distinguishing himself which had been prodding him on ever since his early manhood began gradually to coalesce with his enthusiastic championship of the national cause in politics and culture. Tracing the path of this process is extremely difficult because it is so largely hidden from sight, one's views of it never more than oblique, restricted by lack of pertinent information and obstructed by Whitman's later policy of rewriting or distorting the record. Outwardly, his habits during these years remained fairly constant: flexible working hours, long walks through Brooklyn, summer excursions to eastern Long Island, frequent trips across the river to New York, exciting hours at the opera and theater, broadly eclectic reading – although now there was also the keeping of notebooks into which he poured his thoughts, ideas, and observations. Even his family, with whom he had lived in close quarters since 1848, did not discern any change in him, did not think him "more abstracted than usual."[16] The changes overcoming Whitman were all internal, and they are therefore not to be seen so much in his public behavior and activities as in his miscellaneous writings of the early 1850s: specifically, in his journalism, notebooks, and marginalia.

I remarked earlier on the decreasing frequency of Whitman's journalism after 1850, decreasing partially because he was becoming professionally frustrated but also because in his notebooks he now had an alternative place in which to express his mind. What little journalism there is, however, attests to a certain maturation in his taste and sensibility. It was primarily an impressionistic cultural journalism that he was now writing, the record of his reflections and opinions about the various arts with which he was conversant and which he was obviously attending now with heightened discrimination. His tastes were becoming more clearly decided, and his concern with aesthetics, more primary. In the occasional article he was publishing, he was now championing aesthetic principles which he would soon be honoring in the practice: the importance of uniformity of effect, the primacy of nature over art, the beauty of the human form.

Although as preoccupied as ever with the theoretical basis of the arts in a democratic society – why else commit his thoughts publicly to the press – he was now writing demonstrably with a greater degree of specificity, from a position located closer to his own aesthetic development (although how close, one can only speculate). When he wrote in late 1850, for example, that "poetry exists independently of rhyme," he was simply restating the lesson he had recently labored to teach himself.[17] It was only earlier that year that he had taken definitively to writing his own poetry in a free-verse, colloquial style, which can be seen in the series of slashingly aggressive, partisan political poems he published in Bryant's *Evening Post* and Greeley's *Tribune*. Although they unquestionably sound, as Paul Zweig has said of one of them, like "angry editorials," they place Whitman for the first time beyond the conventional verse he had been writing and publishing right through the 1840s, and they offer one more clue about the degree to which his *Leaves of Grass* poems were influenced by his experience in journalism.[18] When he was invited by his artist friends in the spring of 1851 to address the newly formed Brooklyn Art Union, he concluded his remarks on the preconditions for artistic creativity by reading from one of these experimental poems, "Resurgemus," which he still thought highly enough of in 1855 to include with his more recent poems in the first edition of *Leaves of Grass*.

But I do not believe that in 1851 he was as yet prepared or preparing to come out programmatically with his poetry. That idea was still two or three years ahead of him. Until 1855, in fact, he was curiously silent publicly, especially for one previously so voluble, about the twin subjects of poetry and the poet. He apparently felt more confident commenting journalistically in the intervening years about painting, photography, drama, and – his new passion of the early 1850s – opera. Privately, however, he was pouring his personal thoughts, ideas, opinions, ideals, hopes, and beliefs into his homemade notebooks and into marginal comments he wrote onto the many and varied clippings he was collecting from his periodical and book readings. In these various notebooks and marginalia, one can see the clearest reflection of Whitman's self-transformation.

Whitman had been an eclectic reader from his early youth, and his training and experience as a printer and journalist could only have hardened this tendency into a habit. Put simply, he read in a manner remarkably analogous to the way he would write: extemporaneously, selectively, and subjectively. He had had access to circulating libraries in his teens, and as books and periodicals became more inexpensive and numerous thereafter, he had been able to supplement their holdings with his own occasional purchases. But the main supplier of his reading through the 1840s came from the editorial offices of the newspapers he served, which received review copies of books and magazines on exchange from publishers throughout the United States and Britain. Many of these, naturally, he reviewed editorially in his paper, but those which were most interesting to him he also reviewed in his more searchingly personal fashion.

His manner of reading and commenting, surely one of his most distinctive customs, was as idiosyncratic as was the writing it helped to inspire. As he frankly admitted from his editorial chair at the *Eagle*, he was forced by the time pressures of his profession to be an outright skimmer of print; but what Whitman did not mention was how nicely this manner of reading also suited his personal needs. He had neither the training nor the obligation to read books, like the scholar, holistically, systematically, or objectively. He read, rather, at all stages of his life, selectively and impressionistically, his purpose to satisfy his own interests. Even his staying power suited his personality; he read best in bursts, chapters or articles at a time.

He would soon be urging readers of his own books to read, above all, actively, which is exactly what he himself was already doing. He read, as nearly as one can, physically; like the printer he had once been and the maker of books he would soon be, he went through texts, as it were, with scissors in one hand, pen in the other. Passages or pieces which deeply interested him he marked or cut, treating printed matter, perhaps as a result of his training, much as a printer would handle proof. He also developed a system of markings to highlight what was to be restudied and possibly reused: in order of ascending importance, marginal brackets, underlinings, hands with pointing index fingers, or some combination of these for passages requiring particular attention.[19] In the case of unusually thought-provoking passages, he often added his own thoughts and ideas in the margins.

Likewise, he worked freely with his scissors, clipping out articles from newspapers and magazines or chapters from books, which he desired to file or recombine in units more serviceable to his own needs. Some of these clippings he allowed to lie loosely or bound indiscriminately in bundles, while others he preferred to assemble systematically, often among and between pages of his own thoughts, in homemade bindings or in the skeletons of published books whose pages he had removed. In this manner, he manufactured in the early and midfifties a variety of makeshift scrapbooks and textbooks for his general self-education and blank notebooks for his poetry. Unknowingly, he was already anticipating in several ways at once the manner by which he would "make" the 1855 *Leaves of Grass*.

These clippings survive in the hundreds, the majority from the decade and a half preceding the Civil War, which was the period in which Whitman read most intensively and creatively. Their range is impressive; they cover a breadth and variety of fields more befitting the curriculum of a modern university than that of a college of his own day – a measure not only of the range of his interests but also of the variety of influences pouring into his poetry. Because of Whitman's customary procedure of reading (and sometimes annotating) them repeatedly over the years, it is not always possible to relate specific readings to specific dates in his life. This limitation notwithstanding, one can discern a general pattern by which he read broadly for his self-education in the last half of the 1840s, then gradually in a more directed fashion as he came to focus on matters more specifically related to poetry and culture.

One can get no closer to the budding poet than in his marginalia on poets and poetry. Sometimes, what he did not say in his notes is as important as what he did say. Often, what he took as crucial would with others have been considered extraneous to the craft of the poet; he generally showed a greater interest, for instance, in personality than in poetry. Various writers interested him, some even considerably, but not always for reasons having anything to do with poetry per se. Conversely, he was often impervious to the appeal of writers who might reasonably have been expected to attract him, such as the English Romantics. One thing, though, is patently clear: He found in no single author or style the model of the kind of poet he meant to be or of the kind of poetry he intended to write.

His reaction to Wordsworth, the English Romantic closest in sensibility and theory of poetry to himself, illustrates several of these points. To read Whitman on Wordsworth with the expectation of being lifted to a higher plane of insight is to be disappointed; Whitman was never truly able to step into the imaginative world of Wordsworth (any more, for that matter, than he could into that of Shelley, Keats, or Coleridge). In clipping out the opening and closing pages of a review of the *Prelude* from the 1851 *American Whig Review*, Whitman, as he often did, paid less attention to what was said of the poetry than to the reviewer's brief summary of the poet's life and character – *that* was his primary text. His lone comment was elicited by the reviewer's allusion to Wordsworth's various appointments and legacies: "So it seems Wordsworth made 'a good thing,' from the start, out of his poetry. legacies! a fat office! pensions from the crown!"[20] Similarly, in several other articles about Wordsworth he took the trouble to clip and save, Whitman exhibited a primary (and occasionally rather gossipy) interest in the poet as man – his appearance, manner, and bearing.

He was particularly fascinated by Wordsworth's efforts to overcome public indifference or hostility to his poetry. He underscored, for instance, in a March 1845 article from *Graham's* ("Egotism. As Manifested in the Works and Lives of Great and Small Men"), which he probably read or reread in the early or midfifties, the statement that when Wordsworth "discovered that the regularly constituted arbiters of public opinion on matters of taste, were indisposed to do him justice, he took the task upon himself, and in his prefaces glorified his own powers and works in a spirit of unhesitating self-reliance."[21] When the time came in late 1855 for Whitman to prepare the indifferent arbiters of public opinion in the United States for the second issue of *Leaves of Grass,* he remembered Wordsworth in one of the extracts from reviews he bound in the book for promotional purposes: "The new forms are not to be judged by the old models, but are to be judged by themselves. Wordsworth truly said that every original first-rate poet must himself make the taste through which he is to be fully understood and appreciated."

Whitman read through his books and magazines generally as he read about Wordsworth: for his personal edification, clarification, and inspiration. The forties enthusiast of the *Democratic Review,* one can see vividly in the marginalia, carried his cultural nationalism unadulterated right into the new decade, but infused now with the added excitement and urgency of one who was discovering his own role to play in the larger drama. He was clearly worked up by the remarks of a writer in the January 1851 *American Whig Review* about the preconditions for national literature, bringing in his full array of marking symbols to highlight the following claim: "It is impossible for any but a people whose actions are free and unrestrained, who have great and national purposes, simple and heroic views, and an experience of life, varied upon sea and land, in peace and war, and through the vicissitudes of calamity and brilliant fortune, to produce an original and classic school of poetry." The question the reviewer then raised specifically with regard to America's credentials, for Whitman at least, would have been purely rhetorical: "And will America ever produce great writers and artists who will transmit our glory to future generations, while she is cloyed and debilitated with the sweet and sickly literature of French libertinism and English servilism?"[22]

Whitman took such questions to heart, worked them over in his solitude during the days and years of the 1850s until he had formulated his own creative as well as intellectual position. He would still be asking them – and answering them positively – long after others had stopped, well into the Gilded Age. He was also considering the matter of cultural nationalism from the opposite direction, from the bottom up. He collected during the early and mid–1850s at least a half dozen articles from the press about the state of the publishing and related industries in the United States. He clipped, for example, from Fowler and Wells's *Life Illustrated* of May 31, 1856, the article, "Bookmaking in the United States," which was reprinted widely in American papers and magazines because of its big-numbered, highly complimentary analysis of the quantitative output of publishing houses, booksellers, paper mills, and inventions in the United States.[23] He also clipped out separate newspaper items giving statistics of steam presses and of newspapers and books printed in the country, in each case totaling the sums himself at the bottom. Next to a clipping of "List of Patents Issued from the United States Patent office for the week ending May 12, 1857," he noted: "This list of one week's issue of patents from the National Patent office at Washington illustrates America and American character about as much as any thing I know. – (Remember the show at the Crystal Palace, and the American Institute fairs.)."

He had been entertaining such thoughts about culture ever since the 1840s, but it was only in the early 1850s that he began to see the "advent" of himself as coming into alignment with Emerson's notion that "the birth of a poet is the principal event in chronology."[24] To read through the excited marginalia Whitman was writing during the fifties on poets and poetry is to sense something of the atmosphere of an aspirant actor reading for a desired part, or, the part won, preparing himself to go out on stage. He studied the careers of poets from the time of Chaucer to the present, as though looking for clues to poetic deportment.[25] He noted down in several places the practice of some poets to write self-criticism. He observed variously, most likely with himself in mind, the advice of William G. Simms to young writers to devote themselves single-mindedly to their work (Whitman: "very good"); the claim of a writer in the January 1852 issue of *Graham's* that the features of the landscape would be only "blank conditions of matter, if the mind did not fling its own divinity around them" (Whitman: "This I think is one of the most indicative sentences I ever read"); and the equation drawn by a reviewer of a Keats biography between ill health and poetic genius (Whitman: "?," and on top of the clipping: "The great poet absorbs the identity of others and the experience of others and they are definite in him or from him; but he presents them all through the powerful press of himself."). It was perhaps with a sense of the "powerful press of himself" that he jotted down the thought: "The Poets are the divine mediums – through them come spirits and materials to all the people, men and women."

I spoke of Whitman as though of an aspirant actor, and I used that figure advisedly. The kinds of perceptions and insights that Whitman was able to draw about the "perfect poet" frequently drew on his intuitive sense of the dramatic and corresponded to his continuing interest in the theater and his newfound love of the opera. For all his journalistic interest at this time in aesthetics, Whitman was still more truly an appreciator than a critic of the arts. His receptivity to the arts, especially to the performing arts, I would describe only as prodigious. It was his habit to attend performances usually by himself and to sit in a kind of expectant ecstasy, awaiting the moment to release himself up to the spectacle before his eyes – "to wander out of myself," as he would later describe his manner of response to performance.[26] When he went to a Manhattan synagogue in the early 1840s, for example, he was affected as though in a theater rather than in a house of worship:

> And there we were amid the Jews worshipping in their temple. The
> people of Solomon and Saul, of Ruth and Mary Magdalene, of the

traitor Judas, and John, the beloved Son of God – the people of the very Christ himself – these were they who stood around. And they were speaking in the same tones as those which at night bade the shepherds to follow the guidance of the star in the east – the same tones which Jonathan and Saul used in their beautiful friendship – which sounded out from the plaintive Hagar in the wilderness – through which Absalom, "that too beauteous boy," made rebellion against his father – with which the widow's son, who was dead, and brought to life again, gladdened his desolate mother's heart; – the tones and the native language of the holy Psalmist, the lovely Rebecca of Scott, and the malignant Shylock of Shakespeare...

The heart within us felt awed as in the presence of memorials from an age that had passed away centuries ago. The strange and discordant tongue – the mystery, and all the associations that crowded themselves in troops upon our mind – made a thrilling sensation to creep through every nerve. It was indeed a sight well calculated to impress our mind with an unwonted tone.[27]

Or when he attended a performance of Mendelssohn's oratorio *St. Paul* in 1845, he came out enraptured, using the oceanic metaphor he often reserved for describing his strongest emotional responses: "But who shall define the cabalistic signets of the undying soul? Who shall sound the depths of that hidden sea, and tell its extent from a few dim and dull reverberations aneath its surface? Who shall tell the how and the why of the singular passion caused by melodious vibrations?"[28] A few days earlier, in a distinction of which he was proud, Whitman had come out in favor of what he called "heart music" over "art music."[29] He would later show the same preference in literature.

At this time, Whitman took as his musical ideal the touring family groups who sang minstrelsy and the popular tunes of the day in preference to foreign opera; but by the early 1850s, coincidentally with the enormous success of Italian opera before New York audiences, Whitman reversed himself and began to see the great touring soloists Alboni and Bettini as his exemplars of "heart music" at its best. To listen to such singers, he wrote in 1851, was to be launched into the atmosphere:

Have not you, in like manner, while listening to the well-played music of some band like Maretzek's, felt an overwhelming desire for measureless sound – a sublime orchestra of a myriad orchestras – a colossal volume of harmony, in which the thunder might roll in its proper place; and above it, the vast, pure Tenor, – identity of the Creative Power itself – rising through the universe, until the boundless and unspeakable capacities of that mystery, the human soul, should be filled to the uttermost, and the problem of human cravingness be satisfied and destroyed?[30]

He even came forward, in tones markedly similar to those of the persona of his 1855 poetry, with the offer to share his experiencing of music with his newspaper readers: "Come, I will not talk to you as to one of the superficial crowd who saunter here because it is a fashion; who take opera glasses with them, and make you sick with shallow words, upon the sublimest and most spiritual of the arts. I will trust you with confidence; I will divulge secrets."[31]

Much as this sounds like and close as this takes us to the creative source of the poetry of 1855, it still lacks the power of 1855. Whitman's imagination would have to be superheated one magnitude further before such sentiments could break into the inspired poetry of 1855. Hear, for example, Whitman describing the identical scene in an undated notebook entry, which, to judge from the perfectly modulated rhythm and erotically imaged climax, I believe, could only have derived from a period very close to 1855:

> I want that tenor, large and fresh as the creation, the orbed parting of whose mouth shall lift over my head the sluices of all the delight yet discovered for our race. –
> I want the soprano that lithely overleaps the stars, and convulses me like the love-grip of her in whose arms I lay last night. – I want an infinite chorus and orchestrium, wide as the orbit of Uranus true as the hours of the day, and filling my capacities to receive, as thoroughly as the sea fills its scooped out sands. – I want the chanted Hymn whose tremendous sentiment,/ . . . shall uncage in my breast a thousand wide-winged strengths and unknown ardors and terrible extasies – putting me through the flights of all the passions – dilating me beyond time and air – startling me with the overtures of some unnameable horror – calmly sailing me all day on a bright river with lazy slopping waves – stabbing my heart with myriads of forked distractions more furious than hail or lightning – lulling me drowsily with honeyed morphine – tight'ning the fakes of death about my throat, and awakening me again to know by that comparison, the most positive wonder in the world, and that's what we call life.[32]

This needs only to be set into lines of verse to fit the form and spirit of *Leaves of Grass,* where indeed it was to figure in "Song of Myself."

Whitman would later pass on to his friend and first biographer, John Burroughs, the notion that "many passages of his poetry were composed in the gallery of the New York Academy during the opera performances."[33] This may or may not be only one more of Whitman's after-the-fact autobiographical rationalizations, but I do believe that Whitman often composed in moods of great excitement similar to those in which he took in the opera. I also believe that by the time he wrote poetry featuring "the pure contralto" singing up in the loft he had come to see the performance of the soloist as analogous to the "vocalism" of his own chosen role.

He had, likewise, a rare appreciation for the skill of the stage actor. He had thrilled to the theater from his earliest adolescence, had been left "drunk with pleasure," as he later described it, by his first experiencing of the theater; and for many years thereafter, he considered himself an aficionado of the New York stage.[34] The trips across the river during the years of his apprenticeship were one of the formative experiences of his youth, and even in old age and broken health he could still write about those and later trips to the theater with the old surges of emotion. The flair of the gaslights above and the footlights below, the spread of the assembled crowd, the mood of hushed expectation, the sensation of electricity whistling through the house, the gestures of the actors and the expressions of the spectators – all the old memories came back to Whitman in a flash. Even in years of failing memory, he had the names of favorite actors and actresses at his fingertips; and what he said of one of them, Edwin Booth, he might also have said of the effect the entire profession had had on his life: "His genius was to me one of the grandest revelations of my life, a lesson of artistic expression."[35]

But it was not simply the performance of opera, drama, or any other dramatic art form which most inspired Whitman: It was performance itself. Whitman could respond freely to any manner of performance, secular or holy; and in virtually any setting, indoors or out. Theater, opera house, lecture hall, church or synagogue, exhibition hall, parade, Fourth of July gathering – they all charged Whitman with the magnetic force of the performer and the audience. He had, moreover, the curious ability, as he put it in an 1855 poem, of being "both in and out of the game, and watching and wondering at it," to be both actor and spectator. He had the knack at the theater, when able to detach himself from his own feelings, of watching for the effect of the performance on the audience: "I always scann'd an audience as rigidly as a play."[36] It was perhaps this conspicuously double-sided sensibility which made him as appreciative as he was of the art of the impresario, the art of bringing the two major parties to a performance under a common roof. Indeed, there is something fascinating about watching the future great auto-impresario of *Leaves of Grass* classifying his own favorite impresarios of the early 1850s, such as Max Maretzek and Billy Niblo, the latter the purveyor of Sontag and Alboni, whom he rated over P. T. Barnum, the purveyor of Jenny Lind.[37]

Whitman would later claim that at some unspecified date in the early 1850s he even participated in an amateur acting group which met on Broadway. Although he did not mention what specific roles he played except to say that they were secondary, he did describe

what in any case is more significant, his instinctive relish for the art
of expression:

> And so let us turn off the gas. Out in the brilliancy of the footlights
> – filling the attention of perhaps a crowded audience, and making many
> a breath and pulse swell and rise – O so much passion and imparted
> life! – over and over again, the season through – walking, gesticulating,
> singing, reciting his or her part – But then sooner or later inevitably
> wending to the flies or exit door – vanishing to sight and ear – and
> never materializing on this earth's stage again![38]

He returned to this idea one more time in one of his pre–*Leaves of Grass*
notebooks, this time with himself out front under the lights: "Now I
stand here, a personality in the Universe, a personality perfect and sound;
all things and all other beings as an audience at the play-house perpetually
and perpetually calling me out from behind [my] curtain."[39] A more
perfect fantasy for the soon-to-be outsetting bard of 1855 it would be
hard to imagine.

By 1854, he was at work on what would prove to be the prototype
of the mature *Leaves of Grass* poems. Entitled "Pictures," it translated
his long-standing fascination with the new democratic art of photography
and his years of observant street walking into the new idiom of his
experimental poetry. I have already spoken of how Whitman had followed with keen interest the history of the daguerreotype process from
the moment of its earliest introduction to the United States; that interest
intensified during the early 1850s. He would refer several times in his
journalism of these years to his frequent trips to daguerreotype parlors,
his inspection of the daguerreotype gallery at the Crystal Palace, and his
friendships with leading local daguerreotypists. Whitman would one day
be acquainted with and sit for many of the most famous American pho-
tographers of the century, but at this time he was on personal terms
primarily with Gabriel Harrison, whom he thought Brooklyn's finest
daguerreotypist. One hot summer day in 1854, he went to Harrison's
studio and posed for his picture, and with that began Whitman's photographic analogue to the poetic task of self-presentation and self-
portraiture, the two to complement each other in the first and in all
succeeding editions of *Leaves of Grass*.

It was therefore fitting that about the time he embarked on the creation
of *Leaves of Grass,* he began by internalizing his interest in photography
and came up with the first striking trope of his career: his mind as a
camera recording the sights of his world as it passed through his territory.
With the opening lines of this poem, Whitman was unquestionably well
on his way to putting himself, his world, and his sensed experience of
the world, as he would later phrase it, "freely, fully, and truthfully on
record":

In a little house pictures I keep, many pictures hanging suspended –
It is not a fixed house,
It is round – it is but a few inches from one side of it to the other side,
But behold! it has room enough – in it, hundreds and thousands, –
all the varieties;
– Here! Do you know this? this is cicerone himself;
And here, see you, my own States – and here the world itself, rolling
bowling through the air;
And there, on the walls hanging, portraits of women and men,
carefully kept.[40]

He had stated his desire in one of his notebooks to see the universe "pass through me as a procession"; this was, poetically, an important beginning. Supple and capacious enough to encompass any number of word pictures, it also contained one of the photographer-poet himself, his first self-portrait in verse: "– And this – whose picture is this? / Who is this, with rapid feet, curious, gay – going up and down Mannahatta, through the streets, along the shores, working his way through the crowds, observant and singing?"[41] This was quite the picture one might expect of the poet, footing his way as always on the territory of the new poetry, the streets of the city and the alleys of his consciousness, and opening his mind, like a camera shutter, to record a range of subjects beyond that normally available to traditional poetry.

But Whitman did not immediately dare to screen his poem to the general public; the viewing of his "picture gallery" remained for the time being a strictly private function. He may have spoken only a few years earlier in his open letter to Bryant's Evening Post of the "close phalanx, ardent, radical and progressive" of young brother-artists, whom he tended to idealize, as he did the young workingmen, as constituting the bulwark of the democracy and his compeers in the construction of America's new literary culture; in actuality, however, he preferred to work in solitude and secrecy, biding his time until the right moment.[42]

By some time in 1854, that moment finally came. He wrote in or around June of that year a poetic polemic denouncing the Anthony Burns affair ("A Boston Ballad"), but unlike the angry political poems of 1851, he chose not to publish this topical piece immediately but to hold it for future use. He had already begun by that time, or would soon thereafter begin, devoting his working time primarily to the conceptualization and composition of a volume of poetry. The real estate boom in Brooklyn had come to an end during the course of the year, and this may or may not have influenced Whitman in his wholehearted dedication to his poetry. Whatever the exact timing or order of cause and effect, the process of composition had its own irresistible logic and psychological momentum, something of whose force is still perceptible in the explosive energy of the opening pages. By the end of the next winter, with the "great pressure, pressure from within" of pent-up creative power, of which he later spoke to his friend Ellen O'Connor, at last releasing itself into manuscript pages, the book must have been rapidly approaching completion.

One day that spring, he took his completed manuscript to the District Court of Manhattan and registered it for a copyright. With this act, however, factual information about the publication of *Leaves of Grass* becomes scanty, and one is left mainly to infer about the way Whitman planned to bring his volume, the book with which he hoped to transfigure America, before its public. Did he approach an established publisher? No doubt, he had dreamed of doing so, of handing his volume over to a house such as the Harpers, the firm he had treated with respect bordering on open adulation in his journalism. But I doubt that he would actually have acted on this wish. Devout Methodists and hard-driving businessmen, the Harpers would have rejected the manuscript on the spot. Or he might have offered the manuscript via his friend, the popular lecturer and writer on the sciences Edward Youmans, to his publishers, the Appletons; but this is equally unlikely. The Appletons were backward in publishing belles lettres and deeply conservative and would have rejected the manuscript just as quickly as would the Harpers. So, for that matter, if not on the grounds of immorality, would virtually every major house in New York. Whitman perhaps half anticipated, half feared such a formal reception at the hands of the publishing industry, for in an undated but probably pre–*Leaves of Grass* notebook he speculated, "It would be as though some publisher should reject the best poems ever written in the world because he who brings them to be printed has a shabby umbrella, or mud on the shank of his boot."[43] Whitman, worse yet, should any publisher have cared to notice, was sporting an open shirt and a tilted "wide awake" in his frontispiece photograph.

A more likely scenario and one more in keeping with Whitman's characteristic reserve about initiating contacts is that he might also have considered asking one of his well-placed friends, such as Greeley or Bryant, to act as intermediary with a publisher. It is not likely, though, that he ever attempted this tactic; some rumor or record of such a plan would probably have survived once the reputation of the book spread. Bryant, in any case, was deeply offended by the poetry of the volume; and Greeley, who had used Fowler and Wells as his own publisher, would probably have had no better suggestion to Whitman than to do likewise.

So Whitman was thrown back on his own resources, and with a curious symmetry he returned full circle to the kind of small, local printing office in which he had done his apprenticeship two decades before. He no doubt knew many of the local printers in Brooklyn – he had been competing with them for business as recently as 1851 or 1852 – and from among them he settled on the Rome brothers, immigrant job printers from Scotland specializing in legal texts, to put his manuscript into print. Unaware that this would become the dominant pattern of his publishing career, he consulted with them and advised them about the physical appearance of the volume: typeface, inking, paper, margins, layout. Each morning through the spring, Whitman would walk to their red brick printing shop, seat himself at the sole desk and chair, page through the New York *Tribune,* and read through the proof as it came off the press.[44] He even took an occasional turn at setting his unusually long lines of verse into print (he would later alternately encourage and discourage the idea that he printed the entire volume himself). He also put an important finishing touch on the book at the Romes's: he "hastily" assembled into a prose essay the thoughts he had been pondering for years on the role of the poet and poetry in American life and set the article at the head of the volume.[45]

There was a certain circumstantial (not to mention, poetic) justice in the eventuality which brought Whitman back at this juncture of his career to the printing shop. In an important sense, the compositor in Whitman had always been and would always remain a vital part of the composer of his poems; the typecase was always to be before his eyes as the "latent mine" – a nice pun, if he meant it – of his verse:

> This latent mine – these unlaunch'd voices – passionate powers,
> Wrath, argument, or praise, or comic leer, or prayer devout,
> (Not nonpareil, brevier, bourgeois, long primer merely,)
> These ocean waves arousable to fury and to death,
> Or sooth'd to ease and sheeny sun and sleep,
> Within the pallid slivers slumbering.

("A Font of Type")

It was one of the ironies of his strange publishing career that the first and one of the few times in his life that he appeared in a literary anthology – and Whitman was keenly aware of how fine a measure anthologies are of popular taste and acceptance – was in 1850, when his old Long Island friend and employer James Brenton reprinted one of his stories in a collection of imaginative works by onetime printers. Nathaniel Willis, another of the contributors, was quoted there as saying something which, to my mind, has a particular pertinence to Whitman: "If there were an apprenticeship to the trade of authorship, it would be as essential that a young author should pass a year as a compositor in a printing-office, as that a future sea-captain should make a voyage before the mast . . . There is no such effectual analysis of style as the process of type-setting."[46]

Whitman had written in the lead poem of the new volume going through the press, no matter whether with or without the slightest intent at self-characterization, "My words are words of a questioning, and to indicate reality; / This printed and bound book . . . but the printer and the printing-office boy?" In doing so, he spoke from a position of knowledge about the interconnectedness of the arts of printing and poetry that few but a printer-poet, or more likely yet, that this printer-poet, would have possessed. Both the arts, he well understood, were engaged in an effort to press the stamp of verbal specificity onto the blankness of paper.

Beginning with the 1855 edition and continuing throughout his publishing life, Whitman would write in closer relation to printers and printerly considerations than would virtually any of his more conventionally trained, conventionally published contemporaries. This was, in part, the result of necessity, of his history of troubled relations with publishers; but it was also, I suspect, the consequence of his innermost desire. For one thing, he was personally comfortable with this arrangement. He enjoyed the atmosphere of the printing office and the camaraderie with the workmen. There is a sense of ease and familiarity in the descriptions by friends and acquaintances of Whitman, seated in small printing offices, reading proof and holding court to his friends, that one cannot imagine of him, say, in a library or behind a writing desk. There was, moreover, so strong a measure in Whitman's nature of the quality of the protesting Protestant which Edmund Burke associated with the American character that it is difficult to conceive of Whitman's sending off friendly, little poems to "my Murray" or settling into tight, formal relations with any publisher, however much he appreciated the profession per se.

He was also comfortable with the arrangement technically. A consequence of his training, he preferred to work, whenever possible, from proof. Throughout his Brooklyn years, he had an arrangement with the Rome brothers to draw proof sheets of manuscript poems, which he could then conveniently use for revisions; and in later times he would make similar arrangements with them or with other printers or simply use the previous edition of his work, as in the case of the famous "blue book," as his working copy for future editions. There was also an important aesthetic advantage in this arrangement for Whitman, since it enabled him to exercise a considerable degree of control over the design and manner of presentation of his volumes. In effect, it allowed him to place his highly personal poetry before the public in a more personalized manner than would otherwise have been possible.

In an ironically fitting trope of his poetic career, Whitman, while in Boston in 1881 to oversee the publication of a new edition of *Leaves of Grass,* was invited to tour the famous Riverside Press of Cambridge. There, he was taken around personally by its proprietor, the printer-turned-publisher, Henry Oscar Houghton – Houghton, who might publish Whitman's good friends Burroughs and Trowbridge, but who would formally receive Whitman only as a member of their common fraternity, not as an author.[47]

With no apparent alternative, and yet with no apparent lack of faith in his literary culture and its ideals, Whitman took it upon himself – as a professional bookman, he would have known how – to assume the role of publisher as well as creator of his poetry volume. Once the sheets came off the Rome brothers' press, perhaps even earlier, he completed the arrangements for the volume. He took the daguerreotype of himself photographed the previous summer by Gabriel Harrison to Samuel Hollyer for engraving as the frontispiece to the volume. He contracted with a local workman of his acquaintance, Charles Jenkins, for the binding of the sheets, Jenkins, in turn, after completing 200 volumes, passing on the remainder of the work to a subcontractor, who would more cheaply bind an additional 183 volumes by July.[48] In the meantime, Whitman took out the copyright as the "Author and Proprietor" of Leaves of Grass under the name he had always used for his writing, Walter Whitman.

There remained one last, all-important task. He was too much the experienced literary man not to know that all talk about the "final test" of his book would be superfluous if his book was not widely read. His years of journalism had made him acquainted with the proprietors of various local bookstores, and he managed to convince a few to put the book on their shelves. But with visions of future editions adapted to suit the various regions of the nation and with the knowledge of his own inability to distribute the work on a scale commensurate with this transnational ambition, he offered the task of distribution to a firm of his long-standing acquaintance, Fowler and Wells, the leading phrenologists in the country and the operators of a publishing house of middling size and importance. He had known them personally since the day in 1849 when, ever in search of direction, he walked into their establishment and submitted himself to their psychological examination. Since that time, he had had dealings with them as an agent of their books and magazines through his bookshop and more recently in 1853 had even contributed an article to one of their periodicals. Whitman offered them the opportunity, which they accepted, to serve as the distributor of the volume.

They made a strange but by no means illogical partnership. Fowler and Wells did not publish imaginative literature, but then again, they may have seen Leaves of Grass less in this guise than in one more or less in line with the kinds of works on phrenology, self-culture, health and dietary reform, and workmen's rights in which they specialized. They might even have been flattered by the strong boost given phrenology by the poems, which made an art of their science. Whether or not they realized it, the book was the single best exemplification in its time of the definition that the Prospectus to their 1853 *American Phrenological Journal* gave for "phrenology":

> Phrenology, the science of Mind, includes in its wide domain, a knowledge of all the faculties, passions, and powers of the Human Soul; all the bodily organism over which the soul presides, with its structure and functions; and all the realm of nature to which man is related, and with which he should live in harmony. It includes a knowledge of man and his relations to God, and to the universe. It is thus a central and comprehensive science, beginning with the Constitution of Man, and ending with all his possible relations, Spiritual and Material. It is thus that Self-Knowledge is the basis of all knowledge.

As though in reciprocation to *Leaves of Grass,* the current issue of the journal was running an article entitled, "I Know Myself 'Like a Book,'" which would have made a cogent commentary on the poet and poetry of *Leaves of Grass* and the long period of development necessary to bring them together. As the author of the article said of one of his new converts to phrenology, "He 'knew himself like a book,' but Phrenology taught him to know himself like a man."[49]

Though certainly not organized on the scale of the largest publishers, such as the Harpers or Appletons, the house of Fowler and Wells did a fairly brisk, nationwide business in books and in-house magazines. A puff in the trade magazine described them as follows: "They publish works in Phrenology, Physiology, Psychology, Hydropathy, Phonography, Spirit-rapping and women's Rights. They issue also two or three periodicals which have an immense circulation. As men of liberality, character and energy, they have no superiors among publishers. They also understand the virtue of advertising."[50] They operated bookstores in New York, Boston, and Philadelphia, advertised an extensive network of sales agents around the country, and had a working relationship with a London publishing house. They were therefore in a position to give *Leaves of Grass* at least something of the broad exposure that Whitman himself could not manage alone.

By the beginning of July, the folding and binding of the sheets were finished, and Whitman was able to bring home the first volumes of his book and to go about delivering or sending copies to friends, fellow writers, and editors. And thus, fifteen years after he had first publicly stated his desire to write a "wonderful and ponderous book," the long foreground of his poetic apprenticeship finally having been fleshed out after years of preparation, Whitman set out to engage the American people.

II

Whitman, Leaves of Grass, *and the Reader*

But I alone advance among the people en-masse, coarse and strong
I am he standing first there, solitary chanting the true America,
I alone of all bards, am suffused as with the common people.
I alone receive them with a perfect reception and love – and they shall
  receive me.

> Whitman, manuscript version of "That Shadow My Likeness"

Leaves are not more shed from the trees or trees from the earth than
  they are shed out of you.

> Whitman, "A Song for Occupations"

I teach straying from me, yet who can stray from me?
I follow you whoever you are from the present hour;
My words itch at your ears till you understand them.

> Whitman, "Song of Myself"

Where are we going, Walt Whitman? The doors close in an hour.
Which way does your beard point tonight?
  (I touch your book and dream of our odyssey in the supermarket and
feel absurd.)
  Will we walk all night through solitary streets? The trees add shade
to shade, lights out in the houses, we'll both be lonely.

> Allan Ginsburg, "A Supermarket in California"

5

Intentions and Ambitions

On July 6, 1855, there appeared in Greeley's New York *Tribune,* the favorite newspaper advertising medium for book publishers, a brief, unpretentious advertisement for

> WALT WHITMAN'S POEMS, "LEAVES OF GRASS," 1 vol. small quarto, 2$ for sale by SWAYNE, No. 210 Fulton st., Brooklyn, and by FOWLER & WELLS, No. 308 Broadway, N.Y.

Four days later Whitman lost all or part of his home base when Swayne, who presumably had taken the book sight unseen, saw or heard something about it which caused him to remove his name from the advertisement and the book from his shelves. But there were other stores where one could find the book: at Dion Thomas in New York; at the Fowler and Wells stores in New York, Boston, and Philadelphia; at the famous Old Corner Book Store in Boston; and there may have been other stores as well. Copies of the book were also sent to Fowler and Wells's connections in London, Horsell and Company, and indirectly through them eventually passed on to the British intelligentsia.[1] Fowler and Wells, furthermore, routinely mailed prepaid orders for books to all addresses in the United States. Still, this was hardly the broad base of supply that America's self-declared national poet had envisioned for satisfying the demand of a national reading audience. The reviewer of the book in the January 1856 *North American Review* felt required to explain the tardiness of his review by claiming that the book was simply difficult to find: "It bears no publisher's name, and, if the reader goes to a bookstore for it, he may expect to be told at first, as we were, that there is no such book, and has not been. Nevertheless, there is such a book, and it is well worth going twice to the bookstore to buy it."[2]

Only a small number of people did so, apparently. Whitman would later variously estimate the sales of the eight-hundred-copy first edition, announcing publicly in his open letter to Emerson in 1856 that the edition "readily sold," while telling Traubel in 1888, "I doubt if even ten were sold – even one."[3] The truth probably lay closer to his more pessimistic assertion. However meager the sales may have been, the book did have at least a modest and rather influential circulation, if only because of Whitman's all-out exertions. He publicized it by word of mouth among certain friends and acquaintances, sent out numerous complimentary or review copies to writers and editors, and when interest, judged by his standards, proved insufficient, tried to incite more by writing extravagantly positive self-reviews. Emerson, Longfellow, and Whittier received their copies through the mail; the engraver Samuel Hollyer, the journalist Carolan O'Brien Bryant, and bookman Thomas Danman Smith (and possibly William Cullen Bryant) received theirs in person (as Alcott and Thoreau would receive the second edition in 1856). Moncure Conway and Theodore Parker purchased their copies at bookstores in Boston and John Swinton bought his in New York. Frank Sanborn received his copy from Emerson, as did Carlyle and Arthur Hugh Clough in England; Lowell got his through Charles Eliot Norton. John Trowbridge became an instant Whitman admirer even before setting eyes on either Whitman or the volume when a newspaper review of the book (probably Charles Dana's excerpt-filled notice in the New York *Tribune*) reached him in Paris in the fall of 1855. In Philadelphia, a reading from *Leaves of Grass* was the central event of a Nov. 20, 1855, meeting of reform-minded Quakers and abolitionists.[4] A year later, Whitman was one of the celebrities discussed at an after-dinner gathering of "select company" at a merchant's home in Brooklyn.[5] During that same year, remaindered copies began passing through the ranks of the English intelligentsia, preparing the way for its eventual acceptance in Britain by a small group of well-placed writers and scholars. And by 1857, as the legendary story has it, a copy of *Leaves of Grass* reached the Springfield, Illinois, law office of Abraham Lincoln. Moreover, the first edition was reviewed or noticed by several dozen newspapers and magazines in America and England, including such prominent publications as the New York *Tribune*, *Putnam's*, *North American Review*, *Democratic Review*, *Crayon*, *Criterion*, New York *Ledger*, London *Critic*, London *Weekly Dispatch*, and *Punch* – not to mention the most influential lift to the book's reputation, the private letter that Whitman did his best over the years to transform into the *Emerson Review*.

One can therefore discount Whitman's old-age gripe that the first edition went out into the world unread, unrecognized, and unappreciated. The facts indicate quite otherwise: Within a matter of months, the book had brought a little-known, unemployed printer-journalist-housebuilder to the attention of Emerson, Thoreau, Parker, Alcott, Whittier, Longfellow, Norton, Lowell, and Griswold in America; and within a matter of years, it would transform the anonymous "Walt Whitman," which Emerson initially considered possibly a pseudonym, into one of the most widely known, if not necessarily understood or respected, names in Anglo-American letters. Still, though this was recognition of a sort, it was not at all the kind that the outsetting poet had hoped for. What manner of reception, then, did he hope for? And what manner of reception could he reasonably have expected? These are fascinating and complex questions, questions most readily answered when approached via Whitman's state of mind in the months surrounding the publication of his volume as well as via the state of the literary market at that time.

By the time he published "Poets to Come" in 1860, Whitman was taking primarily the larger view of his poetic career:

> Poets to come!
> Not to-day is to justify me, and Democracy, and what we are for,
> But you, a new brood, native, athletic, continental, greater than
> before known,
> You must justify me.
>
> Indeed, if it were not for you, what would I be?
> What is the little I have done, except to arouse you?
>
> I depend on being realized, long hence, where the broad flat prairies
> spread, and thence to Oregon and California inclusive,
> I expect that the Texan and the Arizonian, ages hence, will
> understand me,
> I expect that the future Carolinian and Georgian will understand me
> and love me,
> I expect that Kanadians, a hundred, and perhaps many hundred years
> from now, in winter, in the splendor of the snow and woods, or
> on the icy lakes, will take me with them, and permanently enjoy
> themselves with me.
>
> Of to-day I know I am momentary, untouched – I am the bard of
> the future,
> I but write one or two indicative words for the future,
> I but advance a moment, only to wheel and hurry back in the
> darkness.
>
> I am a man who, sauntering along, without fully stopping, turns a
> casual look upon you, and then averts his face,
> Leaving it to you to prove and define it,
> Expecting the main things from you.

But back on the eve of the first *Leaves of Grass*, Whitman would have found little consolation in sublimation, in his high hopes and ambitions for himself and his book deferred. The stiff-jointed, stoical warrior fighting a rearguard action for the public acceptance of his work was to be a thing of the future. In 1855, Whitman was looking directly in front of himself, was planning and working for the immediate recognition of his poetry and its immediate impact on Americans and American culture. In the welter of distortions and half-truths made over the years about the book's reception (many emanating from Whitman), it is all too easy today to overlook Whitman's frantically sincere determination in 1855 to be read and – if he had his way about it – read correctly by his contemporaries.

All the thoughts about American writing he had been harboring for years, the hopes he had been entertaining for the creation of a national culture and for his own debut in the role of national spokesman, now came rushing forth in the torrent of prose with which he introduced (and into whose context he set) the poems of the first edition. That excited prefatory credo, the final accumulation of thoughts and ideas gathering for years but committed to print only as his poems were going through the press, was an essay understandably pitched to the superlative. The greatest potentiality for modern man and culture, Whitman claimed with his opening breath, was America; the greatest man among a people was its poet; and the greatest poet was he who most completely followed the prescriptions for poetry set down by the essay. All this Whitman wrote in the third person, but observant readers then had no more difficulty than readers today in understanding the essay as having been written in Whitman's autobiographical third person.

There is something electric even from the distance of the late twentieth century in the prose of Whitman's Preface – its crackling enthusiasm, kinetic energy, sprawling vistas, contagious sense of on-the-spot self-discovery. Original as it seems today, however, in 1855 it was actually something of a straggler in entering upon the well-worn territory of literary nationalism. Other writers before Whitman had competed for bragging rights about American cultural potentiality, and many others – so many that Perry Miller, tired of reading them, labeled them all as purveyors of the "nativist inventory" – had taken to listing the geographical and topographical features which would figure in any national poem.[6] Still, no one, not even Emerson, had succeeded in proceeding with the gusto and compass of Whitman. Gargantua reborn as a modern, he would have his ideal poet "incarnate" the geography and "embouchure" the waters of North America; and as thought to demonstrate his meaning, he indited that task in long-running sentences seemingly as illimitable and inclusive as their subject.[7] But when it came to adding the obligatory, corresponding accounting of leading American writers which normally accompanied the "nativist inventory," Whitman chose to turn his shoulder, even though he was to be punctiliously respectful of the convention for decades after it was no longer de rigueur. In 1855, the omission was, of course, calculated and strategic; at the moment when Whitman, in the flush of self-discovery, stepped forward, all other poets necessarily stepped backward.

"The poets I would have must be a power in this state, and an engrossing power in the state," he wrote in one of his preparatory notebooks, and Whitman never wavered in his assertions – the 1855 Preface is really one long assertion composed of smaller ones – about the proper place for a national poet.[8] Presidents he might provokingly seat next to prostitutes and matrons next to fishermen, but however he shifted the hierarchical configuration of society, Whitman was always certain to position the poet at the center of the new order. He had, like Emerson and other transcendentalists, a pronounced affection for the figure of the circle, and in the ideal state of affairs he liked to think of the poet as the man at the center of things – the focus of the crowd, the midpoint between sky and ocean, the "spanner" of east and west, the "arbiter" of diversity, the "equalizer," the "tallier." One of the most persistent figures of his imagination – a fantasy, no doubt – was of himself, the modern poet, as surrounded by crowds of people, sometimes involved with and sometimes separate from them, but always at their center.

Emerson had said of his ideal poet in "The Poet" that he would have to be possessed of a "centred mind," and no doubt Whitman would have fervently agreed. But where Emerson tended to mean by this the poet's metaphysical relationship with the universe, Whitman would naturally also have stressed the social component, the poet's relation to his time and community. A "bard," he wrote in a central tenet of the Preface, "is to be commensurate with a people," is to be the voice of the common people in their relations to all things – to times past and future, to their and to other polities, to the physical and spiritual universe, to their bodies and minds, and, finally, to their language. Whitman never tired of speaking of the "eligibility" of the people to culture, and reciprocally he saw his ideal poet as their "answerer." The test of the new American poetry, therefore, as he put it near the end of the Preface, was this: Did it "answer"? The stipulated response was, if it was to be the true poetry of its time and place, that it must.

All these things done, all the preconditions that he laid down in the Preface for his new American poet and poetry faithfully met, Whitman was able to conclude with perfectly matched poetic and philosophical balance, poet and people would meet at the highest level of common good:

> An individual is as superb as a nation when he has the qualities which make a superb nation. The soul of the largest and wealthiest and proudest nation may well go half-way to meet that of its poets. The signs are effectual. There is no fear of mistake. If the one is true the other is

true. The proof of a poet is that his country absorbs him as affectionately as he has absorbed it.

What made the 1855 Preface so powerful a document was its underlying faith that this situation of affairs was not only possible but was awaiting its benefactor. If poetry had its "uses," as its nineteenth-century defenders fervently believed, Whitman was confident that his American poet would be the one to put his and his contemporaries' faith to its supreme test.

This may sound like an empty boast today, the kind of inflated patriotism and self-aggrandizement for which Whitman has often been parodied and caricatured, as in Max Beerbohm's cartoon of "Walt Whitman, Inciting the Bird of Freedom to Soar." But in 1855, large statements of this sort would not have sounded as implausible to Whitman's contemporaries as they do to his descendants, nor was Whitman alone in stating them; only the range and style of his rhetoric, not the rhetoric itself, would have singled him out from numerous of his contemporaries in the press and elsewhere. Against the background of the Crystal Palace dinner and the greatest surge of expansion and prosperity in the history of the American publishing industry, this kind of large claim was far from uncommon. The publication of Harriet Beecher Stowe's *Uncle Tom's Cabin* in 1852, the publishing event of the century with American sales running well into the hundreds of thousands during its first year and far beyond that figure overseas, had become a byword about the possibilities of authorship and publishing in an age of mass readership; it put a measure of substance behind the popular advertising phrase, "literature for the millions." Within weeks of the publication of *Leaves of Grass,* the editor of the publishers' trade magazine could refer to the period as an "age of books, where every author, *properly introduced,* is assured of a large circle of readers."[9]

The current bestseller was Henry Ward Beecher's *Star Papers,* advertised by its publisher, J. C. Derby, as "A Book for the Million" and "A Book That Will Live for Generations." Derby was doing his best to push the book along by using advertising tactics he was helping to introduce at that time, such as saturation ads in newspapers, publication of sales figures, republication of snippets from favorable reviews, and direct appeals to potential readers ("Reader, are you of a social turn – given to hilarity and exuberance of feeling? Don't delay to get at once a copy of Beecher's *Star Papers;* and upon making its acquaintance you will thank this advertisement for the introduction"). John Jewitt, still riding high on his success with *Uncle Tom's Cabin,* was currently touting as "The Great Book of the Year" his firm's edition of Margaret Fuller's *Woman in the Nineteenth Century.* T. B. Peterson was advertising as "The Great Book of the Age" a Philadelphia society novel called *Our First Families,* and Bunce and Brother (O. B. Bunce was later to publish O'Connor's defense of Whitman, *The Good Gray Poet,* and to become involved briefly in the publication of *Drum-Taps*) were announcing "The Great Book Is Published" in their *Blanche Dearwood* ("In a few years hence the term 'By the author of Blanche Dearwood' will be as familiar to our lips as 'By the author of Waverly'"). Stringer and Townsend were bringing out new volumes of their popular "People's Edition" of Cooper's works. Miller, Orton and Mulligan, who had had a success the previous year with the second series of Fanny Fern's *Fern Leaves,* were preparing to bring out what they called "The Autobiography of a Self-Made Man," Frederick Douglass' *My Bondage and My Freedom. New York Naked* by George B. Foster was issued in June, and in early July so was James Gordon Bennett's autobiography. Tennyson's *Maud* and Longfellow's *Hiawatha,* the first already out and the other soon to be released, were to be the poetic successes of the year.

Leaves of Grass, by contrast, attracted relatively little notice at first. Fowler and Wells ran the small ad, actually a squib, reprinted above, through early August in the New York *Tribune;* and it was not until July 23 that the first review of the book appeared. It was surely no coincidence that that review also appeared in the *Tribune,* since Fowler and Wells were apparently on good professional (and Wells on good personal) terms with Horace Greeley.[10] Fowler and Wells had been the publishers of several editions of Greeley's *Hints Toward Reforms* and of his edition of Margaret Fuller's *Papers on Literature and Art,* and they regularly used the *Tribune* as an advertising medium for their books and journals (including *Leaves of Grass,* which was the only title they consistently advertised by itself). Greeley, for his part, reciprocated by printing frequent puffs of the firm's books and magazines, and he even wrote an article in the paper in strong praise of Orson Fowler's book on housing for the workingman's family.[11] He had even once sat, like Whitman, for his phrenological examination in their office.[12] Intellectually, the two parties had the considerable common ground of reform, self-culture, and the rights of the workingman between themselves – as well as between themselves and Whitman. Greeley was at the same time also partial to Whitman, whom he had occasionally published in the *Tribune* during the late forties and early fifties. In fact, at some later date in the 1850s – one cannot specify exactly when – he also became an admirer of *Leaves of Grass* (his personal copy of the 1856 edition survives in the Lion Collection of the New York Public Library).

So when he or his managing editor, Charles Dana, authorized Dana's July 23 review of *Leaves of Grass,* there was presumably at least as much of a background to the review as there was to many reviews at a time when book and newspaper publishers were often in relation with one another. But this does not mean that most midnineteenth-century reviews should be discounted as biased. Dana, for instance, was unquestionably following his own well-known, hardheaded judgment in mixing praise and criticism for the book before concluding that it contained "much of the essential spirit of poetry beneath an uncouth and grotesque embodiment."

At virtually the same time, Whitman received the now famous letter of praise written by Emerson on July 21 in response to Whitman's "wonderful gift" of Leaves of Grass. These two important critiques, coming as they did in immediate succession and soon followed by a review in Fowler and Wells's Life Illustrated, must have given a considerable lift to his spirits; but a pair of public responses and one still private, he was too experienced not to know, would hardly have sufficed to launch a book's reputation. When only silence followed them in the following weeks, he decided to take the fate of his book into his own hands by writing anonymous self-reviews and placing them with his editor friends.

There has been a certain notoriety attached to the writing of these self-reviews since the initial revelation of their authorship after Whitman's death. Whitman had himself been an outspoken critic during his editorship of the Eagle of the widespread practice by book publishers and theater managers of placing paid puffs in newspapers, but when it came to his own poetry he looked the other way. I have already spoken of how the practice of self-criticism by various English writers had caught his eye in the pre–1855 period; this practice was also quite widespread in the United States. Poe, for example, excelled at self-promotion, was second in zest and originality in playing the game, as it turned out, only to Whitman. And in the months following the publication of Leaves of Grass, a minor scandal would erupt in the press over the revelation that James Fields, quickly making Ticknor, Fields known as the leading American publisher of imaginative literature, had used his company's influence to seek favorable reviews from newspapers of Longfellow's recently issued Hiawatha.[13] In fact, soliciting positive reviews of his firm's forthcoming works was standard procedure with Fields, as it was with other influential publishers.

Whitman was to the self-promoters among writers as Fields was to publishers; but Whitman, unlike Fields, had no fear of detection. If anything, he welcomed it as a means of gaining additional publicity for his work. Why else would he have been so careless to write his reviews in a prose style so nearly identical to that of the 1855 Preface or to have dropped titillating hints as to the fact of his self-authorship? But if Whitman's practice of self-promotion was not particularly aberrant literary practice for its time, his style of self-promotion was as distinctive as the poetry itself. The reviews, in fact, can be understood as an important extraliterary extension of *Leaves of Grass* itself. Read in this way, they give one an unusually vivid glimpse of Whitman's ambitions and expectations for the volume shortly after its delivery, umbilical cord and all, into the world.

"An American bard at last!" he wrote in the opening words of the first of the self-reviews as though putting to rest any doubts as to the identity between the author of the volume of poetry under consideration and the ideal poet called for in the Preface, "One of the roughs, large, proud, affectionate, eating, drinking, and breeding, his costume manly and free, his face sunburnt and bearded, his posture strong and erect, his voice bringing hope and prophecy to the generous races of the young and old."[14] Describing himself as he would have liked to be seen, Whitman cast himself as the new American bard: "Self-reliant, with haughty eyes, assuming to himself all the attributes of his country, steps Walt Whitman into literature, talking like a man unaware that there was ever hitherto such a production as a book, or such a being as a writer."

At the same time, his corresponding view of the new national poetry was "defiant," even genuinely revolutionary. The new poetry, as he prescribed it, was to do away with decorum, authority, precedents, and rhyme. It was, rather, to be written in a style "simply [its] own style, just born and red"; it was to deal equally with men and women, with the pleasures and attributes of the body equally with those of the spirit; to be organic even to the point of equating the sexual act with the creative act of poetry; to open up poetry to the world so as to make it not only democratically inclusive of all people, occupations, activities, and regions of the country but also consubstantial with life. And at the center of it all, the greatest lover, he placed Walt Whitman.

"Who is it, praising himself as if others were not fit to do it, and coming rough and unbidden among writers, to unsettle what was settled, and to revolutionize in fact our modern civilization?" he rhetorically posed, before answering his question by giving a mannered, thumbnail biography of Walt Whitman. But the man who placed this review with the *Democratic Review* was not the same Walter Whitman who had contributed his moralistic stories years before, nor was this the same dynamic *Democratic Review* of the early 1840s which published them. The *Review* (now known as the *United States Review*) was now under different management since its glory days under O'Sullivan and was an organ of the conservative Democratic establishment with which Whitman had long since broken. But it at least retained a tie to the cultural nationalism of its past, and perhaps for this reason, or perhaps because of a personal connection, Whitman was able to place his boisterous article in the staid confines of the *Review*.

A second, less interesting article, written at virtually the same time and sent to Fowler and Wells's *American Phrenological Journal*, took a different tack in expressing the cultural nationalism underlying his thinking in 1855 by comparing an English against an American poet, Tennyson author of *Maud* and Whitman author of *Leaves of Grass*.[15] Working one of his favorite notions rather hard, an unchanging article of faith with him throughout his life, he crudely divided literature into two seemingly irreconcilable categories, the aristocratic (English) and the democratic (American), each the direct and inevitable offspring of its "national blood." Although he would in later years play the sycophant to Tennyson, in the summer of 1855 he was in no frame of mind to praise Tennyson ("the bard of ennui and of the aristocracy") or any other foreign writer, dismissing them wholesale as the products of an antiquated civilization. About the "new poet," Walt Whitman, he naturally had greater hopes: "He is to prove either the most lamentable of failures or the most glorious of triumphs, in the known history of literature. And after all we have written we confess our brain-felt and heart-felt inability to decide which we think it is likely to be."

The third and most autobiographical of the self-reviews ("To give judgments on real poems, one needs an account of the poet himself") he appropriately placed in the hometown Brooklyn *Daily Times*, the paper he would edit during the depression years of 1857–9.[16] The "man whom our Brooklynites know so well" offered the public an idealized self-portrait painted in conformity to the specifications of the persona he had created in the *Leaves* themselves (especially in the poem he was variously to call, "Poem of Walt Whitman, an American," "Walt Whitman," and finally "Song of Myself"). He characterized himself, above all, as a man of the people, "a man who is art-and-part with the commonalty, and with immediate life":

> Of pure American breed, large and lusty – age thirty-six years (1855) – never once using medicine – never dressed in black, always dressed freely and clean in strong clothes – neck open, shirt-collar flat and broad, countenance tawny transparent red, beard well-mottled with white, hair like hay after it has been mowed in the field and lies tossed and streaked – his physiology corroborating a rugged phrenology – a person singularly beloved and looked toward, especially by young men and the illiterate – one who has firm attachments there, and associates there – one who does not associate with literary people – a man never called upon to make speeches at public dinners – never on platforms amid the crowds of clergymen, or professors, or aldermen, or congressmen – rather down in the bay with pilots in their pilot-boat – or off on a cruise with fishers in a fishing-smack – or riding on a Broadway omnibus, side by side with the driver – or with a band of loungers over the open grounds of the country – fond of New York and Brooklyn – fond of the life of the great ferries – one whom, if you should meet, you need

not expect to meet an extraordinary person – one in whom you will see the singularity which consists in no singularity – whose conduct is no dazzle or fascination, nor requires any deference, but has the easy fascination of what is homely and accustomed – as of something you knew before, and was waiting for – there you have Walt Whitman, the begetter of a new offspring out of literature, taking with easy nonchalance the chances of its present reception, and, through all misunderstandings and distrusts, the chances of its future reception – preferring always to speak for himself rather than have others speak for him.

No doubt, it was the same "easy nonchalance" about his reception which led him two weeks later to play his best trump in handing over Emerson's personal letter of praise to Charles Dana, their common acquaintance, for publication in the *Tribune*.

These brilliant pieces of self-promotion indicate the extent to which Whitman had adopted his favorite Wordsworthian adage about the necessity for the original poet to create the terms for his or her own reception. Using the journals at his disposal, he was going all out in the months following the publication of his work to reaffirm the case he had made in the *Leaves* for a new poetry of cultural democracy with himself playing the leading role of poet laureate of the people. There was something magisterial in the rank egotism with which he went about this business, as he himself must have known:

> What good is it to argue about egotism? There can be no two thoughts on Walt Whitman's egotism. That is avowedly what he steps out of the crowd and turns and faces them for. Mark, critics! Otherwise is not used for you the key that leads to the use of the other keys to this well-enveloped man. His whole work, his life, manners, friendships, writings, all have among their leading purposes an evident purpose to stamp a new type of character, namely his own, and indelibly fix it and publish it, not for a model but an illustration, for the present and future of American letters and American young men, for the south the same as the north, and for the Pacific and Mississippi country, and Wisconsin and Texas and Kansas and Canada and Havana and Nicaragua, just as much as New York and Boston.[17]

This was not purely the stuff of rhetoric, Whitman in an annexationist mood for himself and the country. It was the exhilarating vision he possessed in the summer of 1855 when, perched on high on top of his hard-earned achievement, he looked out onto a spreading nation populated by a coast-to-coast expanse of readers. For one who felt the mythic pull of North America as powerfully as Whitman, the prospect was intoxicating; and Whitman took it in with enormous enthusiasm and inspiration. Within the next several years, he would be considering the possibility of taking his one-man show out onto the open road of America as a "wander-lecturer" and would also be planning on bringing out geographically designed editions of *Leaves of Grass* for the various sections of the country, even rehearsing his manner of invocation in his notebook: "Man! Woman! Youth! wherever you are, in the Northern, Southern, Eastern, or Western States – in Kanada – by the sea-coast, or far inland."[18] If ever an American poet had a personal and national vision on a grand scale, it was surely Whitman in 1855. And by that time, he had developed the poetic means by which he believed he could make his vision a reality.

6

Whitman and the Reader, 1855

I have been arguing so far the case of Whitman's grand – some would say grandiose – aspiration in 1855 to speak as a national poet with *Leaves of Grass*; it remains now to argue the separate but related case of his aspiration to speak as a national poet *in Leaves of Grass*. It has been all too easy for modern critics to see Whitman, as Sartre saw his prototypal nineteenth-century writer, as writing from a situation of "solitude": "He made of writing a metaphysical occupation, a prayer, an examination of conscience, everything but a communication."[1] It is not that Whitman did not do these things also; he wrote, after all, narrowly speaking, in the kind of physical and spiritual isolation that Sartre criticized. At the time of the composition of *Leaves of Grass*, he was sharing a room in the family house with his retarded brother and had neither at home nor in the community the support of like-minded, even partially comprehending family, friends, or colleagues. But it is also true, as I will be claiming, that Whitman had an overwhelming desire and need to communicate to his contemporaries. He would never have thought to say, even as only a whimsical disclaimer, what Hawthorne said in his Preface to *The Snow Image*: "Ever since my youth, I have been addressing a very limited circle of friendly readers, without much danger of being overheard by the public at large." Whitman, by contrast, wrote with the fervent desire and expectation of being read and discussed by the reading public. *Leaves of Grass* without a public, in his eyes, would have been a contradiction in terms.

To put this matter into different words, there was a perhaps surprisingly high degree of congruity between Whitman's ambitions as a private and as a national poet. The most useful discussion of these terms for my purposes was made a generation ago by William Charvat, who distinguished between three basic types of poets: mass poets, public poets, and private poets. Discounting the importance of mass poets to literary history as mere "manufacturers" of verse rather than as "artists," he was left with the more difficult problem of distinguishing between public and private poets, which he did by counterposing their relations with themselves against those with their reading public.[2]

The private poet, he claimed, "is concerned not only to preserve [his or her] personal uniqueness but to intensify it through the writing of verse – even at the expense of being rejected for unintelligibility." The public poet, conversely,

> progressively subordinates or submerges his uniqueness. For reasons which are the province of the psychiatrist-sociologist, his sense of separateness is less strong than his social sense. And though his urge to be a moral leader may be shared by the private poet, his wish to be a *spokesman* is not. A writer may through his works be a leader in his old age and after he is dead, but he can be a spokesman only in his time. Representativeness *in his time,* then, is the differentiating quality of the public poet, and it is the quality that makes the fundamental difference between his verse and that of the private poet.

Charvat also noted that the public poet can reasonably expect to be supported economically by the public for his writing: "He not only believes that the verse he writes to answer a need of his own meets a need of his readers, but hopes that there are enough readers to support him in verse-writing as a way of life."

His representative examples of the private and public poet are Dickinson and Longfellow, respectively – a fair enough selection. Although Charvat was primarily interested in analyzing the connections between nineteenth-century public writers and the evolving literary conditions, institutions, and practices of their time, he was intellectually flexible enough to recognize the fact that his conceptual distinction could not be uniformly maintained in practice. Even the writers he was most interested in, such as Melville and Longfellow, he knew, often waged their own internal battles between their private and public inclinations. Melville, for instance, wrote out of extensive personal experience in creating the extreme representation of the midcentury writer cut off from his receiving audience in his story of the "dead letters" writer Bartleby the scrivener, a story for which he chose magazine publication in *Putnam's.*[3]

Of Whitman, Charvat had curiously little to say, although the few references that he does make suggest that he thought of Whitman, with Emerson and Dickinson, as "an exclusively lyrical (and private) poet."[4] I see Whitman, by contrast, as the most fascinatingly complex, confused, and, finally, significant mixture of private and public impulses in American literary history. His egotism was, of course, formidable; and his best writing, not surprisingly, was normally deeply and searchingly autobiographical. And yet, in 1855 Whitman unquestionably saw himself, in Charvat's phrase, as an American "spokesman," as his Preface, still one of the most impressive American cultural manifestos, makes clear. But he was also an American "spokesman" in the poems themselves, and in order to appreciate this fact one has to broaden Charvat's conception of this term to make it fit the kind of poetic "speaking" that Whitman did in *Leaves of Grass*.

The issue presents itself with the opening poetic lines of *Leaves of Grass:*

> I celebrate myself,
> And what I assume you shall assume,
> For every atom belonging to me as good belongs to you.

Whitman could not possibly have created a more audacious, or a more suitable, opening to his poetry. It is no exaggeration to claim – the notebooks offer clear substantiation – that it took Whitman years of effort, of thought and experimentation, to reach this formulation of his poetic relations with his American readers. It required of him, as part of the general process of inventing a new mode for his poetry, that he create an "I" and a "you" to act in tandem within it. With the aid of the notebooks, which permit one to see the stages preliminary to the published poetry, one can appreciate how assiduously Whitman worked at that strategy.

The central drama of Whitman's life, as Paul Zweig persuasively articulates the matter in his critical biography of the poet, was his "self-making," the cross-fertilization of art and life in the creation of Whitman's identity as a poet and the matching creation of the semiautobiographical persona at the heart of his 1855 poems.[5] I have already spoken of Whitman's gradual personal and professional self-transformation during the late 1840s and early 1850s, and I would like now to show how a similar development overtook his self-representation in his new poems. One can see from his pre–1855 notebooks how carefully gotten up was his new poetic persona, how fully planned and mannered was what Whitman would later attempt to pass off as his "spontaneous me." Numerous entries, in fact, have the sound of a man rehearsing before the mirror before daring to go onstage: "Boldness – *Nonchalant ease and indifference* To encourage me or any one continually to strike out alone – So it seems good *to me* – This is my way, *my* pleasure, *my* choice, *my* costume, friendship, amour, or what not."[6] Throughout the notebooks, he sprinkled reminders and bits of advice to himself which served him, in effect, as stage directions about how to speak, look, act, write – how, in short, to be himself. One of the more fascinating phenomena that the notebooks reveal is his experimentation with resetting into the first person lines originally written in the third person. The famous line, certainly one of the conceptually central ones in the 1855 *Leaves,* "I am the man. I suffered. I was there," he originally conceived as "he is the man;

he suffered, he was there"; and there are other similar shifts of person as well.[7]

This line appears toward the end of a long catalogue in "Song of Myself" in which Whitman's persona identifies itself with the full scope of human activity: I am with the western gold diggers and the southern cotton pickers; I am on the farm with the animals, in the factory with the workers, in the hills of Judea with "the beautiful gentle god by my side"; I am outside under the stars, at sea with fur hunters, in bed with the bride. His "I," in short, is potentially everywhere and everything, is as fluid and flexible as the human scene is broad and open. But in reaching for breadth, it necessarily sacrifices depth; for flexibility, definition. Who, after all, one wonders, is the "real I myself," either in or out of the poem? It is as though Whitman's poems are in a constant search for the *real* — the "real words," the "real literature," the "real thing," the "real body," the "real self," the "real ME," the "real life," the "real war," the "real Union," even the "real real." If Whitman's persona seems elusive, the reason is that it is; there would always be moments when it eluded Whitman himself. Even to read Whitman's notebooks, as Zweig has commented, is to have one's normal expectations of finding intimate traces of personality and revelations of character disappointed.[8] One simply cannot read Whitman in his notebooks as one reads, say, Emerson or Thoreau in their journals for exploration of personal depths; there is surprisingly little to be revealed. Far from being his most private, intimate works, the notebooks are virtually as public as the poetry, leaving one in doubt as to where the private self leaves off and the public one begins. For all the technical modifications and improvements he made between the stage of the notebooks and that of the finished poems, the "I" of the notebooks *is* the "I" of the early poetry, the "performing self" of the one, to use Richard Poirier's term, coexistent with that of the other.[9]

Whitman seems also to have written into his notebooks throughout his career with an exaggerated sense of being observed. Phrases he considered impure he tried to obscure with a scribbling orthography; thoughts or ideas he felt guilty about, with erasures or emendations; his tempestuous relationship with Peter Doyle, with numerical ciphers to cover identities. In later years, he periodically committed papers, letters, and documents — how many and of what sort, we will never know — to the flames. It was as though he felt, or anticipated, the eye of the public boring in on him through his walls. This may not have been all to the good of his personal life, but its service to his poetry was clear. By 1855 he had learned to incorporate his heightened sensitivity to audience ingeniously into the new vocative mode of his poetry. Had he left lines originally written in the third person unrevised, he would have closed off the possibility of a receiving role within as well as without the poetry. The shift to the first person allowed him to insert an "I" to be followed by a "you" into his 1855 poems, opening them up simultaneously inwardly and outwardly; and that pattern was to become one of the central poetic conceptions of his 1855 edition.

Indeed, the "role" of the reader – Whitman thought of it as such – was as carefully theorized and rehearsed as was his own role as persona in the poetry. It had a history as long as, and interrelated with, that of his poetic self-conception. Whitman had been addressing the reader repeatedly, as I hope I have made clear in previous chapters, from the earliest days of his journalism, often in tones nearly indistinguishable from those of *Leaves of Grass*. Even an act so seemingly mundane as the periodic call to Democrats to vote could come out sounding like the invocatory mode he would perfect in the future *Leaves of Grass*: "Democratic readers! *you* whose eyes pass over these lines! have *you* deposited your ballot? If not proceed to the polls, forthwith."[10] Or consider this advisory 1845 newspaper piece, already quoted in Chapter 3, which for the sake of argument I now give set into Whitmanesque lines of verse:

> Boy, or young man, whose eyes hover over these lines!
> How much of your leisure time do you give to *loafing?*
> What vulgar habits of smoking cigars, chewing tobacco, of making
>   frequent use of blasphemous or obscene language have you begun
>   to form?
> What associations and appetites are you idly falling into, that future
>   years will ripen in wickedness or shame?
> Consider these questions as addressed, not to everybody in general,
>   but to *you*, in particular – and answer them honestly to your own
>   heart.
> The one who speaks to you through this printed page, never has
>   spoken, and probably never will speak, to you in any other way;
> But it would be a deep and abiding joy for him to know that he had
>   awakened wholesome reflection in your mind, even if it lasts for
>   only a passing five minutes.[11]

These lines not only convey much more of the rhythm which would characterize the future *Leaves of Grass* poems than do Whitman's early poems, but they also anticipate by a full decade Whitman's fondness for channeling the rhythmic emphasis of his statement into his personal pronouns – or more exactly here, into the relationship between those pronouns.

This mode of address can be understood, at least in part, as Whitman's absorption of the journalistic usage of the age. M. H. Abrams has argued strongly that Romantic poetry typically conceived of no functional role for its audience; but he made his generalization in looking upward to the exclusion of what was transpiring down below, as in the case of an American writer like Whitman, who drew heavily on the journalistic conventions of the time.[12] The journalistic style of intimate address to the reader was extremely common in the midcentury years, particularly in magazine journalism, where it became something of a literary convention. American magazine journalism had inherited the convention of the address to the "gentle reader" from the British; and as one might readily expect, that convention became gradually democratized as the American readership itself broadened and multiplied during the decades of Whitman's early manhood. Magazine editors regularly addressed their readers directly across the "editorial table" in caressing tones designed to cultivate a bond of familiarity between reader, editor, and journal – this, ironically, at the moment when the incipient age of mass circulation was actually putting distance between them.

By the 1840s, it had become one of the standard modes of the journalistic editorial, the common practice of numerous editors. Park Benjamin, Whitman's boss at the *New World,* for instance, was an expert at this mode; but its most masterful practitioner was unquestionably Nathaniel Willis, one of the most resourceful and successful journalistic writers of the 1830s and 1840s. Willis once spoke of the familiar, rambling literary style used to personalize and familiarize reader and writer as "the undress of the mind"; and in the generation before Whitman broadened that phrase to include body and soul, Willis was the most flamboyant journalist writing in the mode.[13] Here, for instance, is a typical Willis tête-à-tête with his reader in the *New Mirror* from the early 1840s:

> Our heart is more spread and fed than our pocket, dear reader, with the new possession of this magic long arm by which we are handing you, one after another, the books we have long cherished. Almost the first manifestation of the poet's love, is the sending of his favorite books to his mistress... The Mirror becomes, in a manner, our *literary parish* – we the indulged literary vicar, with whose tastes *out* of the pulpit you are as familiar as with sermons of criticism when *in;* and you, dear reader, become our loved parishioner, for whom we cater, at fountains of knowledge and fancy to which you have not our facility of access, and whose face, turned to us on Saturday, inspires us like the countenance of a familiar friend.[14]

More typical of this editorial mode of address was this refined sales pitch made by the editor of one of the new monthly magazines of the 1840s in its opening issue:

> We as good as give away our Magazine, and only charge an inconceivably low price for the information which we impart under the head of Topics of the Month, which will not be found a mere essay, to be

read by nobody in particular, but a private letter addressed by the Editor to each reader of our Magazine personally; so that every one who subscribes to Holden's Dollar Magazine, will be sure of receiving a monthly letter from a very sincere well-wisher.[15]

Even writers less confident of the public or more removed from the conventions of journalism than Whitman, such as Hawthorne, Melville, and Thoreau, were openly engaging their readers, at times even putting the "reader" into their works in the early 1850s – Hawthorne sent the reader into *The Scarlet Letter* holding a wild rose, Melville had Ishmael conduct the reader on a tour of a whaler and through the intricacies of the whaling life, and Thoreau rigorously lectured the reader, New England–style, on the conduct of life. The prevalence of such literary strategies at this time was no mere coincidence. As the rapidly changing conditions of midcentury literary culture forced all the partners to American letters to redefine themselves and their relative positions, American writers, good and bad alike, found it a necessity of the highest order to stake out their grounds anew vis-à-vis their readers.

With Whitman, however, the engagement of the reader was more dynamic and lasting than it was with his major contemporaries, and more sincere and serious than with journalistic usage. A typical early Whitman poem, as I will soon be showing more closely, opens with an address to his reader which it then becomes the poem's task to sustain, an indication of how close the idea of "making" poems was with Whitman to an act of vocal address. Indeed, Whitman's need for "contact" with his readers – to use a term which habitually gets his poetic accentuation – was an obsession. One normally thinks of it as the reader, eager to touch his or her fantasy, who is the one to cross the line separating literary relations and situations from their real-life equivalents; but in the case of Whitman, the first step (and the resultant confusion it caused) was often his. At times, in fact, the early poems seem addressed less to impersonal readers outside the reaches of the poem than to unidentified friends and lovers located within the imaginary plane of the poem. A typical instance of this manner of address is this, from the opening to the second poem of the 1855 edition:

> Come closer to me,
> Push close my lovers and take the best I possess,
> Yield closer and closer and give me the best you possess.
>
> This is unfinished business with me .... how is it with you?
> I was chilled with the cold types and cylinders and wet paper
> between us.
>
> I pass so poorly with paper and types .... I must pass with the
> contact of bodies and souls.
>
> ("A Song for Occupations")

Not only were the niceties and conventions of polite literature but literature itself was too restrictive, a sheet of paper too thick and resistant to allow him the face-to-face, body-to-body immediacy he claimed to desire in these poems. Clearly, Whitman's was one "print-based authorial identity" which needed to extend its muscles to the outermost limits that print allowed.[16] A more cautious Whitman would later remove these lines from the poem, but in 1855, his fervor far outpaced his common sense. In writing a poetry which was purportedly to transcend the physical means of its production and the literary conventions of its transmission, Whitman would be pursuing a literary strategy which would bring extraordinary pressures to bear not only on its readers but also on its creator.

This need for contact is perhaps most idiosyncratically reflected in his poetic vocabulary; here is a brief Whitman lexicon of terms expressing union: "interchange," "interlink," "interlock," "intertwist," "interpenetrate," "intertwine," "interwet," "intercommunication"; "hub," "ensemble," "plenum," "congeries," "clusters," "melange," "compend of compends"; "integral," "omnivorous," "omnigenous," "inseparable," "indissoluble," "banding," "blending," "knitting," "twining," "cohering," "spanned," "tallied," "immerged," "interveined," "joined." He even looked into the foreign languages ("attache," "vis-a-viz," "entourage," "camerado") in his voracious search for a poetic language of human connection; and as I will soon be showing, he worked hard and effectively in the midfifties with his new poetics to devise techniques for expressing this theme in verse.

I spoke earlier of the audacity of the opening lines of "Song of Myself," and perhaps now I can make my meaning clearer. It would be one thing, a mere presumption perhaps, to declare as a matter of democratized physics that my assumptions are your assumptions because we share the same physical universe. But when Whitman proceeded to transmute the shared physical space into a poetic space and to furnish it with his personal ideas about value, belief, behavior, and sexuality; and then, worse yet, when he attributed them to his readers, he overstepped the bounds not only of accepted literary but also of accepted moral conventions.

All this could not but have had a significant effect on his public reception in 1855, as an experienced literary professional should have been aware; but I do not believe that Whitman created his poems in the 1850s with an eye so much to his actual reader as to his idealized conception of his reader and of the new literary culture he hoped to create for and through that reader. He had clearly been giving the matter deep thought for some time before committing himself to print in 1855. By the time he finally reached a mature position about his own role in his poetry, he also reached a considered position about the corresponding role to be played by his reader; they were, in fact, interrelated parts of his larger poetic conception. And just as he worked nervously and tirelessly throughout the second half of his life at his ambition of creating the ultimate version of *Leaves of Grass,* so he formulated and reformulated what he hoped would be a final statement on his desired reader reception right up until the appearance of his farewell "A Backward Glance O'er Travel'd Roads."

In a wide variety of notebook entries, journalistic pieces, self-reviews, and "official" critical statements, Whitman espoused the idea of the reader of his poetry as being a vital agent coequal with himself both existentially and creatively. If he himself was "both in and out of the game," so the reader was both in and out of the game, or to shift the metaphor, was both in and out of the text. One can trace the forerunner of this activistic, participatory conception of the reading process at least as far back as 1845 to his analogous view of the educational process. In one of the articles he wrote in the local newspaper, the ex-teacher gave his towns-people a lesson in pedagogy by deploring the ignorance of many Brooklyn teachers of "the essential spirit of education, which is clearing and freshening and strengthening and properly stimulating the pupil's mind."[17] The following year he told readers of the *Eagle:* "We consider it a great thing in education that the learner be taught to rely upon himself. The best teachers do not profess to *form* the mind, but to *direct* it in such a manner – and put such tools in its power – that it builds up itself. This part of education is far more worthy of attention, than the acquiring of a certain quantity of school knowledge."[18] Ever since his editorship of the New York *Aurora,* it is clear, his journalistic position had been basically that of an instructor of the people; and so it was a natural habit of mind with him even through several changes of profession that he remained predisposed to see himself as a teacher, no matter in what guise or medium of expression.

In considering the way poetry – his poetry – should ideally be written and read, Whitman found a focus in the fifties for bringing together the varied, loosely organized ideas he had long held in mind about such diverse matters as nature and nurture, education, self-improvement, individualism, democracy, and cultural nationalism. Although it was not until much later that he was to speak of "the modern intelligent reader (a new race unknown before our time) [who] can take and adapt and shape for him or herself" final meanings from the raw materials of print, he had already by 1855 reached this functionalist conception of the ideal reader of *Leaves of Grass* and of the reading process it required.[19] The idea of the necessity of a new kind of reader for a new kind of poetry, the one shaped along the same activistic, democratized lines as the other, was to be a critical position he articulated consistently throughout a lifetime of writing in his prose and poetry alike. It was one of the crucial factors on which he based his faith in what he was later to call "the poetry of the future": "The poetry of the future aims at the free expression of emotion, (which means far, far more than appears at first,) and to arouse and initiate, more than to define or finish. Like all modern tendencies, it has direct or indirect reference continually to the reader, to you or me, to the central identity of everything, the mighty Ego."[20]

A firm believer in "the never enough praised spread of common education and common newspapers and books" and the mass literacy they spread, Whitman came to believe in the "eligibility" of the mass public to receive his idea of reformation.[21] As he gradually lost faith in the political system during the decade of dispiriting infighting between sections and parties leading up to the Civil War, which left him in effect without a political option, he naturally transferred his fervor from the medium of politics to that of literature. The great, the exclusive, arena, for him, now became the literary; and by about 1856 he had come upon a metaphor to describe the idealized terms on which he saw himself as meeting his readers: "Of me the good comes by wristling [sic] for it. / I am not he bringing ointments and soft wool for you, / I am he with whom you must wristle. . . . I am / The good of you is not in me. . . . the good of you is altogether in yourself. / I am the one who indicates, and the one who provokes and tantalizes."[22] He liked the metaphor so much that he was still using it after the Civil War to describe reader-writer relations:

> Books are to be call'd for, and supplied, on the assumption that the process of reading is not a half-sleep, but, in highest sense, an exercise, a gymnast's struggle; that the reader is to do something for himself, must be on the alert, must himself or herself construct indeed the poem, argument, history, metaphysical essay – the text furnishing the hints, the clue, the start or framework. Not the book needs so much to be the complete thing, but the reader of the book does. That were to make a nation of supple and athletic minds, well-train'd, intuitive, used to depend on themselves, and not on a few coteries of writers.[23]

Whitman's remarks on the participatory role to be played by the reader in the construction of the artifacts of culture – indeed, of culture itself – sound strikingly modern, remind us in yet another way of how many-sided was his anticipation of the forms and modes of cultural expression in our own day. They bring out starkly into the open the reasons for the mutual antagonism between him and Matthew Arnold: Theirs was nothing less than a fundamental difference over the nature of culture and the manner of its transmission. It was not only that Whitman was locating the center of culture in himself – "trad[ing] merely on his own bottom," as Arnold called it – in the process, transferring cultural authority from the past to the present and from external to internal sources and thereby scrambling accepted notions of the content and character of culture; but that he was also shifting emphasis from the "what" to the "how" of culture.[24]

Whitman was always far ahead of his time in his insights into the "mediumship" of culture. Culture, for Whitman, was more a condition than an achievement, an open, evolving process rather than a formed or finished product at its end. His lack of formal education and the loose-patterned nature of his personal experience left him insensitive to, or even prejudiced against, the virtues of an ongoing cultural tradition. But his lack of immersion in the forms and manners of the past also freed him to overstep traditional boundaries of genre and to seek new subjects and shape new patterns of expression such as he chose out of the raucous, bustling society around him. It would be purest Whitman to characterize the muse of the Old World as come to America and "install'd amid the kitchen ware." Arnold was unquestionably justified from his perspective in seeing Whitman as slighting the inheritance of the past, but Whitman's thinking was geared precisely to emphasizing the presentness of the present. Culture, for Whitman, was *now*. Beginning with the 1855 *Leaves of Grass*, Whitman would attempt to open art radically to his world, to bring down the barriers between the poem and the world and between the poet and the reader.

For every remark about the role and responsibility of the reader, there was bound to be its like for him. Whitman's commitment to the vocation of the poet, through hard times and changing conditions, was unfaltering. One record of his self-dedication is his poetry; another is his notebooks, which contain an endless series of reminders by Whitman to himself about the function of the poet. In a notebook entry written in or around 1856, he stated his view most tersely: "All my poems do. All I write to arouse in you a great personality."[25] Other poets' poems *were*, he claimed; his *did*. Other poets were literary; he was natural. Other poets wrote for the few; he, for the masses. Other poets communicated with their readers across the high walls of conventions and traditions; he communicated directly, person to person. Other poets wrote *for* a passive, seated audience; he wrote *to* a more mobile reader, easily set in motion with himself. As to the identity of "other poets," that was easy enough for Whitman; "they" were European or British, men of the past; or increasingly as he grew older, they were imitative, puerile American writers. Which conveniently left him (and his hypothesized followers, the "poets to come") to be called American and modern.

Whitman was not normally given to expressions of sarcasm; but by the time of *Leaves of Grass*, the onetime defender and exponent of popular middle-class culture was almost invariably irritated to contempt in describing what he considered the "dancing masters" and the prettified, ornamented books of verse and fiction they turned out for the entertainment of their genteel readers. By contrast, he thought of his own contract with the reader, as his wrestling metaphor aptly expresses, as requiring of each labor and struggle, of locking author and reader into a rigorous mental activity whose resolution would eventuate in the transformation of each and of their society. In his mind, that relationship could be consummated only if it was conducted as a joint effort; as he told Traubel thirty-odd years later, "I like the feeling of a general partnership – as if the Leaves was anybody's who chooses just as truly as mine."[26] Activity, or better yet, shared activity, was everything; and so when Whitman came out in the 1850s with Leaves of Grass, with his reader positioned in a critical role, the emphasis of the poetry was shifted from content, where it had been in his reflexive, imitative poetry of the 1840s, to process.[27]

He not only formulated a critical theory of the reader's role for the 1855 Leaves of Grass; he carefully and persistently presented it to that supposed reader in the poetry, beginning with the stanzas prominently placed near the opening of the lead poem:

> Have you reckoned a thousand acres much? Have you reckoned the earth much?
> Have you practiced so long to learn to read?
> Have you felt so proud to get at the meaning of poems?
>
> Stop this day and night with me and you shall possess the origin of all poems,
> You shall possess the good of the earth and sun . . . . there are millions of suns left,
> You shall no longer take things at second or third hand . . . . nor look through the eyes of the dead . . . . nor feed on the spectres in books,
> You shall not look through my eyes either, nor take things from me,
> You shall listen to all sides and filter them from yourself.
>
> ("Song of Myself")

Far from being aberrations or digressions, such passages, planted throughout the volume, were of the very essence of Whitman's poetics in 1855. This passage was to be only one of many instances in the 1855 Leaves in which Whitman would pull the reader behind the looking glass of his poetry, but it is one of special importance, for it reveals how Whitman, the proto-modernist, could link the absoluteness of the poetic act in this (or, theoretically, any other) one moment of poetry making to the activity of the reader as its potential coparticipant.

Whitman would learn to take a pleasure, the slightly perverse pleasure of the creative writer before his critics, in eluding their attempts to pin down his identity. In passages such as the above, one can readily see how permeable Whitman would be to the usual distinctions erected by critics, both of his day and of ours, and how complicated, as a result, would be the task of literary criticism. Where D. H. Lawrence warned readers to trust the text rather than the author, as though the choice presented were one between the lady and the tiger, Whitman complicated matters for his readers by insisting that the text and the author were interchangeable, and more confusing yet, that both were in some way interchangeable with the reader. A necessary fiction, this conflation of relations contributed significantly to the breakthrough which enabled Whitman to write *Leaves of Grass.*

Taken as a whole, the 1855 *Leaves of Grass* was from beginning to end – from theory to composition, from design to promotion, from opening to closing poem – an ingeniously conceived, reader-directed venture. There had been nothing quite like its remarkable figuration of author-persona-reader interplay at least since the appearance of Rousseau's *Confessions,* a work with which Whitman's had strong (although, in 1855, independent) affinities. The 1855 *Leaves of Grass* was a major literary marker in the history of modern sensibility, and one of the features which made it so was its genuinely radical notion of the reader and the reading process. This was not simply or exclusively a matter of philosophy, but equally one of poetics, of what perhaps began in the former finding its expressive form in the latter.

I have spoken of the philosophical radicalism of the I-you formulation of the opening stanza of "Song of Myself," and I would like now to examine the way the poem gives artistic shape to that philosophical construct. Much of the originality of Whitman's poetics, as Sculley Bradley has argued, derived from his practice of detaching the meter of his verse from its traditional (and for the young poetry-writing Whitman of the 1840s, its unquestioned) basis in regularized syllabic patterns, measured in feet, in favor of a meter created by a freer, more flexible fall of points of stress over a line or series of lines.[28] The practical difference when Whitman moves between these two modes of versification is the classic one between a writer constricted and a writer liberated by form. Here is a parallel instance of Whitman's writing before and after the remaking of his verse:

> When painfully athwart my brain
>   Dark thoughts come crowding on,
> And, sick of worldly hollowness,
>   My heart feels sad or lone –
>
> Then out upon the green I walk,
>   Just ere the close of day,
> And swift I ween the sight I view
>   Clears all my gloom away.

For there I see young children –
  The cheeriest things on earth –
I see them play – I hear their tones
  Of loud and reckless mirth.

And many a clear and flute-like laugh
  Comes ringing through the air;
And many a roguish, flashing eye,
  And rich red cheek, are there.

O, lovely, happy children!
  I am with you in my soul;
I shout – I strike the ball with you –
  With you I race and roll. –

Methinks white-winged angels,
  Floating unseen the while,
Hover around this village green,
  And pleasantly they smile.

O, angels! guard these children!
  Keep grief and guilt away:
From earthly harm – from evil thoughts
  O, shield them night and day![29]

("The Play-Ground," 1846)

I go from bedside to bedside . . . . I sleep close with the other
  sleepers, each in turn;
I dream in my dream all the dreams of the other dreamers,
And I become the other dreamers.

I am a dance . . . . Play up there! the fit is whirling me fast.
I am the everlaughing . . . . it is new moon and twilight,
I see the hiding of douceurs . . . . I see nimble ghosts whichever way I
  look,
Cache and cache again deep in the ground and sea, and where it is
  neither ground or sea.

Well they do their jobs, those journeymen divine,
Only from me can they hide nothing and would not if they could;
I reckon I am their boss, and they make me a pet besides,
And surround me, and lead me and run ahead when I walk,
And lift their cunning covers and signify me with stretched arms,
  and resume the way;
Onward we move, a gay gang of blackguards with mirthshouting
  music and wildflapping pennants of joy.

("The Sleepers," 1855)

Both poems express Whitman's habitual identification with things external to his own self, but to entirely variant effect. In the earlier poem,
Whitman's self is essentially static, outside the action of the poem; the

poem's regular iambic rhythm obstructs rather than advances the idea of the oneness of the speaker with the children. In "The Sleepers," by contrast, the self is accented and volatile, is made to twist and turn with the poem's own highly modulated movement.

One can speak broadly of Whitman as having learned by 1855 to employ his metrics to give full expression to his sense of life as an act of verbal unwinding, of the modern self launched into the "strange, unloosen'd, wondrous time" of the midnineteenth century. By the time he had worked out the general mode of his new poetics and had begun to put it extensively into practice, Whitman naturally came to favor several particular kinds of metrical techniques and the verbal effects they allowed him to produce, especially those techniques through which he could give most vivid expression to his sense of the self.

Perhaps the most fundamental metrical effect that Whitman learned to work through his poetics was that of establishing rhythmic balance, whether within or between individual lines. Whitman was, simply, a master of poetic balance. I believe that it was in order to achieve this effect that he tended to use ellipses as a kind of idiosyncratic caesura in the 1855 edition, the rawest form in which his poetry was to be published, and to position them strategically at the joints of his long lines. He set them down virtually instinctively, using nothing more systematic than the test of ear in determining when they were necessary for rhythmic purposes:

> A Jew to the Jew he seems . . . . a Russ to the Russ . . . . usual and
> near . . removed from none.
>
> > ("Song of the Answerer")
>
> A show of the summer softness . . . . a contact of something unseen
> . . . . an amour of the light and air.
>
> > ("The Sleepers")

More often than not, the effect was a more musical rhythm than he would have been able to produce by punctuating with conventional points. His favorite place – as well as the natural one – of setting his point of balance, with or without the aid of ellipses, was toward the center of a verse. The effect, as in the lines below, was often the creation of a sense of marching and matching parts:

> Out of the dimness opposite equals advance . . . . Always substance
> and increase,
> Always a knit of identity . . . . always distinction . . . . always a breed
> of life.
>
> > ("Song of Myself")

There is good reason to believe that Whitman, no less than a more conventional poet, composed his poems essentially in units of a line.

Enjambment was all but nonexistent in his poems, and line closure was virtually automatic: a comma (or, infrequently, a semicolon or question mark) for each but the last verse of a stanza, followed by a period (or question mark) at the end of the stanza. In giving his primary attention to the pattern of the line, Whitman was particularly given to producing the effect created by matching the rhythm of the line to its idea. If one thinks of his poetry as being a poetry of mediation, as one which typically brings his persona into contact with the world of man and nature, Whitman's poetics were ideally suited to performing the matching operation. He did this with considerable effectiveness throughout his poems, coupling the I variously with itself, with the reader, or with the world. The first and, to my mind, the most important instance of this coupling technique in *Leaves of Grass* is the opening stanza of "Song of Myself," already quoted. The rhythm of that pronoun-laden stanza was calculated to stress, first, the existence of the I, and then the existence of the I and you together and to set them into a balance, a balance simultaneously poetic and existential. And once he had established that poetic relationship, Whitman was careful to develop and nurture it through the course of the poem, right up to the corresponding stanzas at its close.

I do not mean in saying this to load the entirety of the poetics of the volume on the back of this one relationship or on any other single feature of Whitman's thought. One of the virtues of Whitman's poetics was precisely their extreme flexibility; they allowed him to fashion a suppleness of effect in his poems to a degree incomparably beyond what he had previously been able to manage in conventional verse. In the post–Civil War period, both he and his use of the new metrics were to grow rigidified; but in the early editions he was able to command patterns of verse as fluid and protean as those of any poet of his time. Whitman could pair off as readily between lines as within them; and, as in the well-known series of stanzas about the child and the grass, he could extend his balancing technique over a long stretch of verse.

Although the most important matching operation he produced in his poetry was that of the I and the you, Whitman could also pair off things not normally associated with one another, his I with virtually anything external to himself, sometimes with no immediate or apparent connection to the I-you relationship. The presumed equality, not to mention, identity of the I and the you was, in any case, as I have said, a necessary myth, a myth probably for both sides better left unexamined. The central or initiating presence in the poetry, there should never have been any doubt, was that of the persona. Life in Whitman's poetry typically began (and ended) with his persona. That persona could just as easily turn in one direction as in the other; toward the reader one moment, toward the barnyard or the heavens the next – which is precisely what he habitually does. Or he could simply dote on himself, or break himself into two equal halves and put them into relation, as in the well-known stanza recounting the union of his body and soul.

Indeed, the slipperiness of his persona was one of the most distinctive characteristics of his poetry, as in this important passage:

> Trippers and askers surround me,
> People I meet .... the effect upon me of my early life .... of the
>   ward and city I live in .... of the nation,
> The latest news .... discoveries, inventions, societies .... authors
>   old and new,
> My dinner, dress, associates, looks, business, compliments, dues,
> The real or fancied indifference of some man or woman I love,
> The sickness of one of my folks – or of myself .... or ill-doing ....
>   or loss or lack of money .... or depressions or exaltations,
> They come to me days and nights and go from me again,
> But they are not the Me myself.
>
> Apart from the pulling and hauling stands what I am,
> Stands amused, complacent, compassionating, idle, unitary,
> Looks down, is erect, bends an arm on an impalpable certain rest,
> Looks with its sidecurved head curious what will come next,
> Both in and out of the game, and watching and wondering at it.
>
> ("Song of Myself")

The character of the new prosody becomes immediately apparent, as the opened rhythm allows the "Me myself" or the "I am" to hop loosely, unfixedly through the lines of poetry, just as Whitman conceived the self as passing through modern life.

Another favorite, self-centered poetic technique that Whitman worked with his poetics was to construct his sentence-stanzas out of a series of like grammatical units (verbs, participles, prepositional phrases, or dependent clauses), built with or without the use of his beloved connecting "and." These conjoined units he strung out over virtually any length of text, from a few lines to the longest catalogue, and connected to a subject, most often his I. Grammatically speaking, these spasmodic bursts of language could not exist independently of the subject-I and its attendant verb; and they became, in effect, the connecting tissue between the I and the world. By placing this subject-I either toward the beginning or the end of the stanza, Whitman was able to channel through it a long-flowing series of accumulating stresses, not compromising but in fact intensifying its autonomy, as here:

> What is commonest and cheapest and nearest and easiest is Me,
> Me going in for my chances, spending for vast returns,
> Adorning myself to bestow myself on the first that will take me,

Not asking the sky to come down to my goodwill,
Scattering it freely forever.

("Song of Myself")

Using this technique of transference, he was able to build blocks of self-intense verse ranging in nature from the supposedly objective catalogues of the surrounding world to his most I-centered passages, such as the superb opening stanza to "Out of the Cradle Endlessly Rocking." The figuration of the self arising "out of" or "passing" through the world and its verbal equivalent was to arrest Whitman's attention throughout his life, recurring in his best poetry from "Song of Myself" and "The Sleepers" through "When Lilacs Last in the Dooryard Bloom'd." Eventually, the technique, kept in full supply and easily pulled out of his deep pockets, was to deteriorate into one of the stock mannerisms which contributed to the heavy-handed quality of much of his late prose and poetry.

The glory of Whitman's early poetry was its freewheeling I. Ever since Rousseau, Western writers had been theorizing and writing about the age of the I. Emerson, the most articulate theorist in America of the self, had written of the modern man, "His experience inclines him to behold the procession of facts you call the world, as flowing perpetually outward from an invisible centre in himself, centre alike of him and of them, and necessitating him to regard all things as having a subjective or relative existence, relative to that aforesaid Unknown Centre of him."[30] Whitman seems to have had an instinctive grasp of this "Me in the centre," as he called it in *Democratic Vistas;* and in his poetry he created a medium of expression as free and fluid in its rhythms and contours as was the unfettered self to give expression to its center. The process of sounding out that personality, and by doing so of giving it poetic and human shape, was to become the true subject, if one can speak of a process as being a subject, of his poetry, beginning with the remarkable "Song of Myself."

Intensely private, the celebration of the self, the process becomes simultaneously collective with the opening lines of the poem, the celebration of me and the celebration of you. That fact does not change even when the persona soon breaks free and goes his separate way because of the fact that he is, and sets himself up at every possibility to be, representative. Everything that his "I am" is, so is that of the reader – sometimes by implication, and sometimes by statement. What it sees, feels, touches, thinks, experiences of the surrounding world is what all men and women see, feel, touch, think, experience – such is the statement and such often the rhythm of the poem. "These are the thoughts of all men in all ages and lands, they are not original with me, / If they are not yours as much as mine they are nothing or next to nothing," the persona claims outright at one point; but in truth this is implicitly under-

stood at all times in the poem. Just the same, from time to time there
are scattered throughout the poem words more directly for the reader:

> Do you guess I have some intricate purpose?
> Well I have . . . . for the April rain has, and the mica on the side of a
>   rock has.
> Do you take it I would astonish?
> Does the daylight astonish? or the early redstart twittering through
>   the woods?
> Do I astonish more than they?
> This hour I tell things in confidence,
> I might not tell everybody but I will tell you.

Or later in the poem, not far from its end:

> I teach straying from me, yet who can stray from me?
> I follow you whoever you are from the present hour;
> My words itch at your ears till you understand them.
>
> I do not say these things for a dollar, or to fill up the time while I
>   wait for a boat;
> It is you talking just as much as myself . . . . I act as the tongue of
>   you,
> It was tied in your mouth . . . . in mine it begins to be loosened.

The poem is filled – odd feature in poetry – with rhetorical questions
of this sort, most addressed by the persona to the reader but others
addressed to himself, to persons real and imagined, to animals, even to
inanimate objects. John Stuart Mill's distinction between "eloquence" as
emotional discourse "heard" and "poetry" as that "overheard" would
have been entirely out of place with Whitman. According to Mill, "All
poetry is of the nature of soliloquy. It may be said that poetry which is
printed on hot-pressed paper and sold at a bookseller's shop, is a soliloquy
in full dress, and on the stage . . . But no trace of consciousness that any
eyes are upon us must be visible in the work itself. The actor knows that
there is an audience present; but if he act as though he know it, he acts
ill."[31]
It would be hard to imagine poetry which more consciously and bla-
tantly violates this notion than does the 1855 "Song of Myself" (as, for
that matter, do many of the other poems of the volume). Like most
Whitman poems, it is a poem conceived more nearly in Mill's terms to
"eloquence" than to "poetry," its poetic act one of the persona "speaking" to an on-the-spot communicant. The self-exhibitionist persona of
"Song of Myself" who struts across the stage of the poem not only
knows that an audience is present but insists on dragging that audience
on stage alongside himself. One can see here vividly how close the poetic

act is with Whitman to the act of the orator or the dramatist, with their acute sensitivity to audience, performance, and address, and how these forms of expression could serve as a closer analogue to his writing than did the forms of literature with which he was familiar. Even as Whitman's persona goes "afoot with my vision" across North America, ostensibly the most solitary of trips, the reader is spokenly or unspokenly with him. Indoors and out, in bed and out, on the road and in the city, the reader is his companion – such is the communicatory dynamic of the poem, cultivated from the start and closely maintained thereafter, joining reader and writer in the same verbal act with which it attaches the persona to his world.

Both as regards its reader and its world, the art of the poem was essentially an art of inclusion, the art of a "putter inner" conducted, here, with a sense of mission. The mission, should any of his contemporaries have needed help in identifying it, was there to be seen, stated forcefully and explicitly, in the book's Preface, which quickly came out and claimed, "The United States themselves are essentially the greatest poem," and then sent out the aspirant poet to prove the assertion. This Whitman did throughout the volume with undisguised pleasure, and nowhere more conspicuously than in his extensive use of the cataloguing technique, which provides so much of the verbal substance of the poem.

The America he exerted himself to work into his catalogues was one which, in the unflattering description of Mrs. Trollope, "may be said to spread rather than to rise." A typical Whitman catalogue likewise tends to spread rather than to rise, and there were good reasons for this. For one thing, Whitman clearly took the purest pleasure in putting the expanse of North America and the breadth of its characteristic activities and peoples into verse via his catalogue technique; even contemporaries who could make little or no sense of his verse could readily perceive that. I understand this, at least in part, as a matter of sensibility, as an act of poetic pleasure by an immensely language-sensitive man in putting his world as directly as was given to a poet to do into words.

But there is more to the phenomenon of Whitman's catalogues than this, and more than the painstaking concern with craft that it took a generation of critics trained in the formalist concerns of the New Criticism to have observed in his cataloguing technique. There was also a decided commitment to the world as he and his contemporaries knew it. Whitman wrote his catalogues with his compatriots in mind, and the intense personal pleasure that he took in writing them had also its social function. Whitman would have known as well as anybody that Americans of his "manifest destiny" generation took an intense interest and pride in their land, and his catalogues were designed to satisfy a pride which he could reasonably have expected to be widely shared. Even his manner of presentation had its carefully worked out communicatory outlet; he presented his catalogues in such a way as to keep his and his readers' common paternity passing before their eyes, whether through his representative I in "Song of Myself" or even through his representative you in "A Song for Occupations." To have kept such an intense source of pleasure and pride to himself would have been worse than pointless; given his view of the role of the poet, it would have been self-defeating. Besides, Whitman had all too deep (and, no doubt, all too intimate) a knowledge of the power of exclusion; the worst fate "Song of Myself" was capable of envisioning was exclusion in one of its various forms – ostracism (the runaway slave, the prostitute), isolation (the twenty-ninth bather), or alienation (the living death of those who walk through life with dimes on their eyes).

Having said this about the timeliness and groundedness of the poem, I am tempted to speak of the "itinerary" "Song of Myself" traces as it moves forward; but in fact the trope is badly misleading. No poem was further from the linear conception of time and form that this trope implies, and no poem was further from the bathetic literal-mindedness with which Whitman has often been charged.[32] One of the peculiar paradoxes of Whitman's art, whose implications he was never able to sort out, was its simultaneous involvement with and escape from the conditions of the present moment. With his hearty appetite for the here and now, Whitman may seem the last person to share the position of Poe of being a poet "out of space – out of time"; and yet the impulse of his poem was to move beyond the historical present moment to the more lasting security of the artistic present, to make art and life one. By the time the long, loping epic journey of the self approaches its conclusion, Whitman circled round, as it were, to his starting point, a point not temporal or spatial but communicatory. He departed from the poem as he entered it, with the reader in tandem:

> I depart as air . . . . I shake my white locks at the runaway sun,
> I effuse my flesh in eddies and drift it in lacy jags.
>
> I bequeath myself to the dirt to grow from the grass I love,
> If you want me again look for me under your bootsoles.
>
> You will hardly know who I am or what I mean,
> But I shall be good health to you nevertheless,
> And filter and fibre your blood.
>
> Failing to fetch me me at first keep encouraged,
> Missing me one place search another,
> I stop some where waiting for you

Air, sun, earth, flesh, and blood – out of such elements and their circular flow has Whitman created his far-reaching poem of being and selfhood.

But in saying this, I should point out that the poem is designed in such a way as to show that the persona's being, central fact of life though it be, is alone not self-sufficient; it is only with his sharing of all life's vital elements with the reader that the poem reaches its close. That is, if one can speak of the poem as ever reaching its close, since the one unstopped line of the poem is the poem's last, Whitman's open-ended statement of the nature of life and art and of the reader-writer relationship through which he joined them.

In still another sense, the poem does not end here. There were contemporary critics who referred to Whitman's book as a "poem"; and although this may or may not have been simply the critical usage of the day, I do believe that Whitman approached the 1855 volume with the idea of designing an unusually holistic work. He deliberately left the individual poems without titles of their own, designating each one in its turn merely under the common rubric of "Leaves of Grass." What to many seemed – and seems – disorganization in a volume of poems, twelve poems arranged with apparently little sense of sequence and no sense of proportion (the first poem is longer than the other eleven together), was in fact the natural consequence of the way Whitman saw the poetic process in 1855. The opening poem with its sweeping compass naturally set the remaining poems in its periphery and in many cases even set for them the same roles and relations for reader and writer that it enacted for itself. It did more than that: It established itself as Whitman's prototypal poem of the New World, the poem which integrated within itself the processes of living, writing, and reading in the open-ended manner Whitman conceived as essential if art was to meet the conditions of modern, democratic society.

Thus, the second poem, later titled "A Song for Occupations," opens, like "Song of Myself," with an invocation to the reader set in the same kind of balanced rhythm Whitman favored throughout the volume ("I will be even with you, and you shall be even with me") and continues to engage the reader in a postulated poetic dialogue to its end. The persona is again the teacher and instructor, the reader his initiate learning the lesson that all truths "exurge from you." Whitman would later revise this poem so as to make it more of an objectified local color poem; but in 1855 all external reality was pliant and flexible before persona and reader, the long catalogue of nineteenth-century professions and their end products more a medium of exchange between them than the fixed facts of their surrounding world. "The paper I write on or you write on .. and every word we write .. and every cross and twirl of the pen .. and the curious way we write what we think ... yet very faintly" – that paper and that writing, and everything else contained in the catalogue, are the currency of the poetic transaction Whitman makes with his reader.

If the poem seemed like a paler version of the preceding poem, as of course it is, this was a risk that Whitman necessarily ran in reusing the poetic strategy and technique he had already used on a larger scale. "A Song for Occupations" was to suffer the fate of several other of the weaker poems of the volume of seeming to be one of the smaller units, nearly interchangeable, which Whitman could just as easily as not have incorporated into the opening poem.

Other poems in the invocatory mode, by contrast, were more successful. One of them, "To Think of Time," provides a good marker for the improvement in Whitman's art since the period of his poetic apprenticeship. A reader-assisted meditation on death, it surpassed the maudlin graveyard poetry he was writing and publishing in the 1840s, in part because it was no longer so narrowly and exclusively self-centered:

> To think of time . . . . to think through the retrospection,
> To think of today . . and the ages continued henceforward.
>
> Have you guessed you yourself would not continue? Have you
>   dreaded those earth-beetles?
> Have you feared the future would be nothing to you?
>
> Is today nothing? Is the beginningless past nothing?
> If the future is nothing they are just as surely nothing.
>
> To think that the sun rose in the east . . . . that men and women were
>   flexible and real and alive . . . . that every thing was real and alive;
> To think that you and I did not see feel think nor bear our part,
> To think that we are now here and bear our part.

Perhaps in no other poem of the volume, except "Song of Myself," did Whitman exert himself more fully to play the role of persuader, his purpose to use the poem to bring the reader with himself to a reconciliation with mortality. This he accomplishes here, as in many of the 1855 poems, via his reader-address technique, which by the end of the passage quoted above has insinuatingly brought "I" and "you" together as "we." It was entirely characteristic of Whitman's strategy in 1855 that he would turn what is normally the most solitary of poetic activities – meditation – into a shared, participatory one.

Other poems deviated in part or in whole from this mode. The two poems composed prior to 1855, "Europe: The 72d and 73d Years of These States," originally published in the New York *Tribune* in 1850, and "A Boston Ballad," composed during the Anthony Burns trial in 1854, were more strictly politically motivated poems, even though they, too, were written in a highly vocative style. One of the most distinguished of the poems, "The Sleepers," was more purely a lyric, the plane of the poetry unusually self-enclosed for a *Leaves of Grass* poem. Perhaps the purest lyric of the volume, "There Was a Child Went Forth," fell directly in between these categories; and it may be the most illuminating for my purposes precisely because it did so.

It was, on the one hand, the most strictly third-person poem in the volume, the only one lacking even a single use of the first or second person. It therefore lay as far as any of the 1855 poems from the model of the poem as an act of address. Moreover, the receiving self at the center of the poem was not strictly that of the poet or his persona but that of an unspecified child. Still, the accumulating process by which the child "becomes" himself is quickly recognizable as the identifying process used throughout the volume; and the unstated equation made here between the process of living and the process of making poetry, the one brought flush against the other, is that on which the entire volume is postulated. The process of the child's being – the life force itself – is expressed by and equated to the verbal act with which Whitman framed the poem: "There was a child went forth every day" in line one, and "These became part of that child who went forth every day, and who now goes and will always go forth every day" in the penultimate line. Past, present, and future merge in the eternal present of the poem, its lovely vision of the child, some child, always going forth into life – Whitman's ideal for life and art alike. But in 1855, the poem did not end here. In the final line, Whitman extended the plane of the poem outwardly by including a verse he would later choose to cut: "And these become of him or her that peruses them now," in effect, opening the poem's previously closed process, even if only obliquely, to the reader. If nothing else, this slight addition indicates how supple a base his poetry rested on, how fully and willfully Whitman, with a quick flourish of the pen, could shift the direction of his poetry.

One of the most perceptive – and itself, culturally interesting – observations about Whitman's engagement of the reader in his poetry was that of the early twentieth-century English critic Basil De Selincourt. De Selincourt spoke of Whitman's poems as an "impromptu confab, in which equal takes equal aside for a few words (or not so few!)":

> The poem, as Whitman conceives it, is to remain fundamentally a conversation. It is to be the expression by me to you of the feelings which are as much yours as mine, and would undoubtedly have been expressed by you to me but for the accident of my being the more garrulous of the two. It is to act in the field of spiritual needs much as the more modern kind of advertisement does in the field of material needs, button-holing its client, assuring him that he is a brother, and confiding to him its knowledge of the common perplexities of the life of man. How easily this atmosphere of confidence and familiarity raises a smile. It subsists largely upon illusions; but the illusions are harmless, for they deceive nobody; and they are really worth entertaining, even

if they are a little wearisome and over-persistent at times; for with them come large reinforcements of that genuine raciness and diffused good feeling which are part of America's contribution to the civilisation of the world.[33]

De Selincourt was too far removed by time and place and by disposition to have sensed the urgency behind Whitman's mode of address, which he parries with a superior smile; but he did make an important point in remarking that Whitman believed this manner of engaging the mind of the reader "to be typical not only of his country but also of his country's ideals."

There were few things, I hope it is by now clear, that Whitman cultivated more assiduously than his address of the reader, or few things he took more solemnly. De Selincourt was badly mistaken in seeing Whitman as a chitchatty good fellow, a type of the American with his much vaunted good spirits and easy camaraderie breaking into letters; but I think he was exactly correct in seeing Whitman's address of the reader as being in conscious harmony with his conception of a national ideal. That ideal was of a democratized poetry for a democratized "nation of readers." Even as Evert Duyckinck was assembling the best that American poets and poetesses had thought and said in his 1855 *Cyclopedia of American Literature,* Whitman was acting in parallel fashion to give voice to the thoughts and sentiments he believed the American public needed to hear. Had he not had an overriding faith in the democratic readership he had seen grow up, with which he himself had grown up and of which he was a part, the venture of *Leaves of Grass,* its very poetics, would have been futile. Where Wordsworth spoke the opinion of many a Romantic writer in claiming "the poet must reconcile himself for a season to few and scattered hearers," Whitman was conceding nothing.[34] "To have great poets," he would later remark, "there must be great audiences, too."[35]

When I say he acted in parallel with Duyckinck – the two men, though living much of their lives in geographical proximity, hardly ever met – I am speaking of the difference of social class between them.[36] Whitman's perspective on the world was always solidly that of his working-class background. That perspective had long tinged his view of politics, his and his family's allegiance to the Democratic party of Jefferson and Jackson as the party of the common man; and it colored his view of culture as well. His antipathy, as much instinctive as reasoned, to the "feudal" past was itself sufficient to turn him against things European and elitist, just as his native receptivity to the "divine average" was to prove one of his greatest assets in opening up poetry to "what was common" in life and in people. As he wrote into a midfifties notebook, "All others have adhered to the principle, and shown it, that the poet and savan form classes by themselves, above the people, and more refined than the people; I show that they are just as great when of the people, partaking of the common idioms, manners, the earth, the rude visage of animals and trees, and what is vulgar."[37]

This, for once, was Whitman speaking the unadulterated truth. Throughout the mid–1850s he was trying – or thought he was trying – to open his poems as broadly as possible to the world, on the one hand, and to the reader, on the other, trying to do so to a degree to which he found no precedent either in contemporary or in past literature. I have spoken of how he did this both in theory and in practice, and I might now add that he was even considering at mid-decade going to the logical extreme of writing "a poem (or passage in a poem) giving an account of my way of making a poem."[38] Likewise, on the other end of the reader-writer continuum, he contemplated writing a "Poem of Materials" consisting of "the bringing together of the materials . . . yet loose, fluid-like, leaving each reader eligible to form the resultant poem for herself or himself."[39] He never carried out these plans in precisely the manner he stated here, but in fact he had already done as much in *Leaves of Grass*.

There was in Whitman's theory and practice of poetry a magisterial vision of the modern poet and reader and a genuinely avant-garde conception of the terms, tone, scope, and dynamics of culture operative between them; but there was also, of course, more than a writer's normal share of wish fulfillment and fantasy. "Read these leaves in the open air every season of every year of your life" was a tall task, if he was referring, as I assume he was in 1855, to his *Leaves*, and one not easily accomplished unless Whitman's views were genuinely, as he put it in "Song of Myself," "the thoughts of all men in all ages and lands, they are not original with me." Whether this was or was not so was to be the judgment not of the poet but of his contemporary readers.

Figure 1. The Hoe ten-cylinder rotary press (from Ringwalt's *American Encyclopaedia of Printing*, 1871)

Figure 2. (below) Harper's Cliff Street book manufactury (from *The House of Harper* by Eugene Exman. Copyright © 1967 by Eugene Exman. Reprinted by permission of Harper & Row, Publishers, Inc.)

129

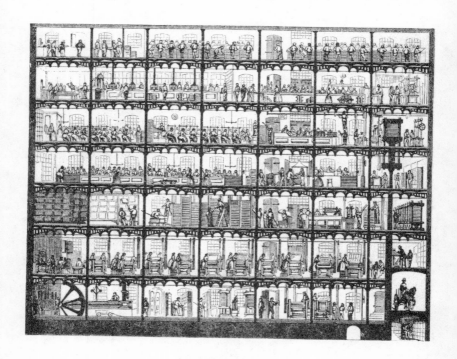

Figure 3. Floor view of the division of labor at Harper's

Figure 4. (below) New York's Crystal Palace

130

Figure 5. Interior of Appleton's famous Broadway bookstore

Figure 6. (below) Printing House Square, New York City

BOOKS FOR THE PEOPLE

PUBLISHED IN EXTRA NUMBERS OF THE "NEW WORLD" NEWSPAPER, AT
NO 30 ANN-STREET, NEW-YORK, BY J. WINCHESTER.

A GREAT REVOLUTION

Has been created in the Book Publishing business by the proprietors of the New World who were the first to introduce the system of printing cheap editions of all popular works, so as to bring within the means of every family in the country works which, in any other form would cost from $1 to $5 each, for the most trifling sums. To this enterprise we have given the expressive designation of

BOOKS FOR THE PEOPLE!

Which truly express the character and design of our publications. These consist of Biographic, Romantic, Scientific, and Standard Works, by the most popular and approved authors of this country and Europe. We are persuaded that no citizen of the United States, who shall become acquainted with the great enterprise which we have established, and are endeavoring to carry into extensive practical operation; but will give us their cordial aid and approval. For how insignificant and trifling a sum can every family be supplied, wet from the press with all the choice, popular, instructive and entertaining works of the most eminent and talented authors, both of this country and Europe. Ours is emphatically an enterprise for the times—tending to bring to every man's door that mental aliment which gives to life its keenest relish and enjoyment; and at a price within the means of his humblest to incur. And we have no doubt but that the people will extend to us a most liberal patronage and support. We respectfully ask them to aid in making known the merits and extreme cheapness of the New World and its Extras, and in obtaining for them the subscriptions of every person who desire a good family paper, and books so cheap that none should be without them.

☞ These Extras are now published in a beautiful octavo form, for preservation and binding.

NEW AND INTERESTING WORKS ALREADY ISSUED.
American Notes for General Circulation,
BY CHARLES DICKENS, ESQ

Of this work, which has created so much sensation throughout the country, we have struck off 53 000 copies, and shall continue to issue successive editions till the whole country is supplied. It is the most extraordinary book of the day and is creating an immense sensation among all classes, everywhere like wildfire, and numbers in this country. Terms—12½ cents single; Ten copies for $1—or $8 per hundred, for twenty-five or over.

The Neighbors, a Tale of Every Day Life.
TRANSLATED FROM THE SWEDISH, BY MARY HOWITT.

"So truthful, so instructive, so high-toned and thoughtful a romance of daily life is rarely found among the treasures of any language, and the translator has done the whole domain of 'Saxedom,' as Carlyle has it, an essential service by rendering it. If perused by every winter fireside, its influence in promoting love, peace and joy, with a truer idea of the aims and ends of life, would be most beneficial."—[N. Y. Tribune.

Terms—Single copies 18¾ cents; Seven copies for $1, or $12 per hundred It is published in a double number, octavo form.

Letters of Mary Queen of Scots,
NOW FIRST PUBLISHED, WITH AN INTRODUCTION,
BY MISS AGNES STRICKLAND.

No work has appeared, for many years, which has excited such general attention and admiration. In the fate of the beautiful and unfortunate Queen of Scots, all the civilized world is to this day deeply interested; and here is the correspondence which actually passed between herself and Queen Elizabeth, and here, also, are her private letters on numerous topics, now first brought to light and edited by an accomplished lady. "There is this attractive feature" says Miss Strickland, "in all the letters of Mary, Queen of Scots, they are full of domestic traits and the natural feelings of the heart. Trifles from her pen assume a grace, and delight us, because of the unaffected simplicity with which she writes." Embellished with a portrait of the Queen.

☞ Price 25 cents; Six copies for $1, or $16 per hundred,

Franklin Evans, or the Inebriate.
A TALE OF THE TIMES.—BY WALTER WHITMAN.

This novel, which is dedicated to the Temperance Societies and the friends of the Temperance Cause throughout the Union, has created a sensation, both for the ability with which it is written, as well as the interest of the subject, and will be universally read and admired. It was written expressly for the New World, by one of the best Novelists in this country, with a view to aid the great work of Reform, and rescue Young Men from the demon of Intemperance. The incidents of the plot are wrought out with great effect, and the excellence of its moral, and the beneficial influence it will have, should interest the friends of the Temperance Reformation in giving this tale the widest possible circulation. Price 12½ cents; ten copies for $1, $8 per hundred.

PAULINE, a Tale of Normandy.

Translated from the French of Alexandre Dumas, by a Lady of Virginia; Dumas is one of the most brilliant and popular French writers, and "Pauline" is a production of great power and interest, and justly sustains the reputation of its author. It is beautifully translated, and cannot fail to give satisfaction to all lovers of romance. Single copies 12½ cents—ten copies for $1.

Percival Keene,

A new and very popular Sea Novel, by Capt. Marryat, author of "Peter Simple," "Jacob Faithful," &c. Price 12½ cents single; nine copies for $1.

Letters from the Baltic,

Illustrated with four beautiful engravings. This is one of the most entertaining works we have ever read, descriptive of the manners, customs, &c. of the people of the Russian Provinces on the Baltic, and the brilliant Court of St. Petersburg. Price 12½ cents; nine copies for $1.

Lives and Times of the United Irishmen.

This excellent historical work is published in three numbers of the New World. It is replete with the most interesting information, and gives to the world many valuable documents now for the first time brought to light Price 25 cents single; five copies for $1.

Morley Ernstein,

James's last Novel, and his best, for only 18¾ cents; six copies for $1. A few copies may yet be had.

Life of Henry Clay.

With a large engraving, published in one Extra New World. Price 6¼ cents sixteen copies for $1; $5 per hundred.

The Western Captive, or Times of Tecumseh.

An original novel, by Mrs. Seba Smith, one of our most popular and talented authors. It is a beautiful story, and should be purchased by every lady in the land who honors the gifted of her sex. Price 18¾ cents. Six copies for $1.

Godolphin,

One of the best of Bulwer's novels, and (like all the works of this great author) evincing the vast powers of his mind. Price 12½ cents; nine copies for $1.

The Conspirator,

An original American Novel, founded on the conspiracy of Aaron Burr. It is a tale of high-wrought interest—written by a lady. An edition of twenty thousand has already been sold. Price 12½ cents; nine copies for $1.

Liebig's Agricultural Chemistry.

This is a most important and valuable work, especial to all who are engaged in Agricultural pursuits. No Farmer, who has the slightest knowledge of the value it is of to be derived from it, can fail to possess a copy. It is issued in a double octavo number, at 25 cts. per copy only, or five copies for $1.

NEW WORLD ANNUAL.

A few copies on hand, at a reduced price—12½ cents each—Ten copies for $1. This splendid Extra contains 64 large octavo pages, and FORTY-NINE SUPERB ENGRAVINGS. The literary contents are of the highest merit, by the best authors, and will give more satisfaction than anything yet issued. Order should be early.

LIVES OF THE QUEENS OF FRANCE.
WITH NOTICES OF THE ROYAL FAVORITES.

Here we have one of he most interesting and valuable works which has appeared during the season. The "MEMOIRS OF THE QUEENS OF FRANCE," possesses all the charms of the most thrilling romance. The history of their loves, the intrigues, the jealousies, and the exciting personal adventures, which are to be found in the lives of ONE HUNDRED AND THIRTY QUEENS and royal favorites, from the foundation of the French kingdom to the present time, forms a book which will be sought after and read with avidity by all classes of people.

The authoress, Mrs. Forbes Bush, has embodied a mass of historical incidents of the deepest interest in the compass of two volumes, which can be found in no other work, and which must have cost immense labor and research.

Term.—Single copies, 25 cents; 5 copies for $1; 25 copies $4; and in large proportion for a larger number.

The Nautilus, or Tales of the Sea,
INCLUDING A NARATIVE OF THE MUTINY OF THE BOUNTY.

This work is very interesting—full of thrilling adventures of a Sea-faring life, accounts of Shipwrecks, Mutinies, Piracy, &c. &c. Double number—price 12½ cents—ten for $1—$8 per hundred.

☞ The above works are published in single, double and treble Extra Numbers, and are subject to newspaper postage, only by a decision of the Post-office Department, dated April 26, 1842. ☞ All Post-masters who shall remit to the amount of One Dollar, or over, for New World Extras shall receive a gratis copy for each dollar remitted, of such work as may be designated. Those giving a standing order are supplied at a discount of 33 per cent. from retail prices. Address as above.

RING'S MEDICATED CANDY.

For the cure of Consumption, Bronchitis, Asthma, Whooping-Cough, Colds, spitting of Blood, &c. &c. &c. This well known and popular preparation of medicine has now been three years before the public, and has not only sustained its reputation, but is now used more extensively than ever before. It is acknowledged, by all who have taken RING'S MEDICATED CANDY, that it is vastly superior to any other, for the cure of

COLDS, COUGHS, AND CONSUMPTION,

and all complaints of the Liver, Lungs, or Bronchial Tubes, &c. &c. This candy is prepared from the formula of one of the first medical men of the day, who has found the ingredients very efficacious in diseases of the lungs, but on account of their disagreeable taste, in a liquid form, particularly to children, could not so generally prescribe them; but now that they are in the composition of Ring's Cough Candy, those objections are removed. While this candy acts as a gentle expectorant and cathartic, it will be found a powerful bracer of weak constitutions.

☞ Sold, wholesale and retail, by J. C. WADLEIGH, 409 Broadway, corner of Grand; also at 641 Broadway; H. G. Daggers, 30 Ann-st. Green, 69½ Fulton-st. Brooklyn; Burgess & Zieber, Ledger Buildings Philadelphia; Redding & Co. State-st. Boston. Agents supplied at a large discount for cash. Address, post paid, as above.

Figure 7. Park Benjamin's advertisement for *Franklin Evans* in the *New World* of Feb. 1, 1843 (courtesy of Rare Books Division, Library of Congress)

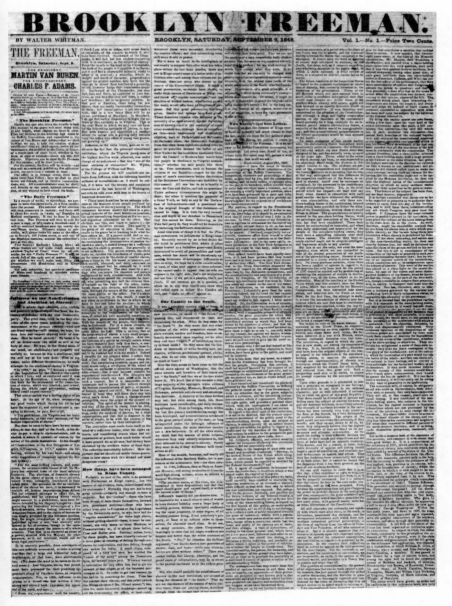

Figure 8. Front page of Whitman's Free Soil newspaper, the Brooklyn *Freeman*, Sept. 9, 1848 (courtesy of Department of Rare Books, Perkins Library, Duke University)

Leaves

of

Grass.

Brooklyn, New York:
1855.

Figure 9. Title page and frontispiece of 1855 *Leaves of Grass* (courtesy of Alexander Library, Rutgers University)

Figure 10. (below) Title page and frontispiece of 1860 *Leaves of Grass* (courtesy of Rare Books Division, Library of Congress)

COUNTER-JUMPS.

A POEMETTINA.—AFTER WALT WHITMAN.

AM the Counter-jumper, weak and effem-
    inate.
I love to loaf and lie about dry-goods.
I loaf and invite the Buyer.

..m the essence of retail. The sum and result of small profits
    and quick returns.
..e Picayune is part of me, and so is the half cent, and the mill
    only arithmetically appreciable.
..e shining, cheap-woven sarsnet is of me, and I am of it.
..d the white bobinet,
..d the moire antique, thickly webbed and strown with impossible
    flowers,
..d the warm winter gloves lined with fur,
..d the delicate summer gloves of silk threads,
..d the intermediate ones built of the hide of the Swedish rat,
..l these things are of me, and many more also.
..r I am the shop, and the counter, and the till,
..t particularly the last.
..d I explore and rummage the till, and am at home in it.
..d I am the shelves on which lie the damaged goods ;
..e damaged goods themselves I am,
..d I ask what's the damage ?
..m the crate, and the hamper, and the yard-wand, and the box
    of silks fresh from France,
..d when I came into the world I paid duty,
..d I never did my duty,
..d never intend to do it,
..r I am the creature of weak depravities ;
..m the Counter-jumper ;
..ound my feeble yelp over the woofs of the World.

OUR LAW INTELLIGENCE.

TOUJOURS SPURGEON.—An interesting case, involving the whole
.w of Sacred Sweetmeats and Clerical Comfits, has recently been
..cided in London. Mr. Watkins was persuaded by his wife to
..ve an evening party, and we need hardly say, yielded to the
..m and importunity of his better two-thirds. Mr. Watkins com-
..anded a supply of bon-bon for the hilarious gathering. The spirit
..the age is pictorial and biographic ; and Mr. Watkins, therefore,
..dered portraiture bon-bon—expecting, of course, quite a gallery,
.. rather tray-full of the gallant, the gifted, the good, and the
..eat in counterfeit presentment. The confectioner sent home the
..riegated delicacies. The guests gathered ; the voice of the violin
..s heard in the drawing-room ; the floors trembled to the dancers
..ncing in tune ; young Meerschaum was in his maddest, mirthful
..ood ; Beauty beamed upon Bravery ; music arose with its volup-
..ous swell, when from one gay group to another ran the welcome
..armur—" Supper !" The bon-bon were distributed. What anx-
..y is depicted upon that fair young face ! With what a gentle
..emor do those taper fingers untwine the fringed and golden en-

velope ! How those lake-hued eyes brighten, as the lake-hued lips
whisper—" Mario, I hope—D'Orsey, perhaps—Spurgeon, good gra-
cious !" Yes, it was he ! Not the romantic visage of the dulcet
and delicate tenor—not that head of the late Count, so suggestive
in its hirsute luxury of brushes by the wagon load, and of Macassar
by the puncheon—but the lineaments of the Rev. Mr. Spurgeon !
From one end of the board to the other flew the exclamation,
" Spurgeon !" Everybody had drawn Spurgeon, not to quote pro-
fanely, it was :

Spurgeon su—Spurgeon cxin—
Spurgeon qua—Spurgeon la !

We would not speak disrespectfully of the great preacher, but we
just don't think he has a nice face for an evening party. His best
friends, the lithographers, although they have everything their
own way, and a wayward way it sometimes is, do not attempt to
present Mr. Spurgeon as the Rev. Apollo Belvidere. We are not
sworn believers in that Philosopher of Figure Heads and Monarch
of Mugs, Dr. John Caspar Lavater. In spite of his facial flabbiness,
the Rev. Mr. Spurgeon is, no doubt, a gentleman, an orator, and a
scholar. But he does not engrave well for bon-bon wrappers.
Such a good man is altogether too good for the goodies ; and any
young lady who has seen the pious portrait in the shop-windows
for an age—we mean a certain age, of course—may be pardoned for
seeking a less familiar countenance in the haunts of fashion and
festivity. Besides, how might that severe face put the fiddler out of
tune, and discourage the most enthusiastic and long-winded cornet-
a-piston ! How might it bring heaviness to the lightest and most
fantastic toes ! How might it bring the German to an untimely
end, in spite of its natural longevity ! Mr. Watkins, justly indig-
nant, refused to pay the artist in sugar, and bade him go to the
deuce with his confounded tray. Of course, thus requested, Mr.
Watkins went to law. The Court, being a jolly Court, non-suited
the serious-minded confectioner, who will probably, hereafter, confine his portraits of Spurgeon to the Bronchial Comfits which he
tenderly and scientifically prepares for sore-throated exhorters, and
the " organs" of young ladies who sing in Don Giovanni at the
Opera House, and in Elijah at Exeter Hall.

REV. THEODORE PARKER'S NIGHTMARE.

It is not in the nature of some men to keep still under any circumstances. You might pile a family of quiet hills on the head
and shoulders of Etna, but still that mountain would blaze and bel-
low. The same may be said of the Rev. Theodore Parker, who is
a moral Etna in a chronic state of eruption. We are therefore not
surprised to find in the Boston papers a second letter from him on
the subject of John Brown, written in the shadows of St. Peter's,
amid the colossal grandeurs of Rome. We have all given up J.
Brown in these parts. He is not mentioned unless it is absolutely
necessary. The national air is clearer for that great thunder-bolt
propelled into it by a strange destiny. The people everywhere are
restored to their temper, and their business, and can afford to laugh
at the frights and follies they were betrayed into by one old Round
head, born in a wrong age. Therefore these letters of Mr. Parker
come like dreams of the past, and the only serious thought they
provoke is a sad apprehension that while all this country is smiling
in serene peace and content, the gray ghost of John Brown will be
periodically appearing, stirred by Mr. Parker, far away in Rome,
and moved upon our happy horizon like the most disagreeable of
puppets, controlled by the wire of one man's will. Accordingly
and hence, it may not be indelicate to suggest to the intimate friends
of the Rev. Theodore Parker the propriety of intimating to him in
his classic retirement that his fellow citizens have been thoroughly
done Brown, and that in the way of correspondence nothing is more
interesting to the general reader than graphic descriptions of famous
places and persons, such as the Coliseum (moonlit, if possible,) and
his Serenity, Pius IX.

Yet an appalling doubt will interfere. For we read toward the
close of the epistle these words : " But I did not mean to write you
such a letter as this—*it wrote itself*, and I couldn't help it." If this
letter wrote itself, why should not an indefinite number of letters,
now floating in Mr. Parker's brain, also write themselves ? And
what is to prevent all these letters, after writing themselves, from
coloring themselves Brown ? Indeed a gloomy prospect is before
us, and we do trust that the press of Boston will not fear to offend
Music Hall, but see the propriety of refusing further contributions
from the Rev. Theodore Parker, whose nightmare is Brown.

Seasonable Con.

BY A YOUNG PERSON OF DEFICIENT INTELLECT.

Why is a summer like Pride ?
Because it Goeth before a Fall !

..re 11. 1860 caricature and parody of Whitman in *Vanity Fair* (courtesy of Rare Books
..ision, Library of Congress)

on the other, as published in the report. I have
the best authority possible for this assertion.
General Gillmore is evidently an overrated man.
He may be, or even is, a good second or third
rate artillery officer, as he showed at the shelling
of Fort Pulaski.   I learn positively that some
influential Irishmen from Brooklyn found means
to make Greeley enthusiastic for Gillmore's
transcendent capacities; Greeley communicated
his enthusiasm to Lincoln, and so Gillmore was
entrusted with the command before Charleston,
and succeeded in —— nothing.   (See vol. II,
about the plans of Gillmore being submitted to
Mr. Lincoln and approved by him.)

April 18.— *We are in a state of transition*, say
many Americans, and some of them the loftiest,
the most original and genuine American hearts
and minds.   Such a one is the poet Walt Whitman.   But what is a state of transition? when
and where does it begin, when and where does it
end?   Man as an individual or as a *concreto*, as
mankind, as race, as humanity, is uninterruptedly
growing, developing, progressing.   Stagnation is
death, and *per contra* nothing is done by leaps.
Nature labors uninterrupted by growth and
decomposition; nature uninterruptedly combines
and produces.   So does man; all is change and
transition, from yesterday towards to-day, from
to-day towards to-morrow.   All that grows and
lives, grows and lives through an uninterrupted
chain of formation and transition.   The cells in

Figure 12. A contemporary judgment of Whitman the poet (from the
copy of Adam Gurowski's *Diary*, 1866, in the Spader Collection of Rutgers University Library)

ure 13. Whitman, in his last years, among a lifetime of writings and clippings (courtesy Prints and Photographs Division, Library of Congress)

Figure 14. Modern caricature of Whitman (drawing by David Levine, reprinted with permission of *The New York Review of Books*, copyright 1963–89 Nyrev, Inc.)

7

The Public Response

If Whitman was truly "art and part with the commonalty," as he claimed in his Brooklyn *Times* self-review, the question naturally arises: How did the commonalty receive their poet in 1855? I have argued that Whitman had the most intense concern about his reception, one transcending the values of status and compensation which one more ordinarily associates with writers in their dealings with the public. He took reader-writer relations so seriously, I have said, as to have gone to one extreme in rendering reader response a built-in aspect of his poems and to another extreme in resorting to whatever extraliterary means were at his disposal to defend, explain, and promote those poems. The mission he began in the summer of 1855 of creating an audience for his poems was actually to preoccupy him throughout the remainder of his life. But what did his readers have to say for themselves? This question is not easily answered, and it cannot even be properly considered until one reconstructs as nearly as possible the conditions of literary reception at the time.

There has developed over the years an aura surrounding the appearance on the shelves of certain bookstores of the first *Leaves of Grass* as for no other American book, but this is the view of the present on the past. How might contemporaries have perceived the slender, oversized book of poems and the provocatively dressed and posed figure staring self-assuredly out of its covers? And who, for that matter, would have been most likely to patronize midnineteenth-century bookstores and the writing of their time? The most likely answer to the latter question, to judge from the titles in publishers' catalogues, surviving prints and photographs, and critical statements, was the middle and upper-middle class, no doubt predominantly female (although Fowler and Wells was clearly an exception in gearing its book list toward a more male-oriented, working-class audience). Whitman himself, though not given to frequent purchases of books, was well acquainted with the bookstores of Brooklyn and Manhattan, which he had periodically covered as part of his newspaper beat; and he, too, tended to perceive their clientele in these terms. One such bookstore which he recommended to his readers was that recently opened in Brooklyn in 1847 by Thomas D. Smith,

> a gentleman whose cultivated taste and long experience in the book business, render him eminently qualified to conduct a literary depot, so much needed in the central part of the city, where ladies and gentlemen may find an early supply of all the new and standard productions of the day, as they appear – also, school books, juvenile books, plain and fancy stationery, music, etc. . . As we walked past Mr. S.'s place an evening since, and saw the elegant display in the windows, and a crowd of fashionable ladies looking over the music and the gilded volumes, it was plain to us that the store was to be *stamped with public approval*; for do not the ladies "lead" in such matters?[1]

One cannot, of course, precisely visualize *Leaves of Grass* as it stood on the shelves of contemporary bookstores in 1855; but next best thing, one can at least reconstruct the way the volume was situated among other books in a contemporary publisher's catalogue. In Sampson Low's 1856 catalogue of American books, one would have found Whitman's book – starched, ironed, and folded into bibliographical shape – listed as *"Leaves of Grass*. With Portrait of Author. By Walt Whitman. (Brooklyn, N.Y., 1855.) Impl. 8vo., cloth, 7s 6d." If shelved alongside other volumes in the catalogue, it would have stood on the book shelves of the belles lettres department of the store surrounded, in the order of the catalogue, on one side by editions of the works of Poe and of Richard Henry Dana, a biography of Mary M. Chase, Prof. Schele de Vere's *Stray Leaves from the Book of Nature,* a recent edition of Longfellow's *Outre-Mer,* several books of nature sketches by Susan Cooper (daughter of the novelist), Harry Penciller's *Rural Life in America,* Grace Greenwood's *Greenwood Leaves* and *A Forest Tragedy,* Lydia Sigourney's *Olive Leaves,* Frederic S. Cozzens' *Sparrowgrass Papers;* and on the other side, by Minnie Myrtle's *Myrtle Wreath; or Stray Leaves Recalled,* Thoreau's *Walden, Hermit's Dell* "from the Diary of a Penciller," *Summer in the Wilderness* by Charles Lanman (future partisan of James Harlan in the controversy over Whitman's dismissal from office in 1865), followed at intervals by Lowell's *Bigelow Papers,* Curtis' *Potiphar Papers,* and a collection of Lewis Gaylord Clark's *Knicknacks* from the pages of the *Knickerbocker.*

Taken strictly in this company, Whitman's book might have seemed to be one with its age, one leaf among the many ("inter folia fructus" was to become the house motto of the Appletons). Poets bearing alliterative, garden names and putting the leaves of nature into the leaves of print were all the fashion of the midfifties. In fact, the high priestess of the cult, Fanny Fern, authoress of several best-selling editions of *Fern Leaves* and one of the most popular writers of the decade, was to put her private and public blessing on Whitman the following year: "You are *delicious!* May my right hand wither if I don't tell the world before another week, what one woman thinks of you," she wrote him in a letter.[2]

But this view of its kinship with its age has its obvious limits. As Whitman himself knew and desired, his "singular-looking volume," as one reviewer referred to it, was certain to stand out conspicuously, inside and out, from other volumes of poetry. Objectively described, the volume was a thin quarto of 95 pages bound in dark green cloth, the title stamped in gilt in flowery, Victorian lettering into its covers and spine and its covers embossed with ornamental leaves. A person opening the book would have paged from the marble end paper to the title page, giving the title of the book in large, bold letters and below, the place and date of publication. On the verso was the copyright statement taken out by "Walter Whitman," the only external identification linking him or anyone else as author, publisher, or proprietor to the book. Facing the title page, however, was a three-quarter-length picture of a casually dressed, robust-looking workingman, which some reviewers were quick to recognize as the "idealized" pictorial signature of the author.

The design of the volume was no less provocative. A reader looking through it would come across, without the mediation of a table of contents or formal introduction, an untitled prose essay written in sprawling sentences, punctuated irregularly, primarily by ellipses, and printed tightly in small double-columned type more befitting a newspaper than a book of poems. That fourteen-page essay was followed by a series of untitled, undivided, undifferentiated, and uncommonly long-lined poems. All in all, it was an understatement to call it a "singular-looking volume," and merely to glance through it was to see that its contents rivaled its physical appearance for peculiarity. Even its price, at two dollars, and its quarto format set it apart from the normal run of poetry volumes.

Such was the 1855 *Leaves of Grass.* During the weeks and months immediately following its publication, Whitman moved decisively to create a reading audience for it. One of the most obvious ways to do so was to mail out copies to writers and editors whom he respected. The first response he received in return, with fine poetic justice, was the one he cared most about: Emerson's. Writing in the first blaze of his enthusiasm, Emerson saluted his "benefactor" with unreserved praise:

> I am not blind to the worth of the wonderful gift of "Leaves of Grass." I find it the most extraordinary piece of wit & wisdom that America has yet contributed. I am very happy in reading it, as great power makes us happy. It meets the demand I am always making of what seemed the sterile & stingy Nature, as if too much handiwork or

too much lymph in the temperament were making our western wits fat & mean. I give you joy of your free & brave thought. I have great joy in it. I find incomparable things said incomparably well, as they must be. I find the courage of *treatment*, which so delights us, & which large perception only can inspire. I greet you at the beginning of a great career, which yet must have had a long foreground somewhere for such a start. I rubbed my eyes a little to see if this sunbeam were no illusion; but the solid sense of the book is a sober certainty. It has the best merits, namely, of fortifying & encouraging.[3]

It is not hard to imagine what this letter meant to Whitman; it brought him high praise from, in his hero-worshipping eyes, the highest source. Not only high praise but the right sort of high praise, its terms covering what Whitman considered the genuine criteria of poetry: "the best merits . . . of fortifying & encouraging," "courage of *treatment*," "free & brave thoughts," "large perceptions," "incomparable things said incomparably well," the giving and taking of joy.

That letter was to reaffirm to Whitman the authenticity of his genius and ambition; but even in the unlikely eventuality that he needed external support to go on with his plans, this was at first a private matter. It was not until October that he passed the letter on to Charles Dana of the New York *Tribune* and through Dana to the public. But by that time, reviews of *Leaves of Grass* were already appearing in the press, beginning with Dana's in the *Tribune;* and I would like to discuss the views and opinions of the most important of the 1855–6 reviews in their chronological sequence.

Dana's review opened with his half-mocking response to the striking engraving of the author:

From the unique effigies of the anonymous author of this volume which graces the frontispiece, we may infer that he belongs to the exemplary class of society sometimes irreverently styled "loafers." He is therein represented in a garb, half sailor's, half working man's, with no superfluous appendage of coat or waistcoat, a "wide awake" perched jauntily on his head, one hand in his pocket and the other on his hip, with a certain air of mild defiance, and an expression of pensive insolence in his face which seems to betoken a consciousness of his mission as the "coming man."[4]

He then passed on to Whitman's theory of poetry, citing from the Preface, which he compared to Alcott (whom he could not take seriously) and to Emerson (whom he could) in its insistence on a prophetic American poetry, before commenting on the poetry itself.

Dana was obviously baffled by poems which he described as having "been shaped on no pre-existent model out of the author's own brain." On the one hand, he was offended by them:

His independence often becomes coarse and defiant. His language is too frequently reckless and indecent, though this appears to arise from a naive unconsciousness rather than from an impure mind. His words might have passed between Adam and Eve in Paradise, before the want of fig-leaves brought no shame; but they are quite out of place amid the decorum of modern society, and they will justly prevent his volume from free circulation in scrupulous circles.

At the same time, he recognized a peculiar but genuine poetic power in the verse:

They are full of bold, stirring thoughts – with occasional passages of effective description, betraying a genuine intimacy with Nature and a keen appreciation of beauty – often presenting a rare felicity of diction, but so disfigured with eccentric fancies as to prevent a consecutive perusal without offense, though no impartial reader can fail to be impressed with the vigor and quaint beauty of isolated portions.

After giving extensive citations from several of the poems, he concluded on a note of guarded praise: "The taste of not overdainty fastidiousness will discern much of the essential spirit of poetry beneath an uncouth and grotesque embodiment."

I quote Dana's remarks at length not because they were unusually original or perceptive but because, on the contrary, they were in many ways representative of the broader nineteenth-century critical reaction to follow. Like Dana, other contemporary reviewers, regardless of their estimation of Whitman, typically read the prose Preface as a gloss on the intent of the poems, and in doing so many were as predisposed as Whitman to see cultural nationalism as an issue. They were also inclined to follow Dana in his ad hominem approach to *Leaves of Grass,* an approach common in nineteenth-century criticism generally and one obviously invited by Whitman, the very conventions of whose work made himself, or the representation of himself, a primary issue. Not surprisingly, criticism of Whitman, pro and con, would be pointedly personal throughout the century.

Dana's extensive citations from the book, though perhaps in this case a service rendered Whitman by the *Tribune,* were typical not so much of his own period's review style as of the review style of earlier nineteenth-century criticism, before books had become widely available; but the way he quoted is broadly revealing. In order to make his citations more palatable to the public, he felt compelled to package passages from Whitman under titles of his own invention. Future critics would follow Dana's cautionary example at least to the extent of citing from the book with extreme care. But more than anything else, Dana's uneasiness before the book, both moral and aesthetic, prefigured the reaction of the contemporary reading public in general, although not every reviewer to follow would be as generous in stretching his or her imagination to meet a book evident even at first glance as not fitting to be placed at the center of the Victorian household.[5]

Within a week of Dana's review, there appeared a notice in Fowler and Wells's *Life Illustrated* (for which Whitman would begin writing in November).[6] Declaring *Leaves of Grass* "like no other book that ever was written," the reviewer felt obligated to depart from usual critical fashion in order to describe the appearance of the book:

> It is a thin volume of 95 pages, shaped like a small atlas. On the first page is a portrait of the unknown author. He stands in a careless attitude, without coat or vest, with a rough felt hat on his head, one hand thrust lazily into his pocket and the other resting on his hip. He is the picture of a *perfect loafer;* yet a thoughtful loafer, an amiable loafer, an able loafer. Then follows a long preface, which most steady-going, respectable people would pronounce perfect nonsense, but which free-souled persons, here and there, will read and *chuckle over* with real delight, as the expression of their own best feelings. This remarkable preface is something in the Emersonian manner – that is, it is a succession of independent sentences, many of which are of striking truth and beauty. The body of the volume is filled with "Leaves of Grass," which are lines of rhythmical prose, or a series of *utterances* (we know not what else to call them), unconnected, curious, and original . . .
>
> The discerning reader will find in this singular book much that will please him, and we advise all who are fond of new and peculiar things to procure it. We may add that the book was printed by the author's own hands, and that he is philosophically indifferent as to its sale. It pleased him to write *so,* and the public may take it or let it alone, just as they prefer.

Public reaction after these two notices was too slow to suit Whitman's charged expectations, which induced him to accelerate the book's reception by initiating his own well-known, one-man promotional campaign that August and September. But by the beginning of September, *Putnam's Magazine,* a leading monthly which Whitman himself sometimes read, was out with an unsigned review of *Leaves of Grass* by Charles Eliot Norton.[7] Norton's enthusiasm for the volume would have surprised not only his friends and family but also Whitman, who would have expected nothing but prejudice and abuse from someone of Norton's background – the inheritor of Boston's bluest blood as the son of Andrews Norton, the conservative Unitarian theologian and Harvard professor who had been Emerson's chief antagonist in the Divinity School Address affair. Many years later, Whitman, without knowledge of the authorship of the review, would categorize Norton as "the type of scholar who is bound to distrust a man like me."[8]

Like Dana, Norton was clearly dazzled, even a bit blinded, by what he instantly recognized as "a new light in poetry"; and again like Dana, he tried to overcome his initial confusion by reading the Preface against the poetry for an explanation of Whitman's theory and practice. The author of this "curious and lawless collection of poems" he described as "a compound of the New England transcendentalist and New York rowdy," who managed to "fuse and combine with the most perfect harmony" the most and the least fragrant of American ideas. Though ill at ease with Whitman's crudity and vulgarity, which he claimed made the book unfit "to be read aloud to a mixed audience" and which decided him to quote selectively from the poems, he found in Whitman a genuinely American poet endowed with "an original perception of nature, a manly brawn, and an epic directness."

This was Norton's opinion in public; in private, he was less guarded, his skeptical distance considerably shortened. He attempted later that month to interest his friend James Russell Lowell in *Leaves of Grass* and even bought him a copy, believing that Lowell would also see through what was "disgustingly coarse" to passages of "most vigorous and varied writing, some superbly graphic descriptions, great stretches of imagination."[9] Lowell, however, would have none of this, countering Norton's praise with his own view that Whitman's "originality" carried him beyond the pale of genuine verse.[10] More privately yet, Norton paid Whitman the highest honor of imitation. While still under the influence of *Leaves of Grass,* Norton wrote his own "A Leaf of Grass," which attempted to translate "Song of Myself" into a poetic idiom he could more easily understand:

> I will pluck a leaf of grass and give it to you to look at.
> It is made of sunshine and rain, of the dew in the evening and of the
>   cool air of the still starlighted night,
> It springs from the earth as fresh as the first blade that tinged the
>   brown soil with green
> When the world was young, and each day a new miracle to eyes not
>   blinded with the dust of accustomedness.
> . . . .
> I go to a factory; the whirling wheels, the noise and jar of the
>   spindles, the rush of the steam make me proud of myself
> And I think all this I have made with my head and my hands.
> A band that I see not catches the skirt of my coat,
> The cloth will not yield, and I am pulled in between rollers and
>   come out flat and what is called dead,
> But I look down with disdain on the poor flattened carcass
> And laugh for death did not flatten my soul.[11]

For anyone interested in proving the frequently asserted judgment that Whitman's influence on his imitators has been bad, there is hardly a more appropriate place to begin the argument than with Norton.

A more interesting and perceptive review of *Leaves of Grass* than either
Dana's or Norton's – made all the more intriguing by its source – was
the September 15 notice written by an unnamed critic for Whitman's old
paper, the Brooklyn *Eagle*.[12] Whoever the writer was – and it is not
implausible that he was assisted by Whitman – he saw more deeply into
the poetry than would all but a small number of his contemporaries:

> Here we have a book which fairly staggers us. It sets all the ordinary
> rules of criticism at defiance. It is one of the strangest compounds of
> transcendentalism, bombast, philosophy, folly, wisdom, wit and dull-
> ness which it ever entered into the heart of man to conceive. Its author
> is Walter Whitman, and the book is a reproduction of the author. His
> name is not on the frontispiece, but his portrait, half length, is. The
> contents of the book form a daguerreotype of his inner being, and the
> title page bears a representation of its physical tabernacle. It is a poem;
> but it conforms to none of the rules by which poetry has ever been
> judged. It is not an epic nor an ode, nor a lyric; nor does its verses
> move with the measured pace of poetical feet – of Iambic, Trochaic,
> or Anapestic, nor seek the aid of Amphibrach, of dactyl or Spondee,
> nor of final or caesural pause, except by accident.

He, too, went on to expound Whitman's theory of poetry by way of
the Preface, but unlike Dana and Norton, with none of the resistance of
an alien sensibility.

His selections of passages from the poetry for citation are fascinating.
He chose the "both in and out of the game" passage from "Song of
Myself" as constituting an accurate self-portrait of the author. Did he
know Whitman? (Or did Whitman know Whitman?) He cited a verse
frequently praised in the nineteenth century, "A child said, What is the
grass? fetching it to me with full hands," as unsurpassed as "a poetic
interpretation of nature." He noted the tantalizing suggestiveness of
Whitman's poetic manner and took as a specific instance the passage
about the twenty-eight young men, which left him uncomfortably in
doubt as to its final meaning: "Well, did the lady fall in love with the
twenty-ninth bather, or *vice versa*? Our author scorns to gratify such
puerile curiosity; the denouement which novel readers would expect is
not hinted at." His overall opinion, however, was favorable:

> We have said that the work defies criticism; we pronounce no judgment
> upon it; it is a work that will satisfy few upon a first perusal; it must
> be read again and again, and then it will be to many unaccountable. All
> who read it will agree that it is an extraordinary book, full of beauties
> and blemishes, such as Nature is to those who have only a half-formed
> acquaintance with her mysteries.

After a lull of several months filled primarily by the printing of Emerson's letter in the New York *Tribune, Leaves of Grass* received its first

wholehearted denunciation at the hands of Rufus Griswold.[13] Griswold has come down to us as the malicious literary executor of Edgar Allan Poe who misdirected the course of Poe's reputation for decades, but to his own time he was one of the country's leading literary anthologists and arbiters of taste. His influential *The Poets and Poetry of America* had already been out for more than a decade, but it was clear from his remarks that Whitman would have had a better chance of gaining entrance to Griswold's canon with his poems of the 1840s than with *Leaves of Grass*. Griswold considered the Whitman of 1855 better relegated to the farm than to the groves of genuine poetry. "This *poet* (?)," as he contemptuously referred to Whitman, had invested his "natural imbecility" in a "mass of stupid filth," and he went on to pile Whitman high with abuse. He refused even to give extracts, he claimed, for fear of offending "ears polite," but a secondary reason was that he was only partially concerned with Whitman. Whitman was for him a convenient exemplar of what he considered the transcendental school of poetry, whose indecorum and unrestrained individuality threatened his conservative idea of the "healthy core" of society. And through Whitman, he was able to strike at Emerson, whose letter of endorsement he noted and criticized.

Griswold was the first of many contemporary critics who unloaded their strongest abuse on Whitman, who was obviously vulnerable to attacks for his many and varied freedoms from convention. The Boston *Intelligencer*, for example, agreed so strongly with Griswold as to quote his insults approvingly, adding its own description of the book as a "heterogeneous mass of bombast, egotism, vulgarity and nonsense" and of its author as "some escaped lunatic, raving in pitiable delirium."[14] Whitman was to suffer such personal attacks all his life.

But from the periodical from which one might most naturally expect outright scorn for *Leaves of Grass*, the *North American Review*, there came strong praise.[15] The unsigned writer, Edward Everett Hale, who would in later years take his early support of Whitman as a source of pride, commended the book nearly as enthusiastically as Griswold had denigrated it. Like virtually all his contemporaries, he had to work his way over and through the book's unconventionalisms to make sense of the poetry; but that effort having been made, he liked and praised various aspects of the book's experimentation. What he liked most was the "remarkable power" of the book's rendering of America, both in its Preface ("perhaps the very best thing in it") and in its "prose poetry." Quoting Whitman's lines from the Preface, "What I experience or portray shall go from my composition without a shred of my composition. You shall stand by my side and look in the mirror with me," he saw this as the prophecy of the book fulfilled by its poetry.

He was genuinely amazed at Whitman's ability to render life as art:

"And thus there are in this curious book little thumbnail sketches of life in the prairie, life in California, life at school, life in the nursery – life, indeed, we know not where not, – which as they are unfolded one after another, strike us as real, – so real that we wonder how they came on paper." These remarks were unusually sensitive to Whitman's aesthetics, as was his criticism of the book for its departure from convention. But far from being offended by the book's open disrespect of behavioral norms, he was offended rather by what he saw as the mere posture of disrespect: "It is a pity that a book where everything else is natural should go out of the way to avoid the suspicion of being prudish." Still, one can easily overstate his critical acumen; his remarks were generally un-focused, a sign, I take it, of his lingering intellectual confusion.

Whitman's flagrant irreverence was bound to upset conservatives; and nowhere was the reaction more predictable, as with the Reverend Gris-wold, than among the conservative devout, who were not likely to enjoy being told, "The scent of these arm-pits is aroma finer than prayer, / This head is more than churches or bibles or creeds" ("Song of Myself"). Some liberal churchmen, however, such as Emerson and Hale, could follow him in these sentiments. One other who could was the author of a spiritualist-oriented review in the *Christian Spiritualist,* a paper which matched Whitman for the quirkiness of its views.[16] Seeing the new gen-eration following the period of Wordsworth and Shelley as requiring a new kind of poetry which would elevate mankind to a perception of spiritual reality, as the earlier poets had done for their time, the reviewer acclaimed Whitman's the highly "mediatorial" form of expression he was looking for, one in profound sympathy with the spirit of modern man lifted above conventionalism:

> We cannot take leave of this remarkable volume without advising our friends who are not too delicately nerved, to study the work as a sign of the times, written, as we perceive, under powerful impulses; a prophecy and promise of much that awaits all who are entering with us into the opening doors of a new era. A portion of that thought which broods over the American nation, is here seized and bodied forth by a son of the people, rudely, wildly, and with some perversions, yet strongly and genuinely, according to the perception of this bold writer. He is the young Hercules who has seized the serpents that would make him and us their prey; but instead of strangling, he would change them to winged and beautiful forms, who shall become the servants of mankind.

Curiously, of all Whitman's early critics, this spiritualist interpretation of him as a "mediumship" to the people came as close as any to his own conception of *Leaves of Grass.*

A more disappointing review for Whitman would have been that of

the *Crayon,* to which he sent a copy of the book in late 1855.[17] Other
critics had spoken of and praised Whitman's gift for verbal genre painting;
but the editor of the *Crayon,* the leading art journal in the United States,
did not mix artistic genres in his review. He gave, instead, one of the
more rigorously literary analyses the book was to receive, following the
same method Whitman had himself used back in September in the *American Phrenological Journal* by comparing *Leaves of Grass* with Tennyson's
recently published *Maud.* He, too, found the two volumes adhering to
opposing New World and Old World models of poetry; but in contrast
to Whitman, he found both works to fall short of his standards of true
poetry. Where Tennyson was decadent, Whitman was primitive; where
Tennyson was precious, Whitman was crude. Both extremes missed the
proper middle ground of poetry, one respectful of the gradations of value,
form, and the "dignity of verse." He dismissed them both, finally, as
"irreverent, irreligious."

One of the more historically interesting reviews would have been that
of the publishers through their trade magazine, but the *American Publishers' Circular and Literary Gazette* was silent about the book. The less
prominent *Monthly Trade Gazette,* however, which Frank Luther Mott
describes as a parallel journal serving booksellers and publishers, did
notice the book in early 1856 and was so favorably impressed with what
it saw as to praise it in terms as unstinting as Emerson's:

> Had it been issued in a dress worthy of the matter, it could hardly fail
> of mounting, at a single step, to the topmost floor of Novelty's platform,
> and instantly commanding the public eye. As it is, its success will be
> a work of time. We give a cordial greeting to *Leaves of Grass,* which
> we look upon as the most considerable poem that has yet appeared in
> our country.[18]

Strong praise also came from an unexpected source, the most popular
woman essayist in America, Fanny Fern (Sara Willis Parton, wife of
Whitman's friend, the talented biographer James Parton, and sister of
Nathaniel Willis).[19] She was already famous for her best-selling *Fern
Leaves* when hired by Robert Bonner in 1855 at the unprecedented rate
of a hundred dollars an article to write for his weekly New York *Ledger,*
then beginning its climb into publishers' heaven with circulation rising
into the hundreds of thousands of copies. As the most prominent voice
on his family-oriented, middle-class paper, she was in a position to put
a popular stamp, as Emerson a critical stamp, of approval on Whitman,
which was clearly what she meant to do when she noticed him and his
book in her "Peeps from Under a Parasol." "Walt Whitman, the effeminate world needed thee," she proclaimed, "Walt Whitman, the world
needed a 'Native American' of thorough out-and-out breed – enamored

of *women,* not *ladies* – *men,* not *gentlemen;* something besides a mere Catholic-hating Know-Nothing. It needed a man who dared speak out his strong, honest thoughts in the face of pusillanimous, toadying, republican aristocracy; dictionary-men, hypocrites, cliques, and creeds." Whitman could heartily have agreed with these sentiments, as well as with her characterization of *Leaves of Grass* as being "well-baptized; fresh, hardy, and grown for the masses," even if it meant having to suffer the book's being put through her tepid bath of compliments before being proven safe and sanitary for America's mothers and babes. (By coincidence, the English magazine of humor, *Punch,* was at that moment grouping Whitman and Parton together and consigning them to joint burial: "We can only say that these *Leaves of Grass* are fully worthy to be put on a level with that heap of rubbish called *Fern Leaves,* by Fanny Fern, and similar 'green stuff.' ")

What, then, is one to make of all these reviews of the 1855 *Leaves of Grass?* With no pretense of scientific exactitude about a subject too little known or investigated to bear sweeping generalizations, I would draw a few preliminary judgments about the critical reaction of the time.[20] The most obvious is that a self-published volume issued from a local printing shop by an anonymous author was given a fairly broad and serious public hearing by its contemporary media. That hearing, furthermore, was neither as universally nor as monotonously negative as Whitman would later claim; on the contrary, the reviews were widely various both in opinion and in point of view. Reaction ranged from the abusive to the eulogistic (and on to the hagiographic, if one includes Whitman's own reviews). On the other hand, virtually all reviewers, hostile and friendly alike, registered their shock at the sheer novelty and unconventionality of the volume, inside and out; and all had to exert themselves, as Whitman frequently insisted in his public utterances they would, to come to terms with it. Some managed; others did not. Clearly, the volume presented a major challenge not only to expectations and preconceptions but also to sensibility.

If the reviews of 1855–6 were generally mixed and unpredictable, they did share one important area of consensus – not in their content, but in their status as reviews. I can make this point most graphically by making it indirectly, by reprinting a contemporaneous, journalistic mock-review of *Hamlet* which self-consciously brought the unstated premises underlying the practice of reviewing to the surface.[21] The situation of the parody is that of an official of a country book club whose function requires him to read through book reviews in the press and to present the majority opinion to prospective book buyers of his club. This unnamed critic has a general idea of the state of criticism in his day:

The other evening – when I had been reading up the views taken in a great number of critical notices of the same eight or ten last published works – I fell upon a consideration of the time in which we live, and of the great disadvantage under which our forefathers, both writers and readers lay, when the appeal made by every book was straight home from the writer to the reader, and there were no journals to advise a reader what to think about the works he read, or to instruct a writer, as he went along, by pointing out to him his merits and his faults.

A case in point, he continues, is Shakespeare, about whom he collects a batch of hypothetical reviews to pass on to his club members, and from which I reprint several samples:

Hamlet, Prince of Denmark. A Tragedy. By William Shakespeare. Heart, Soul and Co.

. . . The plot of Mr. Shakespeare's tragedy, though on the whole, well constructed, is exceedingly involved, and it is made more difficult to follow by the circumstance that two of the principal characters are mad, a third is foolish, and a fourth is a ghost. This is a most talkative ghost; the ghost, indeed, of Hamlet's father, who is addressed by his son as a "truepenny," an "old mole," and "a perturbed spirit." The great complication of the plot seems, however, to arise out of the introduction of a King of Denmark, who is a fratricide; and as Hamlet himself is made by the author most truly to say, "a king of shreds and patches." He is called also elsewhere, a "paddock," a "bat," and a "gib"! By the omission of this character of King Claudius the plot would be greatly simplified and the interest of the play would be more strictly centered upon Hamlet. If this play should ever be reprinted (and it certainly has merits which warrants a belief that it may deserve the honors of a second edition), we trust that Mr. Shakespeare will consider it worth while to effect this slight alteration. He would thus obtain space for exhibiting his hero from an interesting point of view, which he has in the most unaccountable manner wholly overlooked. [There then follows a pedantic, excerpt-filled plot summary.]

We lay this work down – immature as it is – not without expression of the pleasure we have had in its perusal. If we have appeared to dwell upon its faults, we have done so because we believe Mr. Shakespeare competent to understand them, and still, with a promising career before him, young enough to succeed in their correction. The tragedy is one that will repay perusal.

Hamlet. A Tragedy. By William Shakespeare

The author of this ill-written play is one of the many instances of young men with good average parts who have totally mistaken their vocation. Hamlet is a melodrama of the worst school. Let it suffice to say that of the dozen characters it contains, exclusive of the supernumeraries, eight are killed by sword, drowning, or poison, during the course of the piece; and one appears as a ghost because he was killed before the play began...

There remain only three persons alive, two of whom are insignificant courtiers, and the third has only been persuaded to postpone an act of suicide that he may remain alive for a time to act as a showman of the dead bodies of the other dramatis personae!...

Beat the drum, Mr. Merryman! Walk up, ladies and gentlemen. To Mr. Shakespeare's Hamlet we believe the public would not often be persuaded to walk up, even were it performed on the only stage for which it is in any degree fitted – that of a booth at Greenwich Fair.

The very conditions of midcentury literary criticism, I hope it is clear, militated against the kind of reception, indeed, against the very conception of the reading act, that Whitman had presupposed in writing *Leaves of Grass*. The coolly reasoned manner, solidly middle-class values, preconceived notions of literary genre and convention, and partially or impartially maintained distance from the book under discussion interposed by the critic between the reader and the text all tended to preclude the rigorous, unmediated interplay Whitman hypothesized between his reader and his book. Strictly speaking, Whitman should never have expected anything more; a book which challenged the conditions and conventions of literary criticism could not reasonably expect an enthusiastic or "correct" judgment from its accused. The kind of criticism best suited to his writing was one which substituted inspiration for propriety, spontaneous response for preconception, unrestraint for balance, the test of empiricism for that of rule – in short, his own, the kind of criticism he had devised, perhaps by plan but more likely by contingency, to meet the demands of his situation. Failing that, he would be better served, from his perspective, by private letters or by pieces of criticism written across the institutional grain rather than by formal criticism. This, too, was closer to Whitman's ideal of reading, and one would ideally like to be able to read the 1855 *Leaves of Grass* against such responses; but in the scarcity of written responses at this stage of his career, such a reading is an impossibility.

8

Whitman and the Reader, 1856

When Moncure Conway, Emerson's first emissary, came down to Brooklyn in mid-September 1855 to visit Whitman, he was directed by Mrs. Whitman to the Rome brothers' printing shop.[1] There he found Whitman – "A man you would not have marked in a thousand; blue striped shirt, opening from a red throat; and sitting on a chair without a back," he reported to Emerson – reading proof. The proof, in all likelihood, was that of a poem or poems he was working on in preparation for a new edition of his poetry. Whitman was still riding the creative surge which had taken him through the first edition and which was now sweeping him uninterruptedly into an enlarged and expanded second edition of *Leaves of Grass*. The completion of the former volume, whenever it was precisely in the winter or spring of 1855 that he put his pen down and decided to bundle his ready poems for the printer, was obviously only a temporary pause in an ongoing venture.

He "advanced" – to use one of his favorite terms for the action of the poet – as was his way, simultaneously on two fronts: with the composition of his new poems and with the promotion of the old ones. Even while he was working away on the texts of new poems for the enlarged edition, he continued his one-man campaign for the acceptance of the first edition. As I have already mentioned, in August and September he published his self-reviews of *Leaves of Grass* and in October passed on Emerson's letter for publication to the New York *Tribune*. Then in November or December, he collected a variety of reviews of *Leaves of Grass* for use as advertisements and placed them at the beginning of a second issue of the book, which he perhaps timed to coincide with the binding of a new batch of copies late that fall. More interested in publicity than in praise, he assembled good and bad reviews indiscriminately, incorporating Griswold's attack and Norton's more favorable review with his own three self-reviews.

He also mixed in with these reviews excerpts from two critical pieces unrelated to *Leaves of Grass,* whose selection reveals something of Whitman's strategic thinking at the time. One was from E. P. Whipple's long 1844 review article in the *North American Review* of Griswold's *The Poets and Poetry of America,* which Whitman's editing made sound like a classic 1840s proclamation of cultural nationalism. The second piece was an article in the 1850 London *Eclectic Review* entitled, "Have Great Poets Become Impossible?" which suited Whitman by answering its own question, with Whitman's silent concurrence, "in truth, seldom had a true and new poet a fairer field, or the prospect of a wider favor, than at this very time." And from what he called "Extracts from Letters and Reviews," he excerpted a passage from what was by now a favorite quote:

> Poetry...must become the exponent of a new spirit through new forms. Such is demanded by authority greater than all the critics of Europe and America, the common sense and common instinct of the people. The new forms are not to be judged by the old models, but are to be judged by themselves. Wordsworth truly said that every original first-rate poet must himself make the taste through which he is to be fully understood and appreciated.

He liked the statement so much that he made it his own for one of the new poems of the 1856 edition: "I myself make the only growth by which I can be appreciated" ("By Blue Ontario's Shore").

At about the same time, he began a semiregular connection with Fowler and Wells's *Life Illustrated,* a popular weekly paper with whose unconventional, reform-minded views (as with those of the parent book publishing house) his own were often in accordance. In the occasional articles he contributed over the next year, he spoke his mind on a wide variety of matters, making comments which bear on some of the ideas which had gone into the first edition and were then going into the new edition of *Leaves of Grass.*[2] If these articles had any point of intersection, it was their common concern, spoken or unspoken, direct or indirect, with the democratization of society and culture. Whitman called in them for better housing for working-class and middle-class families in New York, gave popularized tours of the Egyptian Museum and the Academy of Music (New York's new opera house), analyzed the English language as "America's mightiest inheritance" and instructed the working class on its correct use and pronunciation, and rejected the suitability of Voltaire as a literary model for being an aristocrat. In one article, he told of his recent experience in attending a Christmas concert of sacred music at fashionable Grace Church, at which he became infuriated at having to stand with other nonmembers ("we, the herd") for an hour in the cold "until the lions and lionesses, snobs and snobbesses, had all subsided into the meditative depths of their velvet-cushioned pews." The sermon, he noted, was on the "distinguishing characteristic of Christianity [as] seen in the fact that it brings all men – the beggar and the king alike – to a common level."[3]

Whitman, in turn, came in for increasing support from Fowler and Wells, who used *Life Illustrated* in late 1855 and early 1856 to promote the distribution of the 1855 *Leaves of Grass*. They reprinted Emerson's letter and defended him against Griswold's attack in late 1855, and in 1856 they gradually expanded the scope of their support. Eager to finish with the first edition, they ran an advertisement in late February in the New York *Tribune,* announcing its end: "This work was not stereotyped; a few copies only remain, after which it will be out of print." Several months later, they prefaced Whitman's contribution to the April 12 *Life Illustrated* by announcing his future contributions and praising him inordinately: "Walt Whitman is more a *Democrat* than any man we ever met. He believes in American principles, American character, American tendencies, the 'American Era,' to a degree that renders his belief an originality . . . Emphatically and peculiarly, he is a man of the people."[4] Soon afterward, they reprinted the favorable reviews of *Leaves of Grass* by William Howitt and by Fanny Fern.

There was talk of an American era, too, in the center of the book publishing industry. Whitman could have found general support for his ideal of a broad-based national culture, had he needed to look for it, in the popular and professional magazines and newspapers, where there were still brash pronouncements about boom times for books. The organ of the New York Publishers' Association, for instance, ran an upbeat, three-part series on American publishing during November and December, which characterized the present as the age of promise fulfilled for book publishers:

> Whatever, in the shape of a book, is printed here, will find a market if at all respectably meritorious. When we remember that to sell ten thousand copies of the best work of fiction, in Great Britain and Ireland, is among the unprecedented events in the life of an author or publisher; and that behind this public, lies, at least, four centuries of a growing civilization: it may startle the uninitiated to be informed, that, with but little more than fifty years behind us, since Mathew Carey gave the first impulse to the sale of books, to dispose of *fifty thousand* copies, of any moderately good book, is among the ordinary events which every American publisher deems himself entitled to anticipate; and that such a sale (if the work is meritorious) will not surprise any intelligent man![5]

Looking to the future, the writer predicted, "ere half a century rolls by, [the publisher] will have a reading empire to supply with books, the like of which the sun never shone before upon."[6]

The hucksterish talk emanating from the parlors of Broadway may seem far removed from Whitman's garret perch in Brooklyn, but there is good reason to believe that Whitman had an ear tuned to such claims as he worked away at the promotion of his old work and the composition of his new. On December 7, he wrote to his United States Senator, William Seward, to request the latest Census statistics; and he most likely received by return mail the Census Compendium of 1854, itself in its fifty-thousand-copy edition a sign as well as an interpreter of the expansion in the bookmaking and other American industries.[7] Some of his clippings on American book and periodical production also seem to derive from around this period. The statistics he received from the Census Compendium and from newspaper clippings he put directly to use to prove the existence (or potential existence) of a national culture in the new ideological declaration he wrote for the second edition and in the prose proclamation he wrote at about this time, *The Eighteenth Presidency!*. More importantly, the idea of a national culture remained as crucial a part of the literary conventions and overall literary strategy of the second edition as they had been of its predecessor.

I say this with no intention of minimizing the effect of Whitman's personal incandescence on the new poems of the new edition; it was, as biographers and critics have long assumed, the primary agent involved in the creation of his work during these, the most creative years of his life. I say this only with the intention of pointing out that Whitman was still able to proceed in 1856 with an assumed identity between his personal and national roles. His varied writings that year reveal his continuing conviction in himself as a national poet. One of the best indications of this was his work on an idiomatic dictionary of the American language he seems to have worked on most intensely around this time. Although he was, of course, ill suited by temperament and training for a systematic project of this sort, his enthusiastic notes for the project indicate something of the way his authorial position through the first two editions of his poetry mixed personal and programmatic elements.

His notes for the projected *Primer of Words* reveal even more explicitly than does his poetry the electrifying effect of language on Whitman's personality. Names came like "magic" to him; the talk on the street and the new terminology coming out of the workplace excited his imagination; the landscape around him charged him with its verbal potentiality. Words were for him, as for few writers of whom I know, living things. Listen to Whitman describe "night": "How vast, surrounding, falling sleeping, noiseless, is the word Night! – It hugs with unfelt yet living arms. –"[8] Or "Mississippi": "Mississippi! – the word winds with chutes – it rolls a stream three thousand miles long."[9]

It is only a relatively short distance from this idea of language as a living, changing entity to a position in which the word becomes detached from the world and becomes a potentiality unto itself – the direction of Poe and the French Symbolists. This was precisely the road Whitman did not and could not travel. He had too great an attraction to the "thisness" of the world to have allowed language such a degree of autonomy; his own words, by contrast, as he never tired of saying, derived from the materiality of the world. *"Factories, mills, and all the processes of hundreds of different manufactures,* grow thousands of words," he noted down in the wordbook, although in reading the new edition of *Leaves of Grass* one could also see how rich and various were the verbal sources from which Whitman would draw for his new poems.[10] Whitman's idea of language, rather, was one which anticipated the pragmatism of James and Dewey. He was inclined to see language, like poems, as an instrumentality. Words were acts designed to fulfill functions: "A perfect writer would make words sing, dance, kiss, do the male and female act, bear children, weep, bleed, rage, stab, steal, fire cannon, steer ships, sack cities, charge with cavalry or infantry, or do any thing that man or woman or the natural powers can do."[11]

"The Americans are going to be the most fluent and melodious voiced people in the world – and the most perfect user of words," he jotted down in his notes; and it was the ideal poet – himself – who was going to be the instrumentality of this national goal.[12] Whitman's idea at this time was essentially to pass all of the new reality of the country under the pen of the poet – the "perfect user of words," as he had taken to calling him. Names of cities and states were to be rephrased; idiomatic expressions from the streets, the workplace, the home, the new technological processes were to be absorbed; foreign languages and native dialects were to be combed for colorful coinages; new concepts were to be matched to new terms – these were the tasks Whitman assigned to the American poet. In short, language, like the poetry, the culture, and the people it served, was to be Americanized.

The freedoms Whitman – but not only Whitman – was able to suggest and take with regard to language remind one of how open were the linguistic vistas before a writer of his generation. The "language experiment" of *Leaves of Grass,* "the attempt to give the spirit, the body, the man, new worlds, new potentialities of speech – an American, a cosmopolitan (the best of America is the best cosmopolitanism) range of self-expression," would have been inconceivable at any previous time in the United States.[13] But if Whitman was a daringly original theoretician and user of words during the mid–1850s, it would be misleading to think of his experiment with language independently of the larger experiment he was making with the dynamics of poetic communication. The challenge to the American writer, as he understood it, was to reshape not only language but also, through language, the relations between readers, writers, and culture.

His continuing concern with the interrelated roles of writer and reader and with the conditions for reader reception in America were especially clear in the fascinating notebook he kept from the fall of 1855 into mid–1856 and used specifically for the preparation of the second edition of *Leaves of Grass*.[14] The centerpiece of this notebook was unquestionably early versions of passages from the new "Sun-Down Poem" ("Crossing Brooklyn Ferry"); but there were also numerous of Whitman's usual self-directed, diary-style hints, reminders, and musings, which he jotted down randomly as they occurred to him. Here is a medley of those notations, which I give as a reflection of his thinking at the time:

> Not only American literature, but the structures of American social intercourse are household life, are growing up in total severance from the roots and trunks and branches
>
> Ideal to pervade largely / Eligibility – I, you, any one eligible to the condition or attributes or advantages of any being, no matter who, –
>
> To produce such a public that great performances will not be received with noisy applause but as matters of course
>
> *Gist of my books* To give others, readers, people, the materials to decide for themselves, and *know,* or grow toward *knowing,* with cleanliness and strength.
>
> The best   Only first rate poems have the quality of arousing in men and women who hear them or read them those thoughts effects that no words can even describe – effects which themselves cannot be described – great effects, proportioned to the ideas, images, and characters of the poem. –[15]

By the spring of 1856, Whitman considered the new poems he had been working on ready for publication and was able to proceed, unlike in 1855, with a working relationship with a publisher intact. His relations with Fowler and Wells had apparently tightened early that year, as he became a more regular contributor to *Life Illustrated* and as they reciprocated by increasing their journalistic support of his writing. Despite his mixed feelings about the outcome of the previous edition, he proposed to them the idea of a Fowler and Wells edition of *Leaves of Grass*; and on June 7 he received a formal response from Samuel Wells, the pragmatic business manager of the firm who oversaw its book publishing operations:

> After "duly considering," we have concluded that it is best for us to insist on the omission of certain objectionable passages in Leaves of

Grass, or, decline publishing it. We could give twenty reasons for this, but, the *fact* will be enough for *you* to know. We are not in a position, at present, to experiment. We must not venture.

Again, it will be *better* for *you* to have the work published by clean hands, i.e. by a House, not now committed to unpopular notions. *We* are not in favor, with the conservatism, and a more orthodox House would be better for you. Try the *Masons,* Partons publishers, (They publish Fanny Ferns works.) They are *rich* and *enterprizing,* and I guess would publish Leaves of Grass, on fair terms.[16]

Wells's reluctance to publish *Leaves of Grass* because of its supposed obscenity was to become a common theme of Whitman's relations with publishers throughout the century; but in this case, the claim was decidedly ironic, since Fowler and Wells was known for its publication of relatively progressive and explicit books on sexual hygiene and conduct. His advice to Whitman, however, to try the Masons, well-respected members and leaders of the New York Publishers' Association, was an intriguing and not inappropriate suggestion. They were, for one thing, the publishers of a considerable number of creative works and had the reputation for promoting their publications aggressively. They were also, as both Wells and Whitman knew, the publishers of Whitman's Brooklyn friends, Sara and James Parton. James was already establishing himself as one of the leading biographical writers in the country, but it was Sara (under her pseudonym of Fanny Fern) who was the most popular and valuable author on their list. When they contracted with her for a novel (*Ruth Hall*) in 1854, they obliged themselves "to use extraordinary exertions to promote the sale thereof, so as, if possible, to make it exceed the sale of any previous work, and will, moreover, use every means in their power to attain that end, therefore."[17] When she came to publish her *Fresh Leaves* with them in 1857, they ran an advertising campaign which cleverly capitalized on her established popularity: "3,427,918,615 copies ordered in advance" and printed on "50,000 power presses" for "the most stupendous work since the flood."[18]

With Sara Parton's active mediation, Whitman might possibly have gotten a full hearing from the Masons; but given his habitual reserve about initiating contacts, it is extremely unlikely that he took even the first step. Instead, within a month or two he managed to overcome the reluctance of Fowler and Wells and reached an agreement with them about the publication of an expanded *Leaves of Grass,* he to retain the copyright in his name and to supply them with an uncensored manuscript and they to publish it from stereotyped plates paid for and controlled by them but to leave their name off the title page. In the August 16 issue of *Life Illustrated,* they announced the work as nearly ready for sale and sent it off with a nice puff:

It is evident that the American people will give a hearing to any man who has it in him to reward attention. Walt Whitman's poems, the now famous "Leaves of Grass," would scarcely have been thought likely to become speedily popular. They came before the public unheralded, anonymous, and without the imprint of a publisher. The volume was clumsy, and uninviting, the style most peculiar, the matter (some of it at least) calculated to repel the class whose favorable verdict is supposed to be necessary to literary success. Yet the "Leaves of Grass" found purchasers, appreciators, and admirers. The first edition of a thousand copies rapidly disappeared, and we now have the pleasure of announcing that a second edition, with amendments and additions, is about to be issued. The author is still his own publisher, and the Messrs. Fowler and Wells will again be his agents for the sale of the work. The new edition will be a neat pocket volume of four hundred pages, price, as before, $1. It has been stereotyped. Copies will be ready about the first of September.

Walt Whitman has thus become a fixed fact. His message has been found worthy of regard. The emphatic commendation of America's greatest critic has been ratified by the public, and henceforth the "Leaves of Grass" must receive respectful mention wherever Americans are reckoning up those of their country's productions which could have sprung into existence nowhere but in America.[19]

On September 12 and continuing for a month, they ran an ad in the New York *Tribune,* announcing the book as ready for sale:

A small, thick Vol., green and gold, 400 pp. 24mo., handy for pocket, table or shelf:

Walt Whitman's "Leaves of Grass"

New Vol. [Thirty-two Poems.]
Dealers, send in your orders. This book will always be in demand. Fowler and Wells, No. 306 Broadway, N.Y.

The book was on sale by the weekend preceding the annual trade sale of the New York Publishers' Association, and an advertising slip inserted by the publishers announced the book as being for sale at Fowler and Wells stores in New York, Boston, and Philadelphia, as well as at bookstores and via agencies throughout the United States and even in Toronto, London, Paris, and Brussels.[20]

The 1856 *Leaves of Grass* stood in sharp physical contrast to the 1855 edition; an unprepossessing small sixteenmo, it was a stocky, undersized volume containing 384 pages of poetry and prose. Although its reduced page size cramped the printing of Whitman's long lines of verse, it compensated by approaching Whitman's personal ideal of books as being pocket-sized – fit for reading on the move, out of doors, or at one's leisure. It was also a plainer-looking volume than its predecessor, bound in a green cloth binding stamped with floral designs slightly toned down from those of 1855. But it, too, had its own stamp of theatricality; Whitman had printed in gold lettering on the volume's spine the best of all possible advertisements: "I Greet You at the / Beginning of A / Great Career / R. W. Emerson."

Inside, the book was also significantly different from its predecessor. The new edition still included the workingman picture of Whitman opposite the title page, with neither Whitman's nor the publisher's names appearing on the title page, although the copyright on the verso of the title page was accredited this time to "Walt" Whitman. There was now a table of contents to introduce the volume, listing in numerical sequence the poems, which had grown, with all the old ones included, from twelve to thirty-two. All poems appeared, in a break with the manner of presentation of 1855, under their separate titles. The 1855 Preface was gone, large parts of it worked into a new programmatic poem called "Poem of Many in One" ("By Blue Ontario's Shore"), a sign of how easily Whitman and his ideas could pass from prose to poetry. And with the expansion of the number of poems, no single poem dominated this volume as "Song of Myself" had done the previous edition.

There were various signs that Whitman attempted to improve the organization of his volume, but he was no more successful in this regard in 1856 than he would ever be. Organization of his individual poems into larger units was never Whitman's strength, and the problem showed badly even in the early editions. He attempted to systematize the poems by giving them each their individual titles, but squeezing each poem into the formulaic "Poem of . . ." – and this from a poet with a talent for naming – was a drab measure, at best. He also tried to find the proper framing device – he was always looking for framing devices both within individual poems an within larger units of poems – for his work by placing what he still considered the most important of his poems, "Poem of Walt Whitman, an American," ("Song of Myself") at the head of the volume and "Burial Poem" ("To Think of Time") at the end, the former to set the tone and pattern for the rest of the volume and the latter to close it on a note of reconciliation with mortality. This arrangement, however, satisfied him no better than any other; within a year he was at work on two new programmatic poems with which he planned to frame the next edition of his poetry.

Whitman had also begun the related business of tinkering with the texts of his poems. I take "Poem of Walt Whitman, an American" as a typical case of Whitman's editorial practice in 1856. Though still not fitted with stanza or section numbers, the poem was slightly regularized; ellipses were gone, a final period added to close the poem, and a title inserted to allow it to stand more independently than in the previous edition. The effect was far from drastic, to be sure, but it did detract marginally from the loose and natural flow of the previous year. The editing he did in 1856, however, was only a prelude to his lifelong attempt to establish "final" texts of his poems.

A new feature of the second edition was the formal inclusion of promotional material – called "Leave-Droppings" but actually a rather clever, self-serving kind of name-dropping – in the back of the volume following the last poem. It consisted of two parts, one the exchange of letters between Whitman and Emerson and the other, the assemblage of "Opinions" on the 1855 edition gathered from the English and American press. He had already collected an earlier set of journalistic opinion in preparing the second issue of the 1855 edition, although now he paid greater attention to foreign voices; but the unsolicited correspondence with Emerson was a novel, impetuous tactic. He not only printed Emerson's personal letter of appreciation of the 1855 edition publicly and without permission, in effect using it as Emerson's blank endorsement of the follow-up volume sight unseen; but he responded to it with an open letter to Emerson, which can be read as his ideological epilogue to the volume.[21]

Whitman's letter to Emerson was an "incongruous hash of mud and gold" – to apply to it the description by which Whitman was to speak that summer in *Life Illustrated* of the contents of the new *Leaves of Grass*. For all its preposterous bombast, it does give a vibrant expression of Whitman's unabated sense of personal and national mission in writing his new volume:

> Here are thirty-two Poems, which I send you, dear Friend and Master, not having found how I could satisfy myself with sending any usual acknowledgment of your letter. The first edition, on which you mailed me that till now unanswered letter, was twelve poems – I printed a thousand copies, and they readily sold; these thirty-two Poems I stereotype, to print several thousand copies of. I much enjoy making poems. Other work I have set for myself to do, to meet people and The States face to face, to confront them with an American rude tongue; but the work of my life is making poems. I keep on till I make a hundred, and then several hundred – perhaps a thousand. The way is clear to me. A few years, and the average annual call for my Poems is ten or twenty thousand copies – more, quite likely.

However manipulated his circulation figures may have been or exaggerated the estimation of his future popularity, the hope he entertained of reaching the mass public was genuine. It was genuine, impersonally considered, because the underlying conditions of American literary culture, as he understood them in 1856, supported such an ambition:

All current nourishments to literature serve. Of authors and editors I do not know how many there are in The States, but there are thousands, each one building his or her step to the stairs by which giants shall mount. Of the twenty-four modern mammoth two-double, three-double, and four-double cylinder presses now in the world, printing by steam, twenty-one of them are in These States. The twelve thousand large and small shops for dispensing books and newspapers – the same number of public libraries, any one of which has all the reading wanted to equip a man or woman for American reading – the three thousand different newspapers, the nutriment of the imperfect ones coming in just as usefully as any – the story papers, various, full of strong-flavored romances, widely circulated – the one-cent and two-cent journals – the political ones, no matter what side – the weeklies in the country – the sporting and pictorial papers – the monthly magazines, with plentiful imported feed – the sentimental novels, numberless copies of them – the low-priced flaring tales, adventures, biographies – all are prophetic; all waft rapidly on. I see that they swell wide, for reasons. I am not troubled at the movement of them, but greatly pleased. I see plying shuttles, the active ephemeral myriads of books also, faithfully weaving the garments of a generation of men, and a generation of women, they do not perceive or know. What a progress popular reading and writing has made in fifty years! What a progress fifty years hence! The time is at hand when inherent literature will be a main part of These States, as general and real as steam-power, iron, corn, beef, fish. First-rate American persons are to be supplied.[22]

More personally considered, what Whitman was describing here was the school of letters in which he had received his education in the 1830s and 1840s and from which he exited the following decade with the ambition to write first-rate poems for first-rate persons.

Throughout this letter, addressed more to the American public than to his so-called master, Whitman could be heard blowing his and the national horn loudly, no doubt with more clamor and less eloquence than he had sounded in the 1855 Preface. The intensity of the new volume's rhetoric, if anything, was even greater than was that of 1855; it would never again reach such a level. This may well have been a result of the continuing fervency of Whitman's sense of mission, made sharper and edgier by the unsatisfying public reception of the past year. But it is more than likely that Whitman was also feeling the pressure of outside forces, as the 1856 presidential campaign brought passions over the increasingly desperate issue of slavery to the fore (the 1856 *Leaves of Grass* would be issued at a time when campaign-related tracts and biographies dominated the lists of new publications). That Whitman was himself hotly exercised by the issues of the time is made clear by the raucous political manifesto that he was writing simultaneously with the poems of the 1856 *Leaves of Grass*; *The Eighteenth Presidency!*, though seemingly far removed from the concerns and territory of poetry, actually expressed in polemic prose a complementary set of ideas to those he was writing into the verse of the new edition.

Subtitled *Voice of Walt Whitman to each Young Man in the Nation, North, South, East, and West,* this strange, idiosyncratic tract was written in the vocative mode that Whitman was also then favoring in his poetry. Strongly first person in its manner of address and second person in the direction of its address, it was the voice of Walt Whitman sent out to slavers, politicians, editors, youth, Fremont of New York, farmers, boatmen, manufacturers. But mostly, it was Whitman addressing himself to the group with which he most naturally identified, the mechanics in the cities and the farmers in the countryside, the young men whom he habitually thought of when he thought of the nation's future. It was they, he asserted in the opening paragraph in response to the opening question, "First, Who Are the Nation?" who constituted the nation, its numerical majority and its spiritual bulwark. And it was they, he went on to argue in the tract, who were most seriously in danger of losing their democratic birthright of home and property ownership should slavery be permitted to expand unchecked into the territories.

The purpose of the tract, of Whitman's acknowledgment of the sad state of current affairs, was expressly to arouse these true Americans to corrective action. But even in his tract, Whitman was not advising a political solution to the nation's political problems. His remarks in the tract made it clear that he considered the majority party candidates, Buchanan of the Democrats and Fillmore of the Whigs–Know Nothings, an equally detestable two of a kind, interchangeable "disunionists" and servants of the slave interest. And as for the newly formed Republican party, despite its opposition to slavery, it was not then and would never be the party of the workingman. Whitman was closer in his views during the late 1850s, if anything, to the Democrat Douglas than to the Republican Lincoln; and even when he became a Republican around the time of the Civil War, he had long since lost all traces of his earlier political idealism. The counsel he offered the young, then, in 1856 was essentially apolitical, to look elsewhere than to established institutions and mechanisms for solutions to political and nonpolitical problems. So here, too, in substance as in style, his poetry and his prose polemic met on common ground.

In the absence of the "Redeemer President" whose coming Whitman vaguely foretold, there was, at least, "the voice of Walt Whitman," and this request "To Editors of the Independent Press, and to Rich Persons":

> Circulate and reprint this Voice of mine for the workingmen's sake.
> I hereby permit and invite any rich person, anywhere, to stereotype it,

or re-produce it in any form, to deluge the cities of The States with it, North, South, East and West. It is those millions of mechanics you want; the writers, thinkers, learned and benevolent persons, merchants, are already secured almost to a man. But the great masses of the mechanics, and a large portion of the farmers, are unsettled, hardly know whom to vote for, or whom to believe. I am not afraid to say that among them I seek to initiate my name, Walt Whitman, and that I shall in future have much to say to them.[23]

Whether by this hint of future communication he was referring to more prose pronouncements or to his new edition of *Leaves of Grass* is not clear; it does not particularly matter, since both, in Whitman's eyes, would serve the identical purpose of individual and societal reform. *The Eighteenth Presidency!*, however, was never to serve anything but a strictly personal function for Whitman; it survives today in printer's proof sheets but as far as is known was never published. Rich persons and editors, apparently, had no need for it; and, in any case, Whitman had a more pressing self-presentation to make in his new edition of *Leaves of Grass*.

The new edition, with no Preface to introduce it, opened without the explicit ideological statement of the first edition. But the national mission of the poetry nevertheless continued strong. In the badly labored poetic successor to the Preface, called in 1856 "Poem of Many in One," as in its philosophical counterpart, the new "Sun-Down Poem," Whitman gave expression to his profound, lifelong concern with tightening the connection between the modern individual and the democratic collective. The prototype of this individual is, of course, Whitman's "I," the poet as everyman, or alternately when he shifts into his favored mode, it is "you," as in this typical passage near the end of the poem:

> O I see now that this America is only you and me,
> Its power, weapons, testimony, are you and me,
> Its roughs, beards, haughtiness, ruggedness, are you and me,
> Its ample geography, the sierras, the prairies, Mississippi, Huron,
>   Colorado, Boston, Toronto, Raleigh, Nashville, Havana, are you
>   and me.
> . . . .
> Past, present, future, are only you and me.

By this logic, all the world – its territory, history, inhabitants – are you and me; and equipped with the cataloguing technique, Whitman did not hesitate to interpose all these things between himself and the reader.

At its most bathetic, as here, this technique risked the vapid, universalist identification which drove D. H. Lawrence, one of Whitman's most serious and appreciative readers, to exasperation: "This awful Whitman. This post-mortem poet. This poet with the private soul leaking out of him all the time. All his privacy leaking out in a sort of dribble, oozing into the universe."[24] While I would not want to be the one to defend

Whitman the rainmaker, this view of Whitman's insistent identification is extremely partial, and with Lawrence, misleading. Lawrence knew best the Whitman of his last years and of his last edition; he had little perception of the urgency or the sense of mission with which Whitman faced the world and his reader in the 1850s or of the way Whitman's poetry, as poetry, was meant to affect its reader.

Marks of Whitman's obsession with a personalized identification with the reader and the world were in evidence throughout the book, in the new poems equally with the carryover poems from 1855. They were in evidence, for instance, in the new "Poem of Salutation" ("Salut au Monde!"), a poem of greetings set into a format of questions and answers, as though some unseen questioner were engaging "Walt Whitman" in a panoramic dialogue. And they were in evidence in the strangely unsettling "Bunch Poem" ("Spontaneous Me"), with its troubled and troubling sexuality:

> Beautiful dripping fragments – the negligent list of one after another,
>   as I happen to call them to me, or think of them,
> The real poems, (what we call poems being merely pictures,)
> The poems of the privacy of the night, and of men like me,
> This poem, drooping shy and unseen, that I always carry, and that
>   all men carry,
> (Know, once for all, avowed on purpose, wherever are men like me,
>   are our lusty, lurking, muscular poems,)
> . . . .
> And this bunch plucked at random from myself,
> It has done its work – I toss it carelessly to fall where it may.

Although he vigorously defended sexuality as a leitmotif of the new American poetry in his open letter to Emerson, this was Whitman taking Emerson's injunction to "give me initiative, spermatic, prophesying, man-making words" more literally than his "master" would have wanted, or even tolerated. But this was not Whitman being a provocateur; it was simply Whitman being Whitman. Ever since his 1855 Preface, he had given the age's veneration of "creativity" and "organicism" his own peculiarly sexual interpretation. Whether this was Whitman speaking out of his mind or through his pores is not, is almost never, clear; but in 1856 the urge to communicate to his readers through such sexual verbal devices seems to have been overpowering.

The open equation between sexuality and poetic communication recurred throughout the volume. In "Poem of Procreation" ("A Woman Waits for Me"), he expressed this idea with particular explicitness: "I shall demand perfect men and women out of my love-spendings, / I shall expect them to interpenetrate with others, as I and you interpenetrate now." In the case of the 1855 poem he now called "Poem of the Body" ("I Sing the Body Electric"), he reached into one of his finest word lists in order to end the poem with a new, extended catalogue of the parts of the body, the most fully realized of his numerous attempts to write his poetry in a kind of body language. And in the curiously named new poem, "Poem of You, Whoever You Are" ("To You"), he addressed his reader at times as though inviting him or her to an assignation: "Whoever you are, now I place my hand upon you, that you be my poem, / I whisper with my lips close to your ear, / I have loved many women and men, but I love none better than you."[25]

In "Poem of the Sayers of the Words of the Earth" ("Song of the Rolling Earth"), he took a different tack in reaching another form of extreme identification, one which brought together poet, reader, and solid earth in the creative act: "Were you thinking that those were the words – those upright lines? those curves, angles, dots? / No, those are not the words – the substantial words are in the ground and sea, / They are in the air – they are in you." Objects as words, the human form as an object of art, sexual intercourse as poetic discourse; life, in short, as art – such were some of the controlling ideas with which the 1856 *Leaves of Grass* was sent out to reach its audience.

Whitman defied the conventional poetic relations between poet, reader, text, and world throughout the volume; but it was in the three new poems he may (or may not) have deliberately positioned consecutively as poems 10–12 that one can see the direction of his ambition and the extent of his achievement most vividly. I have already briefly mentioned the first and least impressive of them, "Poem of You, Whoever You Are," which is really little more than a proem to the two which follow, "Sun-Down Poem" and "Poem of the Road" ("Song of the Open Road"), poems in which the invocatory mode is more successfully integrated with materiality. Lawrence was particularly excited by the trope of the open road, which he interpreted as the ultimate American formulation of life in the modern world: "The true democracy, where soul meets soul, in the open road. Democracy. American democracy where all journey down the open road, and where a soul is known at once in its going. Not by its clothes or appearance . . . Not by anything, but just itself."[26] But Lawrence's open road was not exactly Whitman's. Lawrence's was solitary; Whitman's was one which began in solitude but ended in community – or, perhaps more exactly, in what Whitman considered to be community. Whitman had been contemplating the idea of the journey down the open road ever since his early manhood, but in 1856 he found his surest grounding for it in the idea of companionship through poetic communication, which is the point to which his poem arrives in conclusion:

> Mon enfant! I give you my hand!
> I give you my love, more precious than money,

> I give you myself, before preaching or law;
> Will you give me yourself? Will you come travel with me?
> Shall we stick by each other as long as we live?

A greater expression of Whitman's sensibility and the finest of the new poems of 1856 was the "Sun-Down Poem," a poem in which Whitman managed to balance and integrate the conditions of poetry with the conditions of the material world, and to do so without the stridency of his "Poem of the Road." It, too, is essentially a poem of connection and camaraderie. Its origins are among the most traceable of those of any of Whitman's major poems, deriving in large part from his early and lifelong "passion for ferries."[27] As a boy living near the ferry and prowling the harbor of the East River, as a young journalist shuttling frequently between Manhattan and Brooklyn, as the editor of the Brooklyn *Eagle* from whose office he could look out onto the Fulton Ferry slip, and much later in life as a "half-paralytic" living near the ferry depot and dependent on it for access to the outside world – Whitman lived his life within intimate sight and hearing of the ferry. For many of his Brooklyn-based years, he rode the ferry back and forth between Brooklyn and Manhattan on a daily basis, often riding in the pilot house (much as he rode the city omnibuses besides the drivers) and occasionally taking the passage back and forth simply for the pleasure of it, regardless of destination. These circumstances might have meant little had his "passion for ferries" not pressed down to the quick of his sensibility, but in fact the scene on the river – the kinaesthetic mix of water, air, sun, and glide – excited Whitman to the state of being which he once thought to describe in a poem about "a soul in glee."[28]

One enters Whitman's ferry in medias res; the boat is already in motion on the river and so, too, is the poet, who has set the constituent elements of matter into motion: the sun above, the water below, and himself journeying between. Rather than they fixing him in place, he defines them – in typical Whitman fashion, he apostrophizes them:

> Flood-tide of the river, flow on! I watch you, face to face,
> Clouds of the west! sun half an hour high! I see you also face to face.

Quickly moving beyond his relations with the natural world, he proceeds to extend his relations to the human sphere:

> Crowds of men and women attired in the usual costumes, how
>   curious you are to me!
> On the ferry-boats the hundreds and hundreds that cross are more
>   curious to me than you suppose,
> And you that shall cross from shore to shore years hence, are more
>   to me, and more in my meditations, than you might suppose.

With these opening lines, Whitman immediately balances the poles of human existence, the I and the not-I, effectively bringing himself into "face to face" or "shore to shore" contact with the world of man and nature.

Having staked out these relations in preliminary fashion, Whitman next turns the focus of attention onto his own self:

> The impalpable sustenance of me from all things at all hours of the day,
> The simple, compact, well-joined scheme – myself disintegrated, every one disintegrated, yet part of the scheme,
> The similitudes of the past and those of the future,
> The glories strung like beads on my smallest sights and hearings – on the walk in the street, and the passage over the river,
> The current rushing so swiftly, and swimming with me far away,
> The others that are to follow me, the ties between me and them,
> The certainty of others – the life, love, sight, hearing of others.

The self, as he poses the issue here, is sustained in the world and by the world; but it is not identical with it. It is paradoxically both integral with "the simple, compact, well-joined scheme," and yet "disintegrated," or as Whitman would later carefully phrase it, "a simple separate person."[29] Moreover, what he says about his own self, it immediately becomes clear, he also says about other people's selves ("myself disintegrated, every one disintegrated yet part of the scheme"), and not merely at one but at all times and places ("similitudes of the past and those of the future"). This was, in fact, a restatement of the idea of the unsettled, undefined relations between the individual and modern, democratic society which Whitman assumed and explored throughout the 1856 edition.

His response – poetic and philosophic – in the poem was to create a sliding continuum between the self and the world. Beginning with the self as first fact, he characteristically mobilized it, floating it in and out of, around and through, the sights and scenes of its world. Although the voyage of the self is necessarily lone, Whitman was careful to link its solitary passage to that of each individual ferryboat rider, present and future (and soon to be transformed into the reader). In fact, the urgency of that accompaniment, parallel in spirit though detached in person from the poet, is keenly felt in the clipped, dignified articulation of the last line ("The certainty of others – the life, love, sight, hearing of others") and in the rhythmic transference of emphasis onto the "other," whose emotional and psychological necessity underlies the entire poem.

In the following stanzas, Whitman tightens the relationship between his own journeying self and that of his parallel passenger, and between their respective times:

It avails not, neither time nor place – distance avails not,
I am with you, you men and women of a generation, or ever so
    many generations hence,
I project myself, also I return – I am with you, and know how it is.

Just as you feel when you look on the river and sky, so I felt,
Just as any of you is one of a living crowd, I was one of a crowd,
Just as you are refreshed by the gladness of the river, and the bright
    flow, I was refreshed,
Just as you stand and lean on the rail, yet hurry with the swift
    current, I stood, yet was hurried,
Just as you look on the numberless masts of ships, and the thick-
    stemmed pipes of steamboats, I looked.

Past and present time schemes, my sensations and yours, merge in the
continuum of experience the poet is building.

The self – the poet's and the parallel passenger's – is now psycholog-
ically and spiritually prepared for an expansive interaction with the world;
and this immediately follows in the far-arching catalogue of the scene
on the river, one of Whitman's best bursts of verse reportage, as the poet
looks out onto the spreading field of the river. Only now does the poet
introduce the core "materials" of the poem, his sensory impressions of
them recording a kaleidoscopic vision of the world and its elements in
ceaseless activity: "slow-wheeling circles" flown by sea gulls across the
sky, the poet's head crowned by the sun and reflected back to him by
the water, atmosphere made visible as haze and light made "shimmering"
by dust, ships sailing by with sailors manning the riggings, waves passing
"glistening" by, factory fires burning brightly high into the night sky.
The act of reportage, all worked into one of Whitman's typically long-
flowing sentence-stanzas, is simultaneously personal and conjugate, I and
you bearing witness separately and together to the wonders of the physical scene.

It is the act that the poet performs mentally each time he crosses the
river, and likewise it is the act that each passenger performs whenever
he or she crosses the river, an analogy of action which Whitman sets
into lines of analogous verse units ("Just as you..., I..."). By this
point in the poem, it has become clear that Whitman's ferry is charting
a two-tiered passage: a physical one across the river and a spiritual one
across miles of space and generations of time, the former from shore to
shore and the latter from poet to reader. Perhaps it is this dual movement
which explains why the voyage on the river of time, which might well
have been expected to agonize a Romantic poet, seems instead to exhil-
arate Whitman. Even as the boat is "hurried" forward on the water,
Whitman and his parallel passenger can stand stationary on the firm deck
of the ferry, safely above the "bright flow" of the river's transiency. The

boat offers him an escape from time but only through time; the specific experience of crossing becomes an experience made generic by its transmission through words to future generations of passengers-readers. Whitman can thus speak of his copassengers through time, in a finely symmetrical phrase, as the "others who look back on me, because I looked forward to them."

The terms of the poem's relations having thus been well established, Whitman shifts his focus in the middle stanzas of the poem from the physical passage to the communicatory one. The insinuating quality present in his address to the reader, though present from the start, now becomes increasingly foregrounded. What began as a relationship between "I" and "you" now passes into "we": "What is it, then, between us? What is the count of the scores or hundreds of years between us?" His intensifying intimacy with the passenger-reader necessarily leads him to a deeper exploration of their common humanity, which, as it becomes focused on his own representative self, turns the poem inward. His previous elation now suddenly verges into depression: "It is not upon you alone the dark patches fall, / The dark threw patches down upon me also, / . . . I too knitted the old knot of contrariety, / Blabbed, blushed, resented, lied, stole, grudged." The "dark patches" may refer to the night about to fall on the sunset scene, but they also reflect the hitherto unspoken precariousness of the poet's condition. The solitary voyage on the free-flowing river is undeniably exhilarating, but it is also potentially threatening; it thrills him with the sheer joy of the expansion of personality, but it also reminds him of the corresponding risk which can befall the solitary traveler of becoming "disintegrated" from the "scheme."

This is a paradoxical eventuality for one who so constantly figures himself in the poem (and out of it) as passing into and comprising one of the "living crowd" or being called by his "nighest name." But if the poetic self is in the crowd, it is never genuinely of the crowd, which flits through the poem like the clouds above and the water below.[30] What little actual interpersonal contact there is between the journeying poet and the surrounding mass of humanity is curiously intangible, metaphorical. Should the crowd disappear or should the ephemera of nature suddenly drain away, Whitman knows that that which in any case preceded them, the first fact of the "Me myself" or the "real ME," as he called it in two not unrelated poems, would nevertheless remain.[31]

Still, in view of the poem's unspoken but pervasive concern with loneliness – or with what Sharon Cameron has called its "terror at space that remains unmediated" – Whitman could not possibly have conceived of the crossing as a solo affair.[32] On the contrary, the trip could not have been made without the necessary presence of "others," of fellow passengers, however amorphous they may in fact be, to join him in the crossing. To conceive of human companionship in these terms was to buoy his spirits against the lurking fear of alienation (or what the poem speaks of as "the knot of contrariety").

By expressing his doubts, or more precisely, by sharing them with his fellow passenger, Whitman succeeds in purging himself of them. The immediate consequence is a still tighter intimacy with his communicant:

> Closer yet I approach you,
> What thought you have of me, I had as much of you – I laid in my
>   stores in advance,
> I considered long and seriously of you before you were born.
>
> Who was to know what should come home to me?
> Who knows but I am enjoying this?
> Who knows but I am as good as looking at you now, for all you
>   cannot see me?

The way is now open before him to a heightened appreciation of the beauty of life in all its kinaesthetic splendor, and in the closing stanzas of the poem the poet returns with renewed vigor and confidence to the earlier scene on the river. It has not changed – as elemental process, it never will – but the poet has. Reassured by the companionship of the passenger-reader, without whom there can be no poem or ferry, Whitman launches into a paean of celebration. It begins, as though for psychological reinforcement, with one final, climactic address to the reader, completing the process of "fus[ion]," of "pour[ing] my meaning into you":

> We understand, then, do we not?
> What I promised without mentioning it, have you not accepted?
> What the study could not teach – what the preaching could not
>   accomplish is accomplished is it not?
> What the push of reading could not start is started by me personally,
>   is it not?

The communicatory circuit is now complete; the poet and his passenger-reader have become a composite "we," united before the never-ending flow of the river of time.

Flanked by the reader, the poet now returns to the scene on the river with renewed faith, rerecording it with unrestrained lyrical exuberance: "Flow on, river! Flow with the flood-tide, and ebb with the ebb-tide! / Frolic on, crested and scallop-edged waves! / Gorgeous clouds of the sun-set, drench with your splendor me, or the men and women generations after me! / Cross from shore to shore, countless crowds of passengers!" On and on his enraptured vision passes, sweeping first across the spectacle of the river, as earlier in the poem, then across the full range of the poem's gathered images and even beyond them, beyond New York to all cities and beyond the East River to all "ample and sufficient rivers."

Had Whitman's intentions been more particularist or provincial, the poem might have ended here; but with larger philosophical scope he goes on one step further, closing the poem with one last direct address – this time, not to the reader, who has already been incorporated into the voice of the poet and therefore into the poem, but to the material objects which form man's natural setting. In the restrained tone and ebbing rhythm that Whitman often favored for his closing stanzas, he made his – and his reader's – solemn pact with nature:

> You have waited, you always wait, you dumb beautiful ministers!
>   you novices!
> We receive you with free sense at last, and are insatiate
>   henceforward,
> Not you any more shall be able to foil us, or withhold yourselves
>   from us,
> We use you, and do not cast you aside – we plant you permanently
>   within us,
> We fathom you not – we love you – there is perfection in you also,
> You furnish your parts toward eternity,
> Great or small, you furnish your parts toward the soul.

There is scarcely a more dignified articulation of the availability of the material world to poetry in all of nineteenth-century writing. These lines finally make explicit what Whitman has been assuming all along, the intermediacy of the physical objects of the world – and preeminent among them, the ferry – between him and the highest truths given to man to know. Isolated in their own sphere, these "dumb beautiful ministers" lie inert, mere lifeless objects activated only when the "image-making faculty" of the poet's mind passes over them and animates them as vehicles of communication.[33] Emerson had posed the issue well for literary Romanticism in general – for Wordsworth and Shelley, for Melville and Dickinson – in writing of the relations between the individual self and the world: "A subject and an object, – it takes so much to make the galvanic circuit complete, but magnitude adds nothing."[34] Here was Whitman, in effect, answering in his own name for the whole Romantic era, reformulating the galvanic circuit into his own poetic terms with the familiar Whitman accent on poetry as communication with the world and with the world's audience.[35]

"Sun-Down Poem" stands out as the great vehicle of communication among the new poems of 1856. In no other poem of that edition did he more skillfully integrate art and life, and in the process stand the reader by his side as a bridge between the two. One of the best glosses on the poem, appropriately even if inadvertently, came from Emerson, who had written a decade before, "all language is vehicular and transitive, and is good, as ferries and horses are, for conveyance, not as farms and houses are, for homesteads."[36] Whitman himself in his open letter to Emerson had spoken of their mother tongue as "that huge English flow," and certainly one of the chief contributions to the poem's artistic excellence is the harmony between its conception of language, its central metaphor, and its ideal of poetry. In his old age autobiography, Whitman was to speak of ferries as "inimitable, streaming, never-failing, living poems"; and for him they undoubtedly were the living poems of the modern world: mobile, fluid, material, connective, open and accessible to all.[37] Such was Whitman's 1856 ferry, the poem which came closest among those of the second edition to his poetic ideal of streamlining the world and turning it into a flowing medium between him and his reader.

The second edition has been the most overlooked of the early editions of *Leaves of Grass* in our time, and it was in Whitman's time as well. The first edition had excited a small but intense interest in a few places; the second edition generated all but none.[38] Sales were few and reviews were virtually nonexistent. This should have come as a brutal irony to the aspirant poet of the masses and the champion of poetic communication. If his publishers were correct in their August 16 claim, "the American people will give a hearing to any man who has it in him to reward attention," Whitman had evidently made a serious error in calculation. In the short run, however, his failure made seemingly little impression on the hard shell of his ambition. In 1856, he was in no mood to stop and ponder ironies; already he was making his preparations to go ahead with yet another edition of his poems.

9

"Publish yourself of your own Personality"

In understanding Whitman's ongoing attitude toward his poetry and the public, one can easily misconstrue the nature of the long gap between the appearance of the second (1856) and third (1860) editions of *Leaves of Grass*. Had circumstances permitted, a third edition of his poetry consisting of one hundred poems, two-thirds new, would have appeared in 1857. In a letter of June 20, 1857, to a Philadelphia friend and supporter, Sarah Tyndale, he outlined his plans for this new, expanded edition:

> Fowler and Wells are bad persons for me. They retard my book very much. It is worse than ever. I wish now to bring out a third edition – I have now a *hundred poems* ready (the last edition had thirty-two) – and shall endeavor to make an arrangement with some publisher here to take the plates from F. and W. and make the additions needed, and so bring out the third edition. F. and W. are very willing to give up the plates – they want the thing off their hands. In the forthcoming Vol. I shall have, as I said, a hundred poems, and no other matter but poems – (no letters to or from Emerson – no notices, or any thing of that sort.) I know well enough, that *that* must be the *true* Leaves of Grass – I think it (the new Vol.) has an aspect of completeness, and makes its case clearer. The old poems are all retained. The difference is in the new character given to the mass, by the additions.[1]

In a notebook entry he made at about the same time, he exhorted himself to an even more sweeping challenge, one amounting essentially to a life mission: *"The Great Construction of the New Bible* Not to be diverted from the principal object – the main life work – the Three Hundred and Sixty-five – It ought to be read[y] in 1859. – (June '57)."[2] And on the back of one of his new manuscript poems he spoke of his desire to "extract the thousand poems, (as I now intend)."[3]

In 1857, however, Whitman faced not only the continuing problem of reaching the general reading public but the complication of doing so at an extremely unpropitious time for books of all sorts. A title which had already failed twice, and both times recently, to reach beyond a limited circle of readers had to contend that summer not only with public indifference toward itself but also with a sharp economic downturn, which hit the publishing industry with particular severity. Whitman himself tried to maintain his characteristic public optimism from behind his editorial desk at the Brooklyn *Daily Times,* dismissing through early summer as unfounded widespread reports of an imminent panic, even hinting on July 29 of an "unusual prosperity" soon to come. But by September, even he admitted that the country was in the midst of the worst recession since 1837; and in October he acknowledged that it was affecting the sector which to him then probably mattered most: "Not another trade has sustained so many failures, in the crisis, in proportion to the number of its votaries, as the publishers'. Harpers, Miller and Curtis, Emerson, Putnam, Fowler and Wells, and numbers of others, attest the truth of this remark."[4]

He could not have gone back to Fowler and Wells, which had suspended its publishing operations, even had he wanted to; and his own reputation and the poor prospects for publication generally were enough to eliminate any slim chance he might still have had for commercial publication. His only recourse in 1857, if he was to publish at all, was self-publication; and he apparently seriously explored that possibility during the summer. His own financial state was so constrained that he had been forced to borrow two hundred dollars from James Parton that winter. When unable to repay the loan, he was forced to submit on June 17 to a seizure of property in restitution. To have brought out a new edition, therefore, Whitman would have had to rely on the financial help of friends; and one who was willing to help was the enthusiastic Sarah Tyndale, who sent him a contribution in July toward the purchase of the Fowler and Wells plates.[5] But the proposed, makeshift edition, with the new poems added on after the old ones, was not to appear in 1857; and when a third edition of *Leaves of Grass* finally did appear in 1860, it had clearly evolved far beyond the proposed edition of three years earlier, although how and why that evolution came about has long been one of the prime mysteries of Whitman biography.

In one of the few new poems Whitman composed between the springs of 1857 and 1859, when he resumed wholehearted work on his poetry after an apparent lull of nearly two years, he would advise his reader, "Rest not till you rivet and publish yourself of your own Personality.–"[6] There may also be a lurking "indirection" for the reader of Whitman in this idea, since the best source of information on Whitman around this time is in his published personality. But reading the new poems against the little which is known of Whitman's circumstances during this period is no easy matter, so various are the poems, so shifting are their moods, and so preliminary may have been the ordering he intended to give them in his planned new edition; still, I would hazard a few observations. The first may be the most obvious: for a man whose large-scale hopes for the reception of his poems had been upset twice, Whitman was writing with remarkable pertinacity in 1856–7, was writing in fact more prolifically than at any other time in his life. The number of his projected poems – 100, 365, or 1,000 – really does not matter; what matters is the depth and intensity of his commitment to his vocation. To take him at his word in his letter to Mrs. Tyndale, he was even able in 1857 to attribute the failure of his second edition to his silent publisher rather than to some fault in himself or in the public. But if Whitman continued to write with considerable fluency through the middle of 1857, as though impervious to his past reception, a closer look at the poems themselves reveals subtle changes in his thinking, changes which already point toward the more dramatic transformation of personality that Whitman biographers, working with a scarcity of biographical information, usually date to 1859–60.[7]

In the programmatic poem with which he originally intended to close the new edition, he wrote:

> Throwing far, throwing over the head of death, I, full of affection,
> Full of life, compact, visible, thirty-eight years old the eighty-first
>   year of The States,
> To one a century hence, or any number of centuries hence,
> To you, yet unborn, these, seeking you. –
> When you read these, I that was visible am become invisible,
> Now it is you, compact, full of life, realizing my poems, seeking me;
> If I were with you, I should expect love and understanding from
>   you,
> Be it as if I were with you – Be not too certain that I am with
>   you.–[8]

With all his old love of poetic interchange and reciprocity with the reader, he conceptualized his persona "seeking" the reader and the reader "seeking" him and "realizing" his poems. But the expression of the poem is curiously unhistorical. Were the changed circumstances concerning the "realization" of his poems during the previous two years leading him in 1857 to abstract his hopes from the historical present, a damaging concession for a practicing poet with broad national ambitions? Or was it merely his rhetorical strategy? One cannot be sure. Whatever the explanation, the overall impression generated by the new poems is one of confused and tangled motives, of disparate moods and modes not easily reconciled by a critic – nor, I believe, by Whitman himself.

Though he was not yet thinking in terms of the organizing principle of "clusters," Whitman's 1857 poems included the nuclei of what would become the most dissimilar groupings of his 1860 edition, "Chants Democratic and Native American" and "Calamus." The former consisted of some of the most flaccid poems Whitman had yet written, poems in which he allowed his penchant for poetic rhetoric to lose itself in unsubstantiated assertion. Nothing could have been less convincing or satisfying than the claim with which he opened one of these chants, "Me imperturbe" (written, in 1857, with an exclamation point), since the governing mood of the poems was of boastful personal and national imperialism. In a poem given the "typical" title of "Feuillage," Whitman went on for pages in a manner similar to that with which he opened his chant:

> America always! Always me joined! Always our old feuillage!
> Always Florida's green peninsula! Always the priceless delta of
>   Louisiana! Always the cotton-fields of Alabama and Texas!
> Always California's golden hills and hollows – and the silver
>   mountains of New Mexico! Always soft-breathed Cuba!
> Always the vast slope drained by the Southern Sea – inseparable with
>   the slopes drained by the Eastern and Western Seas.[9]

One can say about this poem what one can say about the Chants more generally: They left Whitman sounding too often like the cheerleader rather than the poet to the people, shouting himself hoarse with his large claims and vaunting suppositions as he strained his repertoire for large effects. The freshness of self-discovery, the fast-paced changes of mood and tone, the contagious excitement of his earlier poems were largely absent here, replaced by a more mannered, monotonic poetry which has the sound of a poet rather unsuccessfully repeating and imitating himself.

The new "Calamus" poems, by contrast, were in the main as reflective and modulated as the "Chants Democratic" were boisterous and expansive. In several of the more pensive of these poems, Whitman examined the shadows of his life, took account of intensely personal depths of his nature with which, I suspect, he may not have been entirely comfortable or conversant. One of the finer of these poems was this, written out already in 1857 in substantially the same form as that in which it would appear in the 1860 *Leaves of Grass*:

> Of him I love day and night, I dreamed I heard he was dead,
> And I dreamed I went where they had buried the man I love but he
>   was not in that place,
> And I dreamed I wandered searching among burial places, to find
>   him,
> And I found that every place was a burial place,
> The houses full of life were equally full of death, – (this house is
>   now,)

> The streets, the shipping, the places of amusement, the Chicago, the
>   Mannahatta, were as full of the dead as of the living, and fuller of
>   the dead than of the living. –
> And what I dreamed I will henceforth tell to every person and age,
> And I stand henceforth bound to what I dreamed;
> And now I am willing to disregard burial places, and dispense with
>   them,
> And if the memorials of the dead were put up indifferently
>   everywhere, even in the room where I eat or sleep, I should be
>   satisfied,
> And if the corpse of any one I love, or if my own corpse, be duly
>   rendered to powder and poured into the sea, or distributed to the
>   winds, I shall be satisfied. –[10]

Likewise subdued and pensive, foreshadowing some of the new lyrics of 1859, was the poem of 1856–7 origin, "I Sit and Look Out," also substantially ready for inclusion in the 1860 volume, where it found its way with few changes into the miscellaneous "Leaves of Grass" section. Such poems revealed a somber side of Whitman not fully visible in the previous editions.

Whitman is not a poet with whom the biographical fallacy is to be taken lightly, but these and other such manuscript poems of late 1856– early 1857 suggest to me a poet who was beginning, at first tentatively and no doubt unconsciously, to change direction. As early as 1857, his ability to coordinate the poetry of the self with the poetry of the nation was showing signs of strain. I would not want to exaggerate the extent of this transformation; the process was only incipient at this time, and it was not to become more pronounced until several years later, when Whitman recommitted himself to poetry and to his ambition of bringing out a new edition of his poetry.

His thinking, moreover, was two-tracked at this time. Whitman seems never to have lacked for ideas about how to reach the broad American public; and one which became increasingly insistent during the period 1856–8, to return to him intermittently thereafter, was the prospect of becoming a "wander-teacher." This was the title of one of his new 1856–7 poems, and the idea entered much of his writing of this time. In a letter or notebook jotting dated July 28, 1857, which if correct, places it within days of his stated self-dedication to the composition of his "New Bible," he expressed this other ambition in the most explicit terms: "I have thought, for some time past, of beginning the use of myself as a public Speaker, teacher, or lecturer. (This, after I get out the next issue of my 'Leaves') – Whether it will come to any thing, remains to be seen."[11]

With what degree of realism he intended to go out on the lyceum circuit, it would be difficult to assess. There was unquestionably a background to his thinking both in his own and in his society's experience. He had given several lectures and public addresses in his earlier years, and that experience might well have left a lasting impression on his thinking. He had also been covering lectures through much of the 1840s during his various editorships in Brooklyn and Manhattan, a practice he resumed in the late 1850s during his editorship of the Brooklyn *Daily Times* – Brooklyn at that time, in his opinion, the city which "above all in the United States is the city for first-class lectures."[12] But this is to be understood not simply as a journalistic interest – such things seldom were with a man of Whitman's powerful, intuitive drives – but rather as yet another manifestation of Whitman's full-fledged sensitivity to the power of "vocalism," to the communicatory power of the word – spoken, written, or sung:

> O the orator's joys!
> To inflate the chest – to roll the thunder of the voice out from the
>   ribs and throat,
> To make the people rage, weep, hate, desire with yourself,
> To lead America – To quell America with a great tongue. – [13]

With such an attitude toward speaker and audience and a tendency to attribute his own receptivity to language to others, little wonder that Whitman invariably placed so high a valuation on the power of communication.

By the 1840s and 1850s, lecturing had become a popular and profitable form of instruction and entertainment in the country, the lyceum circuit reaching further and further into the interior as transportation lines stretched out to serve the growing country. By Whitman's time, a lecturer could make a large geographical arc of the eastern half of the country and receive good compensation (often twenty-five to fifty dollars per engagement) for doing so. Many writers made lecture trips an annual winter ritual, Emerson most famously; but Whitman would have had a certain justification in seeing the role of transcontinental lecturer as being peculiarly suited to a writer of his character and ambitions. The prospect of going out on the open road with his thoughts and ideas, it need hardly be said, had a natural attraction to him; and this idea filled his thoughts as at no other period during the late 1850s, when he contemplated stylizing editions of *Leaves of Grass* and lectures to suit the needs of the various sections of the country. Whitman would likewise have found himself irresistibly attracted to the inherent theatricality of the lecture, whose fit of speaker and audience offered an analogy to that which he attempted to introduce into his own poetry. What one historian of the American lyceum has remarked about the influence of the midnineteenth-century lecture system on literature generally has a particular relevance in the case of Whitman:

> Whatever the literary form, whether popular or unpopular, prose or poetry, one of the most pervasive influences of the lecture system on [literature] was in the awareness of the reader. When the lecturer read his manuscript he had the audience squarely in front of him and probably could not have forgotten its members had he wished. Later, when he printed his manuscript, the same awareness was seldom revised entirely away. The direct address to the reader and the attitude, often, of informality were certainly sanctioned by the tradition of the familiar essay; but they received strong psychological support from the lyceum.[14]

Whitman's notebooks reveal his keen awareness of the compatibility between his poems and his projected lectures. In drawing up a circular or pamphlet in 1858 in which he offered or advertised his services to the public in the dual role of poet-orator, he spoke of the two media as "co-expressions"; and as remarks he made in his notebooks reveal, he prepared himself as carefully for the latter as he had in earlier years for the former.[15] "An orator," he claimed in an observation which would have described his poetry equally well, "should be a perfect posturist"; and he spent hours, as it were, before the mirror, training himself to affect the gestures and intonations of the new oratorical style.[16] In his mind, he saw his oratory as taking place in the same metaphorical forum as that in which he was placing his reader and writer: "Yes, the place of the orator and his hearers is truly an agonistic arena. There he wrestles and contends with them – he suffers, sweats, undergoes his great toil and extasy. Perhaps it is a greater battle than any fought by contending forces on land and sea."[17]

There were also clear stylistic similarities between the two modes of expression. One of the leading elements he conceived for his oratorical style was the strong infusion of the vocative mode he practiced in his poetry, which he now called his "ego-style":

Ego-Style
First-person
style

– Style of composition
An animated *ego-style*, "*I* do not think" – "*I* perceive" –
– or something (involving self-esteem decision, authority)
– as opposed to the current *third-person style, essayism, didactic* –
    removed from animation, stating general truths, in a didactic,
    well-smoothed[18]

And here is another piece of self-advice on the lecture style he was training himself to adopt:

FOR ORATIONS
Talk directly to the hearer or hearers:
You so and so
Why should I be tender with you?
Have you not, etc., etc . . . [19]

His notebooks are full of like-minded remarks on tone, manner, and bearing; taken together, they serve as a cogent counterpoint to the idea of Whitman as an artistic naif. However absurdly self-conscious these remarks may sound when taken out of context, they do demonstrate the degree to which style, with Whitman, in poetry or in oratory, was a matter of extreme cultivation.

"I desire to go, by degrees, through all These States, especially West and South, and through Kanada: Lecturing, (my own way,) henceforth my employment, my means of earning my living – subject to the work elsewhere alluded to [on *Leaves of Grass*], that takes precedence. –"[20] He did not get far, however, in 1857 or 1858 with this plan, probably no further than he had a year before with *The Eighteenth Presidency!*. In his roles as poet, pamphleteer, and lecturer, there was to be an identical incongruity between Whitman privately in his bold imaginings and Whitman in the streets of America. As with Emily Dickinson but without her scintillating self-knowledge, his chief stage performances were normally to be played "among my mind."

It was only much later that he reached the podium, and by that time it was a much older Whitman, long past his creative and imaginative peak, speaking to a hardened, post–Civil War America. His best-known lecture was a nostalgic Lincoln recitation normally given on anniversaries of the assassination, steeped in hagiography and keyed to the tone of "O Captain! My Captain!" – even Whitman sometimes allowed himself to give the people what they wanted to hear. The most important occasion of a Whitman lecture, in his eyes, was the day in 1871 when he was invited to read an original poem at the opening of the fortieth National Industrial Exhibition of the American Institute in New York. Exhibitions of this sort, as I have already mentioned, always drew an excited response from Whitman – he was bitterly disappointed when Bayard Taylor was chosen over him to address the Centennial Exposition in Philadelphia – and this one was no exception. Unfortunately, to some who saw him that day and to most who see it from the present, Whitman on the podium offered the spectacle of camp rather than of high drama.

He chose to read for the occasion his splashily grand, patriotic poem, "After All, Not to Create Only," copies of which he distributed beforehand freely to the press. After the invocatory prayer, Whitman, putting his years of practice to the test, stepped up and recited his poem before the assembled crowd. The result, as reported in the Washington

Chronicle by an anonymous correspondent (Whitman, of course), was the following:

> Imagine yourself inside a huge barn-like edifice of a couple of acres, spanned by immense arches, like the ribs of some leviathan ship, (whose skeleton hull inverted the structure might be said to resemble,) and this building, crowded and crammed with incipient displays of goods and machinery – everything that grows and is made – and a thousand men actually engaged at work, in their shirt-sleeves, putting the said goods and machinery in order – all with a noise, movement, and variety as if a good-sized city was in process of being built.
>
> In the middle of this, to an audience of perhaps two or three thousand people, with a fringe on the outside of perhaps five or six hundred partially-hushed workmen, carpenters, machinists, and the like, with saws, wrenches, or hammers in their hands, Walt Whitman, last Thursday, gave his already celebrated poem before the American Institute. His manner was at first sight coldly quiet, but you soon felt a magnetism and felt stirred. His great figure was clothed in gray, with white vest, no necktie, and his beard was as unshorn as ever. His voice is magnificent, and is to be mentioned with Nature's oceans and the music of forests and hills.
>
> His gestures are few, but significant. Sometimes he stands with his hands in his breast pockets; once or twice he walked a few steps to and fro. He did not mind the distant noises and the litter and machinery, but doubtless rather enjoyed them. He was perfectly self-possessed. His apostrophe to the Stars and Stripes which floated above him, describing them in far different scenes in battle, was most impassioned. Also his "Away with War itself!" and his scornful "Away with novels, plots, and plays of foreign courts!"
>
> A few of his allusions were in a playful tone, but the main impression was markedly serious, animated, and earnest. He was applauded as he advanced to read, besides several times throughout, and at the close. He did not respond in the usual way by bowing. All the directors and officers of the Institute crowded around him and heartily thanked him. He extricated himself, regained his old Panama hat and stick, and, without waiting for the rest of the exercises, made a quiet exit by the steps at the back of the stand.
>
> The real audience of this chant of peace, invention, and labor, however, was to follow. Of the New York and Brooklyn evening and morning dailies, twelve out of seventeen published the poem in full the same evening or the next morning.[21]

Newspaper accounts the following day gave rather a different account. The several thousand people Whitman mentioned were actually several hundred, and they were anything but enthralled. Many, perhaps most, of them could not even hear him; his "magnificent" voice carried barely beyond the first rows. The workmen, if it is accurate that they really did stop working, certainly were not "partially-hushed" to attend the recitation. Workmen, it is true, were usually to receive him freely and warmly; but Whitman was cagey enough to know to meet them on their terms, not his – as a son of the working class, not as a poet. Whitman, in fact, had been invited to read only because Horace Greeley, the first choice of the Institute directors, was out West campaigning for president.

Neither the chimera of national poetry nor that of national oratory was able to sustain Whitman for ever. At some point in the winter of 1857, probably in February and certainly not later than in March, Whitman returned to full-time journalism as editor of the Brooklyn *Daily Times,* a daily paper published not far from his home in the newly incorporated Williamsburg district of the city.[22] His contacts with the paper presumably went back at least to 1855, when he had been able to place his hometown flavored self-review in the paper; and his political views were unquestionably in line with those of the *Times,* an independent paper which had supported the Republican candidate Fremont in the presidential election of the previous year. Whitman had devoted a section of *The Eighteenth Presidency!* to Fremont and may have tried to place that tract with the paper. If so, he was refused; but following the resignation of the previous editor, too busy as a playwright to devote his full attention to the paper, Whitman was offered the job. Although he was at the time still composing new poems and planning for a new edition of his poetry, Whitman accepted the offer, his decision no doubt dictated by financial exigency as well as by the nearly silent reception of his 1856 edition.

It was six years and a change of personal and career orientation since Whitman last worked as an editor, an important six years during which time the "Me myself" had emerged from being a voice within his head to becoming a voice on paper. Since journalism had played a significant role in preparing Whitman for his new career, one takes a heightened interest in the kind of journalism he produced during this period, one of the most important and, except for his work on the paper, one of the least documented of his life. Even after a quick inspection of the paper, one can see how far Whitman had moved beyond the stage when journalism had been a formative influence on his poetry. Though coolly professional, his journalism with the *Times* lacked much of the fire and conviction which had distinguished his pre–*Leaves of Grass* journalism. There was less of Whitman in the paper than there had been of him in his previous papers – less of his personality; fewer of his personal convictions, activities, and stylistic idiosyncrasies; and, most interestingly, none of his creative writings.[23] As far as readers of the paper were concerned, the editor of the *Times* and the author of the volume of poems which had been reviewed in its pages just several months before his accession to the editorship could have been two entirely separate personalities. Whereas Whitman had from time to time republished his poems in previous editorships, he was not to make a single reference to his poetry or to himself as being a poet during his two-and-a-half-year editorial "sit," the longest of his life, with the *Times*.

Although he marched daily into the office in high boots, open shirt, and wide-brimmed hat, the uniform of the workingman, his radical views were becoming more fully sprinkled with conservative stances on various social, political, and cultural matters. The side of his personality which made him a surprisingly good family man and solid citizen was now more fully in evidence than in the past. On most issues his views were not far from those expressed in other contemporary newspapers. He came out in favor of a liberalized Sabbath, but he also counseled against one wholly secularized. He praised the marriage tie as the moral foundation of society. His concern with good health – a clear, pure mind in a clean, strong body – was as conspicuous as ever; good health and good poetry, the flow of one and the flow of the other, were inextricably linked in his mind. He was, as always, the vocal local booster, Brooklyn's champion now of improved municipal waterworks, public transportation on Sunday for the sake of the working class, and a public library for the eastern district of the city. Slavery was more on his mind than ever, but as before the touchstone of his thinking remained the welfare of the white laborer. If blacks, free or slave, were to be excluded from the territories to preserve white liberties, that was fine with him. Although still a progressive social thinker, he found himself unable to keep up with the advanced notions of the new literary magazine of the educated, the *Atlantic Monthly*, which advocated causes, such as female suffrage, with which Whitman was out of sympathy.

There was not only a general tendency toward more conservative views but also a subtle but important transformation in the tone and substance of Whitman's attitudes, one figured most significantly by what I think of as an incipient distancing of himself from his previous identification with the people. His attitude toward the people and toward the polity became more cautious, at times even crotchety. He was manifestly anxious about the state of American society, so much so that a number of his editorials struck a jeremiadlike tone anticipatory of *Democratic Vistas* a decade later. He spoke out angrily about the rise of crime and rowdyism in the streets, attacked the salaciousness of the press and of popular culture generally, and blamed the country's overconsumption and underproduction for the events leading up to the Panic of 1857. He attacked as a primary source of urban disorder "this rum-swilling, rampant set of roughs and rowdies," a far cry from the "roughs and beards" in whom he placed such great hope in 1855.[24] He now accepted an extreme measure of insuring order which he had previously scorned: capital punishment. He still took great pride in public education; but one of its virtues, it now seemed to him, was as a preventative:

> Every popular excitement like that which is now disturbing the peace and endangering the safety of the great metropolis across the river, only demonstrates with more clearness the truth that the one thing still lacking in our large communities, notwithstanding our admirable public school system, our cheap information and our omnipresent newspaper press, is the diffusion of intelligence among the masses. Educate, Educate, – it is the only true remedy for mobs, *emeutes,* wild communistic theories, and red republican ravings.[25]

His attitude toward the mass press changed with his attitude toward the public it served. He no longer spoke unambivalently of the benefit of the press as a democratizing, educative agency in society but increasingly saw validity in the conservative argument that democratic leveling could work to the decline as well as to the raising of standards. A democratic press, he argued, could function on no other level than that of its general public:

> The general public will not – we admit the fact to be lamentable, but it is unquestionable – they will not take any paper which does not "spread itself" on horrible tragedies, great crimes, and the grosser offences against society and decorum. It is all nonsense to blame the editors for inserting long accounts of this class of events – they must either cater to the general taste, or forfeit an extended circulation, or retire from competition with others less scrupulous. It is quite a mistake to charge the press with having "poisoned" the public taste. Such reports would never have been written in the first place, if there had not been a demand for them. The journalist does not and cannot create or form the public taste; all he can do is to cater for it and comply with it; and if he fails (whether from conscientious motives or any other cause) to do this, he is quickly supplanted by some less scrupulous journal, and can never retain a first class position for his paper.[26]

He also questioned the idea of the unlimited power of the press:

> The press has power, it is true; but only among those classes who least need its teachings. Those who are themselves really intelligent, know how to respect, as a general thing, the utterances of the newspaper press, but there is a large and numerous class, aye, the most numerous, especially in the great cities, who are utterly impervious to anything that the press may say, simply because they are beyond, or rather below, the influence of the papers they do not or cannot read.[27]

This has the sound of a man whose earlier "fond[ness] of the press" was beginning to wane. Such statements, translated into his poetry, would have undermined the basis of the relations he professed to be building.

He now covered the cultural circuit of galleries, concerts, plays, and lectures far less frequently than in the past; but his interest in literature and journalism, especially as they related to the people and the society, was still keen. One of the more interesting characteristics of his comments was the pronounced ambivalence which had entered his thinking about the relation between democracy and literature. By 1857, he was no longer able to see them as wholly or even necessarily compatible. While he was still willing to devote a column or two of the front page to fiction serials designed for his "lady readers," Whitman had misgivings about the immensely popular Sunday story papers, such as the New York *Ledger,* and their offer of "mental pabulum" to a romance-hungry public.[28] He worried openly, in his most moralistic manner, that popular culture was being given over to "the indecent, the libidinous, the *spicy.*"[29] Of the class on which he had once set his highest hopes, he now expressed deep doubts: "With any literature except the lowest and most superficial the masses in question are not conversant at all."[30] The young men, it seemed, would rather read the *Police Gazette* than *Leaves of Grass.* From time to time, he expressed his distrust of popular taste, as though believing in the operation of a Gresham's law of poetry: "The poem 'Nothing to Wear' has been published in the newspapers of the Sandwich Islands. The wide spread popularity of this clever but common-place effusion, shows how much more quickly the ephemeral and superficial in literature is appreciated by the public than that which bears the imprint of the highest genius. A hundred persons would read, understand and admire 'Nothing to Wear,' to whom 'Annabel Lee' or 'The Raven,' would be *caviare.*"[31]

At the same time, his own attitude toward the popular media of culture and its productions, as in earlier years, was far from hostile. He considered Whittier's insipid New England idyll, "Maud Miller," "the sweetest, simplest, most pathetic gem of our literature," enthused over Holmes's "Autocrat" articles in the *Atlantic* and over the conduct of the "Editor's Easy Chair" in *Harper's,* and occasionally praised (but also occasionally criticized) the accomplishments of the *Ledger.* He commended the Philadelphia publisher T. B. Peterson for making the standard titles affordable to the masses, gushed over the accomplishments of the Harpers and unvaryingly praised their new books, and followed enthusiastically the course of the leading monthly magazines, especially *Harper's* ("the magazine for the million") and the *Atlantic* ("the leading first class magazine of the country"). He would still have his eye on them in 1860 when he was eager to see the best of his new poems first appear in the magazines.

His editorial policy on the *Times,* in short, was far from unified and contained less of an overall program or commitment to educate the masses than his journalistic work had shown in the past. Whitman's hand remained on the *Times* at least until late June 1859. Whether he was then dismissed or simply resigned of his own accord is not clear. Whatever the case, it is hard to imagine that he left embittered. By the time he left, he had resumed intense work on his poems, had even brought or was soon to do so a large number of poems to the Rome brothers shop for printing. The idea of publishing a third edition of *Leaves of Grass* in the near future was already by then formed or forming in his mind; the unsolicited offer of publication which reached him early the next year was to find him largely prepared for publication.

There is every reason to believe that by the spring of 1859 Whitman was working with renewed purpose and energy on these new poems, pouring into them his deepest thoughts and feelings and probing into his personality with an intensity of self-scrutiny he had never before dared. The result was a formidable achievement, an edition far superior to the one he had planned to bring out several years before and one showing fascinating redirections in self-conception and in sense of audience. It is in this 1859–60 version of his "published personality" that one is to look for the "real" Whitman, if one is to find it at all.

10

1860: "Year of Meteors"

To have judged himself by the standard of public recognition and acceptance, a standard he took considerably more seriously than he cared outwardly to show, Whitman could only have been deeply disappointed by his relations with the American reading public during the 1850s. Two editions of his poetry had been published, but neither in satisfactory fashion and neither received with the kind of popular or critical acclaim for which he hoped. On the eve of the new decade, he would have been justified in seeing his attempt to create his own reading public as having been to date a failure. That failure to reach the general public was, by this time, a personal burden, one to be borne with the rest of his creative history into the composition of future editions of *Leaves of Grass*. Beginning with the third edition and continuing through the three remaining decades of his life, he was to carry that burden, if not always with grace, at least with sheer determination. Rather than lighten, the burden was only to grow appreciably heavier with the passing of the years.

But Whitman had always been able to separate his actual from his ideal expectations; and, in any case, the spurt of renewed creativity he experienced during 1859, resulting in a string of richly conceived and composed new poems, gave a renewed thrust to his literary ambitions. To judge from an anonymous self-review he wrote in the first week of the new decade, Whitman began the 1860s with a new edition of his poems (if still with no publisher) and with renewed hopes of reaching a national reading audience:

> We are able to declare that there will also soon crop out the true "Leaves of Grass," the fuller grown work of which the former two issues were the inchoates – the forthcoming one, far, very far ahead of them in quality, quantity, and in supple lyrical exuberance.
>
> Those former issues, published by the author himself in little pittance editions, on trial, have just dropped the book enough to ripple the inner first-circles of literary agitation, in immediate contact with it. The outer,

189

vast, extending, and ever-widening circles, of the general supply, perusal, and discussion of such a work, have still to come. The market
needs to-day to be supplied – the great West especially – with copious
thousands of copies.[1]

Whitman sprang back into print for the first time, poetically, since the
1856 *Leaves of Grass* with the appearance of "A Child's Reminiscence"
(retitled as "A Word Out of the Sea" in the 1860 edition and as "Out
of the Cradle Endlessly Rocking" in final editions of *Leaves of Grass*) in
the December 24, 1859, issue of the New York *Saturday Press*. He immediately followed up that achievement with a campaign of other attempts at periodical publication of his new poems. In January he
attempted to place "A Chant of National Feuillage" ("Our Old Feuillage") with *Harper's Monthly*, "Thoughts" with the New York *Sunday
Courier*, and "Bardic Symbols" ("As I Ebb'd with the Ocean of Life")
with the *Atlantic Monthly*, as well as several shorter pieces with the *Saturday Press*. A new assertiveness can be found in his terms: forty dollars
for the longer poems, cash down on acceptance; prominent billing for
himself or his poem; and the right – he would always insist upon it – to
reprint his poems in future editions of *Leaves of Grass*. To the editors of
Harper's, the leading monthly magazine in America, he stated his nationalist ambitions with particular forthrightness:

> The theory of "*A Chant of National Feuillage*" is to bring in, (devoting
> a line, or two or three lines, to each,) a comprehensive collection of
> touches, locales, incidents, idiomatic scenes, from every section, South,
> West, North, East, Kanada, Texas, Maine, Virginia, the Mississippi
> Valley, etc. etc. etc. – all intensely fused to the urgency of compact
> America, "America always" – all in a vein of graphic, short, clear,
> hasting along – as having a huge bouquet to collect, and quickly taking
> and binding in every characteristic subject that offers itself – making a
> compact, the whole-surrounding, *National Poem,* after its sort, after my
> own style.
>
> Is there any other poem of the sort extant – or indeed hitherto
> attempted?
>
> You may start at the style. Yes, it is a new style, of course, but that
> is necessitated by new theories, new themes – or say the new treatment
> of themes, forced upon us for American purposes. Every really new
> person, (poet or other,) *makes* his style – sometimes a little way removed
> from the previous models – sometimes very far removed.
>
> Furthermore, I have surely attained headway enough with the Amer-
> ican public, especially with the literary classes, to make it worth your
> while to give them a sight of me with all my neologism.[2]

He did not attain much headway, however, with the Harpers, who turned
down their earliest known chance to publish one of Whitman's "national"
poems for the mass audience of their magazine.[3]

But even without their channel to the broad public, Whitman found himself in early 1860 with a considerably expanded and radically transformed edition of his poems in manuscript and with two sets of publishers, one in New York and the other in Boston, eager to bring him and his writing before the American public. In New York, Whitman had made the acquaintance some time in 1859 of Henry Clapp, Jr., the witty editor and publisher of the New York *Saturday Press*. Clapp had founded the *Press* a year earlier with the hope of establishing it as America's leading weekly literary newspaper, one which would take a different path from that of the popular story papers, such as the New York *Ledger*, by printing only a high level of original prose, poetry, and commentary, along with the sharply edged editorials in which Clapp himself specialized. The social relationship between the two men, begun through their meetings at Pfaff's, the fashionable beer cellar near Broadway patronized not only by them but by many of the leading writers for the *Saturday Press* and *Vanity Fair*, evolved during the last weeks of 1859 and through 1860 into one of Whitman's most important professional connections, as well. Clapp took up Whitman with a purpose. Although he was to write in the September 15, 1860, issue of the *Press*, "It is the painful truth that the authors and the books now most popular with the American People, are, with scarcely a single exception, beneath mediocrity in character," his conduct of the paper during 1860 made clear the fact that he considered the major exception to this rule to be Whitman. By the beginning of the year, he granted Whitman free access to the public through the *Press*, while he himself did his best throughout the year to keep Whitman before the public by printing a wide variety of pieces by, about, and in imitation of Whitman.

At about the same time that he was finding a reputable periodical outlet in the New York *Saturday Press*, Whitman found his first genuine book publishers in the Boston firm of Thayer and Eldridge, two young, enthusiastic radical reformers whose guiding principle, according to Thayer, "was to stimulate home talent and encourage young authors."[4] Best known for their support of radical politics, they sought to become the voice of radical poetry as well as taking up Whitman. On February 10, they wrote him the letter he had in some way been hoping for for five years, tendering an unsolicited offer of publication and expressing their offer in terms of strongest appreciation:

> We want to be the publishers of Walt. Whitman's poems – Leaves of Grass. – When the book was first issued we were clerks in the establishment we now own. We read the book with profit and pleasure. It is a true poem and writ by a *true* man.
> When a man dares to speak his thought in this day of refinement – so called – it is difficult to find his mates to act amen to it. Now *we*

want to be known as the publishers of Walt. Whitman's books, and put our names as such under his, on title-pages. – If you will allow it we can and will put your books into good form, and style attractive to the eye; we can and will sell a large number of copies; we have great facilities by and through numberless Agents in selling. We can dispose of more books than most publishing houses (we do not "puff" here but speak *truth*).

We are young men. We "celebrate" ourselves by acts. Try us. You can do us good. We can do you good – pecuniarily.

Now Sir, if you wish to make acquaintance with us, and accept us as your publishers, we will offer to either buy the stereo type plates of Leaves of Grass, or pay you for the use of them, in addition to regular copy right.

Are you writing other poems? Are they ready for the press? Will you let us read them? Will you write us? Please give us your residence.[5]

This was the kind of excited response to his poems that Whitman had always hoped for; and coming from publishers, it was a double blessing.[6] William Thayer and Charles Eldridge were both to become lifelong enthusiasts of Whitman; and through their firm and their contacts, Whitman was to form other long-lasting relationships with men of talent and vision: with Richard Hinton, journalist and abolitionist, fresh from Kansas and possibly responsible for directing the attention of Thayer and Eldridge in the first place toward Whitman; James Redpath, leading Thayer and Eldridge author and future publisher and lyceum manager, whom Whitman would turn to when in need of a publisher during the Civil War; John Trowbridge, popular writer of children's stories and novels, who would unsuccessfully use his influence to try to place *Leaves of Grass* with a Boston publisher in the 1860s; Frank Sanborn, Concord resident and friend of Emerson, author, editor, and educator, who was to defend Whitman right into the twentieth century; and William Douglas O'Connor, also a Thayer and Eldridge author and quickly to make himself into Whitman's closest confederate and strongest public advocate. This was a crowd of young radicals whose fervent companionship around the issue of John Brown and abolitionist politics was far from Whitman's own touchy sentiments during the precarious year of 1860; but where they warmed to his poetry and character, Whitman found the prime response in 1860 to the poems of comradeship he was about to publish.

After a month of negotiations, Whitman went North to oversee the publication of his long-deferred third edition. The conditions for publication, as he explained them by letter to a family friend, were nearly ideal: "Thayer and Eldridge, the publishers, are a couple of young Yankees – so far very good specimens, to me, of this Eastern race of yours. They have treated me first rate – have not asked me at all what I was going to put into the book – just took me to the stereotype foundry, and given orders to follow my directions."[7] Let loose in the foundry, the well-known Rand and Avery shop from whose presses *Uncle Tom's Cabin* had issued eight years before, Whitman followed his own strong ideas about the layout and printing of the volume, leaving the plant foremen shaking their heads in disbelief. The result, however, was a handsome, distinctive twelvemo volume, professionally made, with its taste for decorative symbols and diverse typefaces running toward the ornate; and a deeply satisfied, gratified author. "Altogether, Jeff," he wrote back to his favorite brother, "I am very, very much satisfied and relieved that the thing, in the permanent form it now is, looks as well and reads as well (to my own notion) as I anticipated – because a good deal, after all, was an experiment – and now I am satisfied."[8] How much relief and satisfaction he was then feeling, as he saw his thoughts and sentiments put to press that spring after all the frustrated hopes and postponements of previous years, one can only imagine.

He had good reason to be satisfied with his treatment. For a writer of Whitman's training and sensibility, which led him to see the "making" of his books as an ongoing process continuing beyond the act of inscription, the authorization by his publishers to exercise a free hand over the creation and production of his volume, inside and out, brought him as close as he could ever have wished to his ideal of bookmaking.[9] Thayer and Eldridge even solicited his opinions and advice about the distribution and promotion of the book. Their respect for Whitman, quickly to grow into open admiration, very likely overtook their business acumen. It is hard to imagine Whitman nonplussed by high-powered advertisements for his work, but Thayer and Eldridge apparently proposed ideas which pushed even the master of self-promotion to discomfort. To appreciate his treatment in their hands and his high expectations for the new volume, one has only to contrast Whitman's situation that spring with that of Melville, who was also preparing to come out with a volume – his first – of poems. Where Whitman was all eagerness about the prospects for *Leaves of Grass,* Melville was thoroughly ambivalent about his volume, keen to see it published by a respectable publisher who would publish it without "clap-trap announcements and 'sensation' puffs" but skeptical about its chances with the public: "Of all human events, perhaps, the publication of a first volume of verses is the most insignificant; but though a matter of no importance to the world, it is of some concern to the author."[10]

Whitman and his publishers had none of Melville's proud reservations about the value of promoting the new *Leaves of Grass.* With his assistance, Thayer and Eldridge brought out with the new volume a pamphlet of advertisements, *Leaves of Grass Imprints,* offered free of charge to help the sale of the new edition. The *Imprints,* consisting of many of the reviews of *Leaves of Grass* over its first five years, represented, in effect, a history of Whitman's critical reception to date. Whitman was so thorough in his collection of reviews, in fact, as to have left behind in the *Imprints* a pamphlet which is still one of the best documentations of his critical standing through 1860. In his usually indiscriminate fashion, Whitman assembled favorable and unfavorable reviews alike with self-reviews old and new, including even the moral attack by his friend William Swinton in the New York *Times* for having written his own self-reviews and for having perpetrated a "literary fraud" by his unauthorized use of Emerson's letter in 1856. Such matters of delicacy could not stand in the way of Whitman's ambition. Placed in his hands, the half decade of reviews served as the loudest advertisement he was able to give his new book. This was Whitman playing out his extraliterary strategy to the full. More interesting, though, is the question of the literary strategy he pursued within the covers of this, the most profoundly interior of all editions of *Leaves of Grass*.

One of the most intriguing of the new poems was the obliquely self-reflective "Calamus 40," in which Whitman spoke his bewilderment about "that shadow, my likeness":

> That shadow, my likeness, that goes to and fro, seeking a livelihood,
>   chattering, chaffering,
> How often I find myself standing and looking at it where it flits,
> How often I question and doubt whether that is really me;
> But in these, and among my lovers, and carolling my songs,
> O I never doubt whether that is really me.

Months before, in a manuscript transcription of this idea, he had described the phenomenon differently:

> Comrades! I am the bard of Democracy
> Others are more correct and elegant than I, and more at home in the
>   parlors and schools than I,
> But I alone advance among the people en-masse, coarse and strong
> I am he standing first there, solitary chanting the true America,
> I alone of all bards, am suffused as with the common people.
> I alone receive them with a perfect reception and love – and they
>   shall receive me.
> It is I who live in these, and in my poems, – O they are truly me!
> But that shadow, my likeness, that goes to and fro seeking a
>   livelihood, chattering, chaffering,
> I often find myself standing and looking at it where it flits –
> That likeness of me, but never substantially me.[11]

Such a confusion of self-images hidden among the shadows! Little wonder why a writer who felt forced to track down his "really," "truly," "substantially" me through the welter of shadows and likenesses should have found his personal and poetic identity so elusive. I would state the matter more broadly: One begins to feel about the 1860 *Leaves of Grass,* perhaps along with Whitman, a certain sense of the evolving volume as itself casting its own shadowy, elusive likeness.

These two versions of "That Shadow My Likeness" signify, to my mind, the Janus-faced character of the author and the divided purposes of his third edition: the poet as "bard of Democracy" versus the poet as private lover. One can of course claim that the sum total of Whitman's individual "lovers" brought him round to the former position, a claim not so facile as it seems when one recalls that this was in one sense the brave, if quixotic, vision he proposed for America later in the decade in *Democratic Vistas.* By that time, his years of hospital service during the Civil War in ministration to thousands of wounded and sick young soldiers allowed him to speak more experientially of "adhesive love" – "threads of manly friendship, fond and loving, pure and sweet, strong and life-long, carried to degrees hitherto unknown" – as binding together into a cohesive social unit his traditionless, centerless people.[12] But this was not the direction given his calamus sentiment in the third edition; there, the calamus impulse of his poetry was private, solitary, exclusive; to the margins, not to the center.

Which was it then to be: toward the center or toward the periphery? The answer given by the 1860 *Leaves of Grass* was, in effect, both. There were, on the one hand, more of his broadly reader-directed, nationalistic poems than ever before, mostly deriving from his creative surge of 1856–7. The obvious signal of Whitman's intentions in this direction was the new opening poem "Proto-Leaf" ("Starting from Paumanok"), which featured Whitman, as in previous editions, up on stage, addressing his American readers: "Free, fresh, savage, / Fluent, luxuriant, self-content, fond of persons and places, / . . . Solitary, singing in the west, I strike up for a new world." The poetic act of striking up for the new world was familiarly that of the poet of the previous editions – the poet " . . . coming personally to you now, / Enjoining you to acts, characters, spectacles with me"; the poet sure of his readers ("For me, an audience interminable") and well-stocked with poems with which to meet them ("For you a programme of chants"); the poet so eager to give and so eager that his offering be taken ("Take my leaves, America!"). Familiar, too, was the mode of poetic address, the poet speaking to his people: "O haste, firm holding – haste, haste on, with me," as, hand-in-hand, they pass into the rest of the volume.

This poem led into the 1860 version of "Song of Myself" ("Walt Whitman"), now numbered, as were all the longer poems of the edition as Whitman continued to search for a principle of order, by stanzas.

Through that second (or double) portal lay the new *Leaves of Grass*. The new edition contained more of Whitman's reader-directed poems than ever before, one section (Messenger Leaves) devoted entirely and another (Chants Democratic and Native American) in large part to them, firm proof of the fact that by 1860 Whitman was thinking of his vocative technique self-consciously as such. Many of these poems, it is true, predated the late–1850s and few were truly consequential; still, as poems which reveal something of Whitman's thinking and strategy at the time, they are worth at least a cursory look.

There was in the lead poem of Chants Democratic, appropriately entitled "Apostroph," the extreme instance of a poem constructed exclusively of bursts of address – Whitman on the line to the universe. Its positioning was strategic, a lead-in to the Chants to follow. There then followed some of Whitman's most broadly nationalistic compositions: "By Blue Ontario's Shore," "Song of the Broad-Axe," "A Song for Occupations," and "Our Old Feuillage." One of the more interesting of the new poems, dating from 1856–7, was the one first published in the January 14 *Saturday Press* under the revealing title of "You and Me and To-day" (later, "With Antecedents"):

> With countless years drawing themselves onward, and arrived at
>   these years,
> You and Me arrived – America arrived, and making this year,
> This year! sending itself ahead countless years to come.
>
> O but it is not the years – it is I – it is You,
> We touch all laws, and tally all antecedents,
> We are the skald, the oracle, the monk, and the knight – we easily
>   include them, and more,
> We stand amid time, beginningless and endless – we stand amid evil
>   and good,
> All swings around us – there is as much darkness as light,
> The very sun swings itself and its system of planets around us,
> The sun, and its again, all swing around us.

This has much the sound of the Whitman of the first two editions, playing with time and space, life and language, as the purest potentiality, plastic material to be stretched by the hands of the poet-fabricator. Ultimately, it was his task to put this potentiality at the service of me and you, as they meet through the mediacy of his poem. For once, the "you" of a Whitman poem was identified, or nearly identified: "(For the sake of him I typify – for the common average man's sake – your sake, if you are he)." Or as he was to characterize the beneficiary of modern life and literature at the conclusion of another of the Chants ("I Was Looking a Long While"): "All for the average man of to-day."

What I would emphasize about the Chants in the context of the third edition is how wholly and purely these poems, despite their first-person manner, were a public performance, how far the public and private were beginning to unravel in Whitman's poetry. These were poems generally of reflex, not of impulse, poems written out of a remembered manner and an ongoing commitment to the nationalist cause. But for all the loud clamor about America, there was surprisingly little of the poet himself in these poems, little of his previous immersion in the life and geography of his land or investment of his own being in their circumstances, which perhaps accounts for their general shrillness and superficiality. There were, of course, exceptions – the most notable being the early version of "I Hear America Singing," a poem only to get better in later editions – but the overall impression left by these poems was one of monotony and failed inspiration. The Messengers Leaves, if anything, were even worse – Walt Whitman's afterthought to The States. These were too obviously leftover thoughts addressed to various personages: the revolutionary, the condemned man awaiting execution, Jesus, the prostitute, the patron, the pupil, the President, and, of course, the obligatory "you."

With what surprise, therefore, one turns to the private poems of the new edition, most of them, we know, the product of the last year. The intensity of his self-absorption in these poems, of his search for the truth of himself, signifies a closing of the circle of his poetry more tightly around himself than in previous editions. The intensely self-absorbed poems and sections of the third edition have been seen by critics of the last generation as the finest of the volume, perhaps in part because they mirror the self-absorbed mood of our own time; but even apart from their congruity with current moods and thinking, as poems which reflect Whitman's ideas of poetry and audience in a crucial stage of flux, they deserve the closest inspection.

The note of introspection begins, actually, with the opening poem, whose vaunting cultural nationalism I have already noted. Some of the passages written in 1859, several years after the conception and composition of the main part of the poem, have the bittersweet, self-suffering flavor of Calamus:

> I will make the song of companionship,
> I will show what alone can compact These States,
> I believe the main purport of America is to found a new ideal of
> manly friendship, more ardent, more general,
> I will therefore let appear these burning fires that were threatening to
> consume me,
> I will lift what has too long kept down these smouldering fires – I
> will now expose them and use them.[13]

The motif of consumption by the inner fires of passion and anguish, far from being particular to this poem, was to figure repeatedly throughout the edition. More broadly speaking, there were numerous signs in the 1859 poetry that Whitman was passing through a personal crisis. The facial pose of the "calm exterior," which Whitman had always liked to turn toward the public world, was being overtaken by inner pressures rising to the surface. Not only do I agree with the widespread critical reading of the 1859 poems as being expressions of Whitman's "pertur- bation" – to use what would later become his code word for a state of extreme anxiety – but I think that Whitman was self-consciously trying to come to terms with it in and through the new poems. As usual, he was living his life most searchingly in his poetry.

Repeatedly in these poems, Whitman was staking out a position far removed from that of the self-confident poet of the people. Indeed, the people, the national collective, were largely absent here, as was the am- bition, through reaching them, of attaining universality. Rather, Whit- man was more concerned in many of the new poems with singling out his addressee or isolating his persona from the crowd. The expansive thrust of his earlier poetry was blunted. Often as not, he was emphasizing the specific – the specific moment, feeling, lover, authorial position – as specific, seldom as pathway to the general. To read the manuscript ver- sions of the 1859 poems and their printed versions of the following year side-by-side with later versions is to see how now-centered Whitman had become during that twelve-month period. A poem such as Calamus 24, which opened "I hear it is charged against me," was moved back after 1860 to the past tense; and its predecessor in the series, "This Moment Yearning and Thoughtful," was rephrased so as to make it less clearly a poem of the present moment than it had been in 1860. Similarly, the poem later to be titled after its opening line, "Out of the cradle endlessly rocking," opened in 1860 in significantly different fashion with the onetime action, "Out of the rocked cradle."

Likewise, the act of making poems was becoming in 1859–60 more strictly a self-enclosed act than in previous years. The motifs of confession and self-revelation were to dominate the new poems of the third edition. This was, by no means, an entirely new phenomenon. Whitman had always taken the keenest poetic pleasure in this act, opening and closing the window on himself as he chose, sometimes even making his poems into an act of cat and mouse between persona and reader. But by 1860, the distance between the public and private aspects of his poems was increasing. One obvious sign of this was his growing use of parentheses, into whose folds he liked to tuck his "I" in isolation from the more public sphere of the poem. This device, rare in 1855 and 1856, became more common in 1859–60 as the need to break away his persona from the crowd became more insistent.[14] Then again, many of the new poems of 1859–60 served the purpose of personal confession or reminiscence in their entirety. This was to be the case in the two major new poems of the third edition, "Out of the Cradle Endlessly Rocking" and "As I Ebb'd with the Ocean of Life," as well as in a number of the new Calamus poems. During the period of their composition, Whitman was finding the need for a reevaluation of his life or for confession a virtual obsession, was opening the window on himself far wider than in the past, although never quite as wide as his statements promised:

> Here the frailest leaves of me, and yet the strongest-lasting, – the last
>   to be fully understood,
> Here I shade down and hide my thoughts – I do not expose them,
> And yet they expose me more than all my other poems.[15]

One mask would peel off, only to reveal, often as not, another one beneath it.

The intensified focus on himself necessarily had its artistic corollary, as Whitman repeatedly turned these poems back inwardly upon themselves. The old expansive thrust of the persona outward toward the world of man, nature, and nation was reversed, was redirected inwardly toward a deeper and more intense self-understanding. One can see this in the settings of his 1859–60 poems; the persona locates himself inside his house, alone on the edge of the seashore, away somewhere near the pond side, off on the margins with his own thoughts – seldom out among, if anything in retreat from, the passing crowds and the sights and sounds of the city. Typical of the mood and setting of many of these poems was the early version of "When I Heard at the Close of the Day," one of the most beautifully phrased and controlled of the new lyrics:

> When I heard at the close of the day how I had been praised in the
>   Capitol, still it was not a happy night for me that followed;
> Nor when I caroused – Nor when my favorite plans were
>   accomplished – was I really happy,
> But that day I rose at dawn from the bed of perfect health, electric,
>   inhaling sweet breath,
> When I saw the full moon in the west grow pale and disappear in the
>   morning light,
> When I wandered alone over the beach, and undressing, bathed,
>   laughing with the waters, and saw the sun rise,
> And when I thought how my friend, my lover, was coming, then O
>   I was happy;
> Each breath tasted sweeter – and all that day my food nourished me
>   more – And the beautiful day passed well,
> And the next came with equal joy – And with the next, at evening,
>   came my friend,

> And that night, while all was still, I heard the waters roll slowly
>   continually up the shores
> I heard the hissing rustle of the liquid and sands, as directed to me,
>   whispering, to congratulate me, – For the friend I love lay sleeping
>   by my side,
> In the stillness his face was inclined towards me, while the moon's
>   clear beams shone,
> And his arm lay lightly over my breast – And that night I was
>   happy.[16]

The familiar Whitman circling action is here all inward, self-contained, the I swept along by the driving rhythm of the poem toward its final rendezvous with the object of its desire. The movement of the poem is from the external to the internal, from the Capitol of the nation to the private sea bath, as the ocean waters nestle up to massage and assuage the anxiety of the soul. As for the friend, the lover – he is a curiously silent presence in the poem, more a projection of the persona than a simple, separate, living personality. To attempt to read into him or into the setting a specific lover or a specific memory is to mistake the poem's thoroughgoing artifice, its character as carefully conceived and executed craft. This poem, like many others in the series, is one which has been worked over with exquisite care and precision, the result an expression which is subdued, modulated, remarkably delicate. No "barbaric yawp" of 1855 here either in claim or actuality – this is a poetic art of unusual refinement of phrasing and tenderness of sensibility.

The change of attitude which moved Whitman closer to being the solitary lover is to be seen most vividly in the string of twelve poems, of which this was one, which he began to compose during the spring or summer of 1859. Under what personal pressure or experience Whitman set himself to their composition – a disappointment in love is the best guess, but it may not be a very good one – one cannot know for certain. The result, however, is clear to see. By nature an impulsive writer given to composition in bits and starts, Whitman had never before dealt with a single theme or mood sustained over a series of poems, as he was to attempt in these Calamus poems. Justin Kaplan has described the series well in calling it "a narrative sequence, like Shakespeare's [sonnets], that dramatizes – not necessarily *recounts* – a passionate attachment to a younger man."[17] Whitman's earlier, process-centered poetry had been generally nonnarrative, but by 1859 the need to tell the story of the self was overpowering. The story which he told, however, as Kaplan notes, is not to be read necessarily as the story of *himself*; it was, in fact, one of the most completely artful self-presentations that this highly artful poet was ever to compose.

The keynote was originally to have been the tall-standing, moss-wrapped oak tree, which, in the fine poem ("I Saw in Louisiana a Live-Oak Growing") stood "all alone" in the landscape:

> Without any companion it grew there, glistening out joyous leaves of
>   dark green,
> And its look, rude, unbending, lusty, made me think of myself;
> But I wondered how it could utter joyous leaves, standing alone
>   there without its friend, its lover – For I knew I could not.[18]

The image of the solitary tree nonchalantly uttering its "joyous leaves" was, and so it must have seemed to the older poet to be, a throwback to his self-image of not so many years before, that of the carpenter-poet standing self-assertively before the nation. In looking at the great hairy oak, standing proud and tall in its self-sufficiency, Whitman was looking at himself as he once was; and the emotion that he registers is one of bemusement, verging on disbelief. His reaction serves to remind us of the extent to which the making of his poems was an act of will, and it testifies to what happened when Whitman's willpower slackened or changed directions. Equally striking was the poetic manner of his self-expression: its quiet restraint, its spare wording, its tight formal symmetry. Such were to be the aesthetic guidelines of the Calamus series in general, as Whitman explored, sometimes with quiet dignity, sometimes with barely restrained anguish, the sources of his vulnerability and suffering.

For some unexplained reason, perhaps because it offered a more available human outlet than did the oak tree or perhaps because he planned to exploit its phallic potentiality, Whitman chose to shift his keynote from the oak tree to the calamus plant, which he had known from his earliest boyhood on Long Island. He had first referred to the plant in the openly sexual passage about the "spread of my body" in the original "Song of Myself," and there is little reason to doubt that he associated the long-horned plant with male and intermale sexuality. To do so, and to do so openly, given his compulsive ideas about physical and moral health and cleanliness, was an act of considerable courage for Whitman, an act he had stifled for years. The ideas of sexuality and artistic creativity had been linked in Whitman's thinking ever since he had equated poetic organicism and sexuality as a theoretical basis of the new poetry in the 1855 Preface, as well as in the poems of that edition. As long as the sexual urge remained intransitive and impersonal, an act of self-incarnation, it had the effect paradoxically of opening his poetry to the world. The power of merging the world with one's self which he attributed in the 1855 Preface to his ideal poet had had at that time its clear relevance to himself: "His spirit responds to his country's spirit .... he incarnates its geography and natural life and rivers and lakes. Mississippi with annual freshets and changing chutes, Missouri and Columbia and Ohio and Saint Lawrence with the falls and beautiful masculine Hudson, do not embouchure where they spend themselves more than they embouchure into him."

But in the Calamus poems, he was no longer able or willing to sustain that universalizing ideal. To parade around in his poems naked and sensual before the world, as he had done in earlier poems, was one thing; to bare himself before a more intimate, potential audience was quite another. In 1859, however, he was determined to do precisely that: to address himself more fully than in previous years to a fit audience of the few, rather than indiscriminately to the large nation of readers. But even this may be understating the degree of Whitman's removal from his earlier position. There is every possibility that Whitman was originally uncertain about whether to come forward publicly with these poems at all. They survive today in manuscript form as leaves torn from a notebook, into which Whitman had originally written their fair copies in – unusual pattern of composition for him – one continuous act. At this stage, they may very well have been for his eyes only – a curious situation for a poet for whom the act of publishing his personality was an act of the highest existential significance.

It was probably only later that he removed these poems from the notebook and rearranged them in a series with other poems written earlier on the common theme of manly love. He called this arrangement a "cluster," and with this he discovered the structuring principle he had been looking for years to work into his book. By 1860 the cluster had grown to forty-five poems, and the task of organizing so many poems written over a three-year period required an act of considerable editing. The subsequent homogenization of the poems necessitated by the editorial process was naturally to obscure some of the differences between the earlier and later poems. An interesting instance of the changes he made was Calamus 13, a poem which, as "Buds," read in 1856–7 like one of Whitman's typical reader-directed ventures:

> Earth's and Mine, offered fresh to you, after natural ways, folded,
> silent,
> Thoughts, says, poems, poemets, put before you and within you, to
> be unfolded by you on the old terms;
> If you bring the warmth of the sun to them they will open and bring
> form, color, perfume, to you,
> If you become the aliment and the wet, they will become flowers,
> fruits, tall branches and trees,
> They are comprised in you just as much as in themselves, perhaps
> more than in themselves,

> They are not comprised in one season or succession, but in many
>   successions,
> They have come slowly up out of the earth and me, and are to come
>   slowly up out of you. −[19]

Its second line makes it sound as though Whitman may even have intended this originally for one of his programmatic statements. When he
revised it several years later for the third edition, he removed this no
longer necessary line and fitted the poem with a new pair of opening
lines designed to serve the purpose of the cluster generally:

> Calamus taste,
> (For I must change the strain − these are not to be pensive leaves but
>   leaves of joy,)

But this free and open interplay with the reader in 1856–7 was no
longer the attitude of the poet in the new Calamus poems of 1859–60,
in which the poet was less generous with the gift of his poetry. A more
typical act of a similar sort to that of "Buds" was that which he made
in the manuscript version of "These I Singing in Spring," one of the
central poems of the Calamus series:

> These I, singing in spring, collect for lovers,
> (For who but I should understand love, with all its sorrow and joy?
> And who but I should be the poet of comrades?)
> Collecting, I traverse the garden, − but soon I pass the gates,
> . . . .
> Collecting, dispensing, singing in spring, there I wander with them
> Plucking something for tokens − something for these till I hit upon a
>   name,
> Tossing toward whoever is near me,
> Here! lilac with a branch of pine,
> Here, out of my pocket, some moss which I pulled off a live-oak in
>   Florida as it hung trailing down,
> Here, some pinks and laurel leaves, and a handful of sage,
> And here what I drew from the water where I waded in the pond-
>   side,
> (O there I saw him that tenderly loves me, and never separates from
>   me
> Therefore this shall be the special token of comrades − this calamus-
>   root shall,
> Interchange it, youths, with each other − Let none render it back,)
> And twigs of maple, and a bunch of wild orange, and chestnut,
> And stems of currants, and plum-blows, and the aromatic cedar,
> These I, singing, compassed round by a thick cloud of spirits,
> Wandering, point to or touch as I pass, or throw them loosely from
>   me,

> Indicating to each one what he shall have – giving something to
>   each,
> But that I drew from the pond-side, that I reserve,
> I will give of it but only to those comrades who love as I myself am
>   capable of loving. –[20]

These love buds are not for everyone. Having begun his poetic career as the celebrator and disseminator of the leaves of grass, chosen precisely for their universality and commonness as the central symbol of both his opening poem and his entire career, Whitman in 1859–60 was reserving the choicest tokens for the exclusive few.

The most significant of the new poems was also the one which featured Whitman writing most immediately to himself about himself, rather than to his reader. "A Word Out of the Sea" ("Out of the Cradle Endlessly Rocking" from 1871 on) has every sign of having been composed out of a frame of mind similar to that of the 1859 Calamus poems; but its depth, intricacy, and story all point to a major effort on the poet's part at self-understanding. It is, in fact, especially in its 1860 version, Whitman's equivalent to a Wordsworthian study of the growth of the poet's mind, although one constructed on a less strictly factual autobiographical basis.

The poem opens with one of the finest of Whitman's blocks of running rhythmic verse, all its mounting energy channeled into his poetic I – or more precisely, into his I's performing the poetic act. That act, stripped of its modifiers, consists simply of a single grammatical statement: I sing a reminiscence. The reminiscence that he sings, whether recalled or invented, is of the singular experience in his childhood which made him the man-poet that he now is and that he expects always to be. By 1860, Whitman had already enough years of life and poetic experience behind him to know that his present and future would also have to take into consideration his past, and so he was now given to reviewing his personal and poetic history. That he was no longer a young man and that he realized it is plain to see in the engraving he used for the frontispiece to the third edition. It showed a man clearly grayer, heavier, and fleshier than the rugged workingman pose he had struck for the two previous editions, a sensitive, vulnerable, inward-looking man rather than the self-confident, assertive man of the people of 1855–6.

The primary direction of this poem, as of its like, "As I Ebb'd with the Ocean of Life," is backward, a search for origins. The search takes him back to the most formative of all natural settings for Whitman, one referred to frequently but rarely utilized fully in previous poems: the seashore, the meeting line between his paternal island and the "savage old mother" of life and death. This was the greatest of all areas of intersection for Whitman, "that suggesting, dividing line, contact, junction, the solid marrying the liquid."[21] It is in approaching this magic dividing line, always in flux, that the mature poet meets his boyhood self, as well as his final adversary, death.

Beginning with its opening stanza, the poem is a symphonic song of oneness and twoness. It opens in the preliminary strophe with a masterly display of Whitman's rhythmic control, all its force transferred late in the stanza into the word pair "boy" and "man" ("A man – yet by these tears a little boy again"), and through their apposition, into the subject-I several lines later. Through this technique of rhythmic transference, Whitman immediately formulated the central issue of the poem, the identity of the poet, to whose making the various motifs of the poem all contribute. The poet's identity will be formed from the interplay of these motifs, introduced in this stanza and to figure prominently in the second part of the poem; but it will emerge even more directly through the mediacy of that element which is common both to them and to him: "the word." The word is to come to the man-child in several forms – first from the song of the mockingbird and later from the "undertone" of the sea.

The mockingbirds come up from the South "two together" at springtime to establish their family. As they sing their song of union, "*Singing all time, minding no time, / If we two but keep together,*" the young boy stations himself nearby, "cautiously peering, absorbing, translating" – that is, performing the three-stage process by which the poet transforms experience into art. The harmonious union of the birds, their twoness as oneness, is disrupted by the disappearance of the female, leaving the distraught "he-bird" to sing its song of loneliness and solitude. The bird's song of desolation, written in 1860 with a two-beat apostrophe designed to reinforce the sense of two together, floats out over the water and in its sweep ties together the elements of the universe, worked up by Whitman's present progressive-dominated language into a state of natural generation, for its ultimate recipient, the enraptured boy.

The effect of the song and setting on the boy, the "outsetting bard," is complete and lasting: it awakens his "sleeping" tongue and arouses him to "the unknown want, the destiny of me." His destiny, it is clear, whatever it will be, will be in language and through language. So that when the mature man, reliving the scene in his mind, looks for the "clew" to the memory's final meaning, he looks for it – and finds it – in the form of "a word." That word is "death," brought to him – or more exactly, brought to his remembering consciousness – by the hissing waves, as they slithered up to his feet and rose up over him to the level of his ears. What Whitman had written earlier in another of his water poems – "That I was, I knew was of my body – and what I should be, I knew I should be of my body" ("Crossing Brooklyn Ferry") – is equally true of the scene here, as the body becomes the conduit to the formation of personality. It was always one of the sources of Whitman's strength as a poet that he thought and composed in closest quarters to his body; when "the word" comes to him here, it naturally comes with the contact of the waves on his body:

> Answering, the sea,
> Delaying not, hurrying not,
> Whispered me through the night, and very plainly before daybreak,
> Lisped to me constantly the low and delicious word DEATH,
> And again Death – ever Death, Death, Death,
> Hissing melodious, neither like the bird, nor like my aroused child's
>   heart,
> But edging near, as privately for me, rustling at my feet,
> And creeping thence steadily up to my ears,
> Death, Death, Death, Death, Death.

> Which I do not forget,
> But fuse the song of two together,
> That was sung to me in the moonlight on Paumanok's gray beach,
> With the thousand responsive songs, at random,
> My own songs, awaked from that hour,
> And with them the key, the word up from the waves,
> The word of the sweetest song, and all songs,
> That strong and delicious word which, creeping to my feet,
> The sea whispered me.

"The sea whispered me" – the formulation is too striking not to draw attention to itself. Whitman was to use rhyme with extreme infrequency during his *Leaves of Grass* career; but when he did, he tended to favor rhymes off of "me."[22] The rhyme used so conspicuously here calls attention to the ambiguity of the line's phraseology, which in view of the phraseology of the previous stanza, I can interpret only as being deliberately ambiguous. Does the sea whisper "to me" (and/or "for me") or does it whisper "me"? The answer, I suppose, is both. The sea whispers to the boy-poet's ears, but it also whispers to his ears his identity (death). From his perspective, it whispers me to me. This is what I meant when I spoke of the closing circle of self in the poems of the 1860 *Leaves of Grass* composed latest. With no reader as intermediary, with no addressee outside of the poem, the lines of the poem are all self-contained. For this reason, Roy Harvey Pearce was right to stress the considerable artificiality on Whitman's part of later interposing between the two last verses the lovely but misleading line, with its universalizing effect:

> (Or like some old crone rocking the cradle, swathed in sweet
>   garments, bending aside,)[23]

It draws attention away from the point where the force of the poem lay in its 1860 version: the vital connection between the "word" and "me." For it is here, in personal identity constructed through language, that the 1860 poem centered and that Whitman, even as he grew older, continued to locate the center of his existence.

I spoke of Whitman's heightened concern with time, the present moment, in connection with the Calamus poems; and I find a similar kind of concern here. This poem was composed with an awareness not only of the spread of his body but with the spread of his body over time. Whitman had not previously been so sensitive to the effect of the past pushing its way into the present, which is why in no other poem since "Crossing Brooklyn Ferry" had he been so concerned to merge time schemes in the present moment of the poem. One can, of course, claim that Whitman's aim, in this regard, was transcendental, that the birds' song of "singing all time, minding no time" was one which Whitman's larger song, through the process of "fus[ion]," necessarily transformed from a specific song and moment into a thousand poems and moments. To this extent, this poem approximates the poetic position of process and potentiality Whitman had favored in his earlier poetry, allows him theoretically to point himself and his poetry toward the future. But this is so only in theory; in actuality, the thrust of the poem is toward consolidation, not expansion; its action, retrenchment, not progression. Particularly in its 1860 form, it was the expression of a man taking stock of his life and art.

If "A Word Out of the Sea" was essentially an elegy, "As I Ebb'd with the Ocean of Life" was the major lament of the third edition. Published first as "Bardic Symbols" in the prestigious *Atlantic Monthly* and then positioned at the head of the Leaves of Grass section of the third edition, it was a poem to which Whitman clearly attached special importance.[24] It, too, is a beach poem, the poet walking the strand alone; and it, too, turns his solitary walk into a retrospective meditation on his life and art. But here, he dares to say what he did not say in "A Word Out of the Sea" or even in Calamus, that his life and art are but a kind of detritus washed up by the waves:

> Elemental drifts!
> O I wish I could impress others as you and the waves have just been
> impressing me.
> . . . .
> As I wend the shores I know not,
> As I listen to the dirge, the voices of men and women wrecked,
> As I inhale the impalpable breezes that set in upon me,
> As the ocean so mysterious rolls toward me closer and closer,

> At once I find, the least thing that belongs to me, or that I see or
>   touch, I know not;
> I, too, but signify, at the utmost, a little washed-up drift,
> A few sands and dead leaves to gather,
> Gather, and merge, myself as part of the sands and drift.

That rather oblique "others" he mentions in the first stanza, the entirety
of which was to be dropped from later editions of the poem, was as
close as he would come to shifting the focus of the poem from himself.
For this was to be a poem, as none of the poems of the previous two
editions can be said to be, whose subject was first and foremost he himself
– his hopes, his dreams, his frustrations. What he sees, therefore, when
he looks at the beach, unmistakably, is the debris of his aspirations and
expectations, figured in his "lines" and "dead leaves" strewn over the
sand. What a sad comedown it must have been for the broad-thinking,
large-intentioned poet of Leaves of Grass, who had placed the faith of his
life in the pun he habitually made on "leaves," now to have figured them
as "dead leaves." Ever since his first edition, he had made the "leaves
of grass" the symbol of the universal gift of life and literature, open and
available to all. Seen against this context, the "dead leaves" of this poem
stand out in the starkest, most unequivocal relief, leaves no longer alive
and translatable to the nation of readers but dead and scattered at his
feet.

Side by side with the remains of his writing he sees strewn on the
beach the remains of himself. The "merge" of himself with the play of
elements on his native shore, the thought and sound of which take him
backward and forward over his life, leaves him with the sad realization
that "before all my insolent poems the real ME still stands untouched,
untold, altogether unreached." Elusive as ever, the search for this postulated, unified self leaves him to poke around among the shreds and
tatters of his life, left behind in the wake of the sea. Perhaps the most
striking thing about this poem is the unrelenting way it takes him down
into the abyss of his discontent, at a moment when the thought of his
own incapacity or failure was virtually unbearable:

> Me and mine!
> We, loose winrows, little corpses,
> Froth, snowy white, and bubbles,
> (See, from my dead lips the ooze exuding at last!
> See – the prismatic colors, glistening and rolling!)
> Tufts of straw, sands, fragments,
> Buoyed hither from many moods, one contradicting another,
> From the storm, the long calm, the darkness, the swell,
> Musing, pondering, a breath, a briny tear, a dab of liquid or soil,
> Up just as much out of fathomless workings fermented and thrown,

A limp blossom or two, torn, just as much over waves floating,
    drifted at random,
Just as much for us that sobbing dirge of Nature,
Just as much, whence we come, that blare of the cloud-trumpets;
We, capricious, brought hither, we know not whence, spread out
    before You, up there, walking or sitting,
Whoever you are – we too lie in drifts at your feet.

There is not much consolation in this position, but Whitman was willing to leave it at this, with himself deposited at the feet of his sole interlocutor, God. We can never know what surge of emotion produced this rare moment of humility, this most open cry of pain and self-doubt – the confession of confessions of the third edition. Was it a doubt about the years of preparation and self-dedication he had given to his role as poet of the people? Was it some epiphanic recognition of the extreme edge onto which he, like so many American artists of vision, had dared to set himself as a creative being, a solitary, externally unsupported figure against the vast oceanscape? Whatever it was, the image of himself laid at the foot of the shore, the passive agent of the wind and waves, was an image which was often to come to him in moments of heightened emotion.[25] It brought him back not only to the sources of his childhood but also to the sources of his creative imagination – at the feet of his "fierce old mother." The dreamy-eyed boy who had walked the shores of his ancestral Paumanok would find to the end of his days the tally to his own surging spirit in the cyclical, elemental drama of the sea and shore played out to the thrilling music of the surf.

But seen against the entirety of the volume, this was merely one brief surge of creativity, one among many in the third edition. Profound though it was, Whitman had too much buoyancy to have been held down for long. Overarching the depression of this poem or of any series of poems were his hopes for the new edition. By the time Whitman organized his manuscripts together in composite form, he was once again looking ahead in his closing poem to a reconciliation with his reader, even if it was with a programmatic poem written in the 1856–7 period:

My songs cease – I abandon them,
From behind the screen where I hid, I advance personally.

This is no book,
Who touches this, touches a man,
(Is it night? Are we here alone?)
It is I you hold, and who holds you,
I spring from the pages into your arms – decease calls me forth.
. . . .
Dear friend, whoever you are, here, take this kiss,
I give it especially to you – Do not forget me,

I feel like one who has done his work – I progress on,
The unknown sphere, more real than I dreamed, more direct, darts
awakening rays about me – *So long!*
Remember my words – I love you – I depart from materials,
I am as one disembodied, triumphant, dead.

("So Long!")

As the 1860 *Leaves* had opened with a poem of address, so it naturally
ended with one; such had been the framing device of the two earlier
editions, as well. But rather than issuing a broadly nationalistic address
to the Union, as he had done in "Proto-Leaf," Whitman had advanced
far enough toward his readership by the end of the volume that he could
safely close on a note of greater intimacy with his "dear friend," employing in the stanzas above one of the most daring, not to mention
presumptuous, figurations of author and reader to be found in literature.

Behind him, his work indeed done, he could leave his third edition,
a volume with which he felt the keenest satisfaction. As the volume
issued from the presses of Rand and Avery in May 1860, he had not only
the services – the combined services, in fact – of Thayer and Eldridge in
Boston and Clapp in New York to promote the book but also their faith
in "the great Poet" (as Thayer and his wife apparently had taken to
calling him at home). Separately and together, they were able to give
Leaves of Grass the strongest promotional campaign it was to receive
during the century. As Clapp wrote to Whitman, then in Boston overseeing the printing of the volume, "What I can do for it, in the way of
bringing it before the public, over and over again, I shall do and do
thoroughly – if the S P is kept alive another month. We have more
literary influence than any other paper in the land, and as your poems
are not new to me, I can say it will all be used for the book – in the
interest of poetry."[26] True to his word, Clapp did everything in his power
to secure the reputation of the new edition.

The outlet he had given Whitman to the public even before the third
edition was a reality became the chief advertising medium for the new
edition in 1860. Clapp's motives in the matter were peculiarly mixed.
His appreciation for Whitman was unquestionably genuine, but he also
saw his chance to turn Whitman's good fortune to his own advantage.
Keeping the undersubsidized *Saturday Press* a going proposition had been
a struggle for Clapp from the very beginning, so that when Whitman
was taken up by his Boston publishers, Clapp hoped to merge forces
with them in the common struggle. With Whitman as a more or less
willing intermediary, Clapp negotiated with Thayer and Eldridge on and
off through the spring and summer of the year for financial help. By late
April, Thayer and Eldridge advertisements were appearing in the *Press,*
while Clapp returned the favor by acting as literary agent for the new

Leaves of Grass, placing review copies with various newspapers and magazines. This satisfactory arrangement led to further negotiations between the two sides during the summer, again with Whitman as go-between, as Clapp's financial position weakened. In August, Thayer and Eldridge wrote to Whitman to ask his opinion before concluding a deal with Clapp to buy his paper but to retain him as editor: "Will you please write us per return mail stating what you know of the affairs of the S.P. – that is, if it can be done without trenching up on your friendly relations with Mr. Clapp?"[27]

That deal was never concluded, but even without their joining forces formally the two sets of publishers were able to push the cause of Whitman more aggressively than had yet been done. Within weeks of its issue, Thayer and Eldridge could write Whitman that, despite resistance to handling it by jobbers and retailers, the book had nearly sold out its thousand-copy first issue and that a second issue was printed and ready for binding.[28] Plans were soon made to bring out a cheaper edition of the *Leaves* as well, and by the fall Whitman and his publishers had discussed and agreed on a new volume of poems, which was already being advertised that fall. William Thayer's final assessment of the volume was that it enjoyed a modest success in 1860: "It did not sell rapidly, but the demand was moderately steady and showed gradual enlargement all the time we had control of the business."[29]

Meanwhile, Clapp was busy playing midwife to Whitman's reputation in New York. He sent out review copies to numerous periodicals and reviewers; printed and reprinted many reviews of the new edition, even soliciting some himself; and printed a wide variety of parodies or imitations of Whitman. This was to be a banner year for parodies of Whitman – "He is more open to parody and burlesque than any living figure," noted one contemporary man of letters – and in all likelihood Clapp's solicitation had something to do with it.[30] These parodies, by contemporary writers such as Bret Harte, William Winters, and Richard Grant White, were one indication of the fact that Whitman was gradually becoming more widely known by 1860, even if not necessarily understood or appreciated by his "average man of to-day."

Clapp was also responsible for one of the most interesting of the reviews of the third edition. Timed to coincide with the May issuing of the volume, it was almost certainly his own. It offered the most obvious response to a question which Whitman and Clapp had presumably often asked themselves, separately and together: Why had Whitman so far failed to capture the favor of the general reading public:

> We announce a great Philosopher – perhaps a great Poet – in every way an original man. It is Walt Whitman. The proof of his greatness is in his book, and there is proof enough . . .

Perhaps the scope and significance of Walt Whitman's poetry may be more clearly indicated by contrasting its character with that of the poetry ordinarily accepted and popular at the present time. The latter is rhymed and measured. It is sometimes powerful with passion and sometimes stately with thought. It is generally sweet and graceful – expressing mild and monotonous sentiments in a thousand respectable ways. It is gay for a feast and sorry for a funeral. It is sweet as to Springtime, and thoughtful as to sober Autumn days. It rhymes "kisses" with "blisses," and expresses its writer's willingness to partake of the same. It mourns persistently for dead infants, for those who are snatched away in beauty's bloom, and for blighted blossoms generally. It has an amatory tendency, of a sentimental description, and wastes a good deal of miscellaneous sweetness. It presents its author as one who desires burial under a sweet-apple tree, and will not have a decent graveyard on any terms; it affects to ignore and despise the human body; it dwells fondly upon the sublime nature and destiny of the soul; and passing smoothly over all that is significant in this actual present life, it hints lugubriously at another and a better world. On the other hand these poems of Walt Whitman concern themselves alike with the largest and the pettiest topics. They are free as the wandering wind that sweeps over great oceans and inland seas, over the continents of the world, over mountains, forests, rivers, plains, and cities; free as the sunshine are they, and like the sunshine ardent and fierce. Nothing in the creation is too sacred or too distant for the lightning glance of their aspiration; nothing that in any way concerns the souls and the bodies of the human race is too trivial for their comprehension. Everywhere they evince the philosophic mind, deeply seeking, reasoning, feeling its way toward a clear knowledge of the system of the universe.[31]

With his usual instinct for the popular jugular, Clapp identified the radical disjunction between Whitman's verse and the popular poetry of the day, even though he himself lacked a conceptual vocabulary of his own with which to describe Whitman's originality.

As matters turned out that year, both Clapp in New York and Thayer and Eldridge in Boston would pay the price for having failed to comply with popular taste and opinion. By December, both sets of publishers were forced to suspend operations in the general financial instability of the months preceding the Civil War. Within a matter of days, Whitman lost his two major outlets to the public, not to mention any chance of bringing out the follow-up volume of poems, already announced by Thayer and Eldridge, which he had been working on through the fall. By mid-December, Thayer and Eldridge were out of business, the plates of *Leaves of Grass* passing out of their hands and the profits of the unlicensed editions printed on them, royalties and all, into those of pirates, who would illegally print out copies of the third edition for years.

"What am I myself but one of your meteors?" Whitman would ponder in a poem he was writing in late 1860, and in truth 1860 was to be his "year of meteors." The glittering prospects with which he commenced the year eventually faded away to naught, and 1860 closed on an all-too-familiar note of hopes deferred and Whitman returned to his "slough" of the previous year, to be revived from it only several years later by the new role offered him by the Civil War. The great excitement of the third edition, the prospective breakthrough which had Whitman and his publishers comparing, even if only by contrast, his book's prospects with those of *Uncle Tom's Cabin,* left him as stranded as ever on the far bank of his dream of a national poetry.[32] The "copious thousands" of copies of *Leaves of Grass* he had called for at year's beginning with which to supply the American market had been only a few thousand in actuality; and by year's end he lacked even an outlet for getting out his program, no less his word, to the American public. The expanding range of the Civil War would eventually reach him in his slough and drive him out of his depression to renewed activity, poetic and otherwise; but by the time it did, he would be an older man, aging rapidly, and he would have to confront cultural conditions significantly altered from those of his creative heyday during the antebellum era.

11

Whitman and His Readers Through the Century

To see the third edition of *Leaves of Grass* as the dividing point in Whitman's career as an active poet is admittedly to engage in an act of radical foreshortening. With only five years and three editions of *Leaves of Grass* behind him, Whitman was yet to follow his calling unswervingly during the three remaining decades of his life, in the process bringing out numerous updated editions of *Leaves of Grass* and volumes of prose. Still, the majority of his poems, especially of his best poems, were already written by this date; and I believe that the remainder of his career as a creative man was one of narrowing horizons, scaled-down ventures, and reduced risks – in short, of consolidation. By 1860, his great creative insights into the rendering of life in verse and his experiments in audience-address and other verse techniques were behind him. I do not mean in saying this to minimize, as I think has become the tendency of Whitman criticism of recent years, his Civil War and post–Civil War achievements. His *Drum-Taps,* the best poems to come out of the war, gave the most concentrated evidence to date of his powers as a verbal genre painter; and, even in the subsequent years of declining productivity, Whitman was to compose such fine poems as "To a Locomotive in Winter," "The Dalliance of the Eagles," "Passage to India," "A Clear Midnight," "Fancies at Navesink," and "To the Sun-set Breeze."

But times were moving on. To take a case in point of how they were changing around him – Clapp's *Saturday Press* was to be reborn for a brief time after the Civil War; and when it was, its new leading voice was Artemus Ward, whose writing typified many of the new currents of American letters. The *Press* was even to have the short-lived success of publishing Twain's "The Celebrated Jumping Frog of Calaveras County" before passing out of print a second and final time. Furthermore, not only were times changing but Whitman was the kind of person who was peculiarly unable to keep up with their changing circumstances. The unyielding, inflexible character which served him so well in allowing him to persevere with his poetic program where others faced with similar obstacles would either have made concessions or given it up entirely, the same pertinacity which made Whitman's commitment to his career virtually unique among American writers of his generation, ironically unfitted him for the changing society which emerged from the Civil War. The aging man of Camden whom Edward Carpenter knew and shrewdly evaluated as "less the river than the rock" found himself increasingly out of his element in his last decades.[1]

Whitman's Jacksonian conception of a nation of independent workers and farmers and of its cultural ideal of a poetry for the people was becoming quickly and pathetically outdated in the Gilded Age. I can give a capsule example of what I mean by citing the lovely canticle of America he had worked over considerably before it reached its final title in the 1867 *Leaves of Grass* as "I Hear America Singing" and its final form in subsequent editions:

> I hear America singing, the varied carols I hear,
> Those of mechanics, each one singing his as it should be blithe and
>   strong,
> The carpenter singing his as he measures his plank or beam,
> The mason singing his as he makes ready for work, or leaves off
>   work,
> The boatman singing what belongs to him in his boat, the deckhand
>   singing on the steamboat deck,
> The shoemaker singing as he sits on his bench, the hatter singing as
>   he stands,
> The wood-cutter's song, the ploughboy's on his way in the morning,
>   or at noon intermission or at sundown,
> The delicious singing of the mother, or of the young wife at work,
>   or of the girl sewing or washing,
> Each singing what belongs to him or her and to none else,
> The day what belongs to the day – at night the party of young
>   fellows, robust, friendly,
> Singing with open mouths their strong melodious songs.

The problem with this otherwise perfectly enchanting vision of a nation of individual workers, each one singing his or her song of contentment, is that, even as an ideal, it belongs to a bygone world of small, independent mechanics, craftsmen, and farmers. That world – the world, not coincidentally, of Walter Whitman, Sr., and for a time of Walter Whitman, Jr. – was being bypassed by the age of mass production and modern technology. Rather than singing Whitman's song of self-contentment and self-help, American workingmen in the period following the Civil War would increasingly be given to chanting the slogans of their emergent unions, a movement, significantly, with which Whitman had little sympathy. A symbolic drama on this theme was to be played out many times in his last years by Whitman and his young friend and amanuensis, Horace Traubel, also a veteran of the printing shop, with the younger man promoting and the older man as obdurately resisting the idea of socialism.

The rigidification of his views generally as he passed into old age had important ramifications for his relations with the reading public. As he became more removed from the current scene, disabled physically and given over increasingly mentally to inflexibility, cracks in his authorial position vis-à-vis his audience, already present before the war, widened into an open cleavage. Whitman had half wistfully sought the patronage of "rich givers" before the war, but it was only in his last years that this was to become an actuality, as Whitman became the beneficiary of Andrew Carnegie and other people of means. The poet of the people was forced to accept the inconsistency – he would never admit to seeing it as the ignominy – of subscription publishing and of subscription contributions, the latter often underwritten by the writers and intellectuals whom he had spent his career demeaning.

Of course, Whitman's relations with the reading public had never been smooth, even before the war, either in theory or in actuality. He had never been able to sort out the paradox surrounding his, the self-proclaimed national poet's, failure to reach the "democratic masses." That problem continued to follow Whitman in the years after the Civil War, even as he receded from the creative edge of 1855–60 to a position closer to respectability. The "good, gray poet" of the postwar era who could turn out "O Captain! My Captain!" or recite, on the few occasions when he read publicly, from a reading book stocked with his own and others' traditional verse knew very well how to please conventional taste and occasionally even condescended to do so. By 1867, he was prepared to present a new face to the public: "The author of Leaves of Grass is in no sense or sort whatever the 'rough,' the 'eccentric,' 'vagabond' or queer person, that the commentators . . . persist in making him. [He is] never defiant even to the conventions, always bodily sweet and fresh, dressed plainly and cleanly . . . using only moderate words . . . All really refined persons, and the women more than the men, take to Walt Whitman. The most delicate and even conventional lady only needs to know him to love him."[2]

From "rough" to graybeard, revolutionary to patriarch within a dozen years – so Whitman was to recast himself in his unrelenting desire for broad acceptance. Likewise, he intensified his effort to make over his early poems in his self-image of later years by putting them through a ceaseless process of editorial revision. Slang was toned down, rough edges were smoothened, a more "aesthetic" tack was taken, and tamer new poems were added. Toward the end of his life, wondering how far this process had actually gone, Whitman would find himself asking whether his old-age writings were still "consonant" with the spirit of the original *Leaves of Grass*.[3] On the other hand, he refused to forswear his earlier poetry or the principles upon which it had been based.

His persistence in going on with his poetry and attempting to create his reading audience for it, despite all the old problems now compounded by the paralysis and other physical disabilities which intensified his isolation, was remarkable. The story of Whitman the literary professional during the three remaining decades of his life, during which time most of his contemporaries, major and minor, either died or ceased to write for the public, is in most respects a continuation of that of the pre–Civil War years. It is a story of troubled relations with printers and publishers, of resort to private publication when commercial publication was impossible, of small editions and small sales, of accusations of piracy and of nonpayment of royalties, of reviews often hostile and uncomprehending mixed with occasional praise and eulogy, of various promotional campaigns managed by himself or by his few but loyal followers. Whitman would pass into, and usually just as quickly out of, publishing agreements in this period with such respectable publishers as the Roberts Brothers and Osgood of Boston and the Bunces of New York; attempts to place his works with such major publishers as George Carleton of New York, James Fields of Boston, and J. B. Lippincott of Philadelphia would fail. Fields, who was not unsympathetic to Whitman, expressed the hesitations of nineteenth-century publishers generally in explaining his own reluctance to publish Whitman: "From mere considerations of policy, I wouldn't put our names to a first edition of Byron or even the Bible. When Walt Whitman has become a standard book like them, as I suppose he will, any firm will be glad to publish him."[4] For the most part, Whitman was a self-publisher during the 1860s and 1870s, overseeing and selling his own works on either a small-scale mail order or subscription basis. Finally in 1882, he was able to make a permanent arrangement with the young Philadelphia publisher David McKay, then only at the very beginning of his distinguished career, for bringing out the works of his last decade.

Even through years of genuine suffering, Whitman staunchly refused to accept the kind of commonsensical conclusion put forth by John Stuart Mill in his *Autobiography* that "the writings by which one can live are not the writings which themselves live, and are never those in which the writer does his best." Despite his best efforts, Whitman was never to become a "standard" or even a widely accepted author during his lifetime; his failure to become so hurt him deeply. Not even the homage paid him in Camden by distinguished visitors from overseas or the plaudits from foreign critics could compensate him for his sense of public failure. In recoil, he began in the late 1860s to fabricate the myth that he was completely ignored, even conspired against, by the American literary establishment. Blaming the establishment, of course, was easier than blaming the people, something which Whitman was unable and unwilling to do. In truth, however, it was never with Whitman, as Melville feared it would be with himself, "Down goes his body and up flies his name."[5] Whitman's name and his poems, articles, and squibs were to appear in American papers and magazines far more often in the postwar period than previously; and the question of his popularity was to become so much a public issue that one contemporary newspaper was to state the matter aptly in 1878 in calling Whitman "one of the most renowned unknowns living."[6] Or as another contemporary newspaper was to claim in a review of the well-publicized Osgood edition of *Leaves of Grass*, "The celebrity of this phenomenal poet bears a curious disproportion to the circulation of his works."[7]

The credit for making the issue of Whitman's reputation into a national, even an international, cause belonged in large part to him and to his loyal band of followers, acting with or without his direction but always with his blessing. They stood guard over his name so relentlessly before his critics that the phenomenon of Whitmaniacs became recognized even during the last decades of their master's life. Their persistent, often exorbitant efforts on his behalf were to goad Bayard Taylor, speaking in 1876 during the *West Jersey Press* affair, to state the belief common among many of Whitman's detractors that "no man in this country has ever been so constantly and skillfully advertised by his disciples as Walt Whitman."[8] Even a reasonable, fair-minded man such as Edmund Stedman, who admired Whitman's poetry, was appalled by the ferocity and extravagance of Whitman's and his followers' promotional efforts. Likewise, the normally equable William Dean Howells was to confess to Stedman that he was "tired of the whole Whitman business."[9] But the Whitman business did not go away; it only intensified during the poet's life. As a result of his and his supporters' combined efforts, aided also by the diminishing shock of his originality and changing patterns of thinking and taste, Whitman's position gradually improved during the last several decades of his life. By the time of his death, his critical reputation was approaching a point of solidification.

But the great breakthrough with the general reading public for which he never entirely ceased to hope was not to come in the nineteenth century. Emerson, Thoreau, Burroughs, Gosse, Wilde, Swinburne, W. Rossetti, Symonds, Buchanan, Dowden, and Carpenter might have read him with excitement, pleasure, even awe; but his more general acceptance remained elusive. An American Pushkin he was never to be. This phenomenon was well analyzed by a writer in the November 5, 1881, issue of the *Critic,* a periodical sympathetic to him, in the course of a review of the newly issued Osgood edition of *Leaves of Grass*:

> One great anomaly of Whitman's case has been that while he is an aggressive champion of democracy and of the working-man, in a broad sense of the term working-man, his admirers have been almost exclusively of a class the furthest possibly removed from that which labors for daily bread by manual work. Whitman has always been truly caviare to the multitude. It was only those that knew much of poetry and loved it greatly who penetrated the singular shell of his verses and rejoiced in the rich, pulpy kernel.
>
> . . . As he stands complete in "Leaves of Grass," in spite of all the things that regard for the decencies of drawing-rooms and families may wish away, he certainly represents, as no other writer in the world, the struggling, blundering, sound-hearted, somewhat coarse, but still magnificent vanguard of Western civilization that is encamped in the United States of America. He avoids the cultured few. He wants to represent, and does in his own strange way represent, the lower middle stratum of humanity. But, so far, it is not evident that his chosen constituency cares for, or has even recognized him. Wide readers are beginning to guess his proportions.

A similar observation was to be drawn by numerous other contemporary writers, some far less close or charitable to him; and Whitman himself, as he could not otherwise have been, was acutely aware of the phenomenon.[10] He had proclaimed himself so often and volubly to be the national poet as to have left himself vulnerable to the incongruity between his claims and his public reception. But more than the public inconsistency, the private frustration was difficult to bear. His very breeding and temperament, not to mention the efforts and ambitions of years of work, protested against his failure; and he must have needed all of what he once called his "immense bufferism" to have held himself up against it.[11] Little wonder that he spent so much time in inglorious pursuit of scapegoats. And little wonder that he reacted so strongly to his reviews, which he read, clipped, and kept scattered around him in his room to his dying day in loose piles and scrapbooks. For a writer who had invested so deeply and inventively in the ideal of reader reception, popular or otherwise, those reviews were to have been the proof that his country had "absorbed" him fittingly.

How did Whitman react in his later years to his failure? His response was as complicated and self-contradictory as was his personality. On the one hand, he courted the good favor of people, such as Tennyson, whom he would earlier have dismissed simply as "dudes of literature." Whitman had always had a deeply ingrained mixture of feelings of inferiority and superiority toward men of learning and cultivation greater than his own, an ambivalence which normally put him on his guard in addressing them. He never overcame this mix of attitudes, which accounts in part for the gaping inconsistency in his formal evaluations of their merits; but his own drift toward respectability led him increasingly in his later years to a public flirtation with them. A visit from Wilde, a greeting from Tennyson, a phrase from Ruskin became endorsements to be used in his ongoing, self-publicizing campaign. On the other hand, he continued to long for a more visceral reception by the common man and woman, even though his post–1860 poetry shows a declining preoccupation with the cultivation of this relationship.

Despite all his disappointments, his instincts for patronage by the many, rather than by the few, remained strong. He never retreated completely from his earlier insights into the changing nature of patronage in his time or from the realization that his own career would be a test case for the status of the American writer as democrat. Horace Greeley, with whom Whitman was compared as often as with any of his contemporaries, once wrote something on this subject which, to my mind, bears interestingly on the issue of Whitman's status as a democratic writer. He noted that the writer's dedication to his patron was no longer in the nineteenth century the essential act it had once been:

> And thus it chanced that the *dedication* of books, now so absurd and unmeaning, had once a real force and significance . . . The Dedication, then, was the author's public and formal acknowledgment of his obligation to his patron, – his avowal that the credit of the work ought to be divided between them, – just as to-day the inventor of a mechanical improvement, and the capitalist who supplies the money wherewith to perfect and secure it, often take out a patent jointly. But the Art of Printing, and the general diffusion of knowledge and literary appetite, have abolished patrons, by abolishing the necessity which evoked them; so that there is now but one real patron, The Public, and nearly all dedications to particular individuals are affected, antiquated, and unmeaning.[12]

Greeley, whose own rise from the farm nearly to the White House was a by-product of the printing revolution he was here talking about, was basically correct in the main line of his thinking. But dedications were not yet dead. Instead of being directed to an individual patron, they were increasingly directed to the democratic public, the new patron of American letters. In this regard, I think of Hawthorne's continuing string of Prefaces addressed to the reader or of Melville's various invocations in his novels as profoundly difficult, creative attempts by the nineteenth-century writer, in Hawthorne's words, to "stand in some true relation with his audience."[13]

Whitman, of course, had been drawing the communicatory lines between writer and reader in his original way ever since the 1855 *Leaves of Grass*. In his earliest editions, he had taken the question of readership so far, I have claimed, as to have incorporated it into his new poetics, treating reader-writer relations as simultaneously a literary and an extraliterary phenomenon. By the late 1850s, however, he had begun to retreat from this reader-in-the-text strategy, and this retreat continued for the remainder of his career. In the last three decades of his career, making poetry out of the idea of persona and reader as "two souls interchanging" became an increasingly uncommon practice; moreover, in numerous instances he would subsequently edit out such passages from his early poems.[14]

Just the same, he continued to invest a considerable portion of his energies after 1860 in pursuit of the reader. If less went into the poems themselves, more went into the external means of their presentation and into the advocacy of their reception. For purposes of self-promotion, the old fascination with the photographic process served Whitman particularly well in his later years. In the period after the Civil War, Whitman began the practice of sending out his picture to friends and readers, often in combination with, and as an extension of, his printed book. "My work is extremely personal," he told an 1876 interviewer, "rightly considered so – and on the fly-leaf of each volume I have put my photograph with my own hand."[15] The selection of portraits for later editions of *Leaves of Grass* remained, as ever, a major creative decision, a key, in his mind, to the manner of his self-presentation. A new strategy of a similar sort was his policy of sending out his later editions with his autograph appended: "as, first, I here and now, / Signing for Soul and Body, set to them my name, / Walt Whitman." Mailings of reviews, articles, poems, pictures, and other forms of memorabilia became the common reward of friends and supporters on the Whitman mailing list.

His most ambitious attempts to define his relations with the public, however, were in the various prefatory pieces he continued to attach to later editions of *Leaves of Grass*. With Whitman, the preface was designed to explain the purpose of his writing both to himself and to his reader; the logic of his authorial position had normally presupposed the mutuality of self-discovery. It was here, therefore, that Whitman was most particularly intent to put or keep the reader in the text, treating him or her to the one-to-one address he had used in his early poems. Often, the most important thoughts of his prefaces were those which could not have been expressed except as addresses to the reader reading: "The reader

will always have his or her part to do, just as much as I have had mine.
I seek less to state or display any theme or thought, and more to bring
you, reader, into the atmosphere of the theme or thought – there to
pursue your own flight."[16]

He was to work away on and off throughout the rest of his life on
the formulation of the supreme statement of his poetic purpose in *Leaves
of Grass* but with particular urgency during the 1860s, by which time,
the years of his most intense creativity already behind him, he was looking to define his achievement. The most sustained product of this ambition was the series of musings, alternately in prose and verse, which
he unsuccessfully attempted over the course of the decade to cohere into
the final preface to *Leaves of Grass*. The manuscripts in which he worked
over these musings, one of the most revealing batches of his papers as
to his method of work, offer an unobstructed view of Whitman's manner
of thinking and composing at this stage of his life. One can see in them
how the same thoughts and ideas, expressed in lines and stanzas which
changed little except for their order or phraseology, were worked over
and over in Whitman's mind for years, as Whitman punctiliously re-
combined parts in the search for the perfect whole. He appropriately
thought of this preface as his "Inscription: To the Reader at the Entrance
of Leaves of Grass," with himself stationed at the meeting point between
life and literature, waiting to receive the reader with opened arms. This
final address to the American reader became the "Inscription" to the
fourth edition of *Leaves of Grass*:

> Small is the theme of the following Chant, yet the greatest – namely,
>   ONE'S SELF – that wondrous thing, a simple, separate person.
>   That, for the use of the New World, I sing.
> Man's physiology complete, from top to toe, I sing. Not
>   physiognomy alone, nor brain alone, is worthy for the muse; – I
>   say the Form complete is worthier far. The female equally with the
>   male, I sing.
> Nor cease at the theme of One's-Self. I speak the word of the
>   modern, the word EN-MASSE.
> My Days I sing, and the Lands – with interstice I knew of helpless
>   War.
> O friend, whoe'er you are, at last arriving hither to commence, I feel
>   through every leaf the pressure of your hand, which I return. And
>   thus upon our journey link'd together let us go.

The familiar Whitman motifs are all there: the individual and the collective, man and woman, body and soul, art and America. And so, too,
is the familiar Whitman ploy of communicating these themes through
reader involvement. But even the appearance of this statement in print

did not satisfy Whitman, who eventually condensed this inscription into the short programmatic poem, "One's-Self I Sing," which was to become the lead poem to all later editions of *Leaves of Grass*. Slim as it was, it contained the kernel of his thinking about the dichotomy in his society between the individual (the "simple separate person") and the democratic whole (the "En-masse").

From its beginning, his *Leaves of Grass* career had been a continuous attempt to provide a creative answer to this duality, to locate the individual – himself – in the national collective. One of his most ambitious attempts to provide an answer was the series of essays he worked on separately during the late–1860s before publishing them collectively in 1870 as *Democratic Vistas*. Even in the book's final form, the formal and intellectual division in Whitman's mind between "democracy" and "personalism" was still evident. So, too, were his accordant fears for the nation and for the individual. Of the former he was to say in that book with great truth, "The fear of conflicting and irreconcilable interiors, and the lack of a common skeleton, knitting all close, continually haunts me."[17] No doubt, the Civil War vividly demonstrated to him the living danger of that thought, although in truth his instincts long antedated the lessons taught by the war. As for the modern individual, he also feared the danger, if taken too far, of the "centripetal isolation of a human being in himself."[18]

Even against the changing context of postwar America with its booming economy, sprawling vitality, and rampant corruption, Whitman was still prescribing the same recipe he had for years prescribed for the national ills: literature. This was the third variable in his thinking, and it naturally became the subject of the third and concluding part of his *Vistas*. Not since the 1855 Preface had he spoken so forcefully about the redeeming force of a national literature. But unlike in 1855, the time for such talk, even by his peers, was past. Contemporary writers had abandoned the national camp and were moving to more regional subjects or more overtly realistic modes of writing, and Whitman was left the rare writer who kept to the old nationalist territory and rationale. If there was a transformation in Whitman, it was primarily that he adhered to the old ideas and themes with an ever-stiffening faith and that he chose to state his position more frequently in prose than in verse.

With his country changing and writers going off in new directions, Whitman remained staunchly what he had been in the fifties: the writer in search of connection. The very cast of his imagination shows the impress of this idea: his constant imagining of himself standing at the center of the crowd, his love of the ferry, his fascination with the strand of beach between land and sea, his enthusiasm for the transcontinental railroad and the transatlantic telegraph cable, his longing for a "passage to India." This quest for connection he was to describe best in a poem of the 1860s which I understand as a model of his conception of the creative artist:

> A noiseless patient spider,
> I mark'd where on a little promontory it stood isolated,
> Mark'd how to explore the vacant vast surrounding,
> It launch'd forth filament, filament, filament, out of itself,
> Ever unreeling them, ever tirelessly speeding them.
>
> And you O my soul where you stand,
> Surrounded, detached, in measureless oceans of space,
> Ceaselessly musing, venturing, throwing, seeking the spheres to
>   connect them,
> Till the bridge you will need be form'd, till the ductile anchor hold,
> Till the gossamer thread you fling catch somewhere, O my soul.
>
> ("A Noiseless Patient Spider")

Whitman was that irreducibly singular, sphere-leaping soul, dropping himself into the void held only by the ceaseless "filament, filament, filament" of his art. He had begun his *Leaves of Grass* career by throwing out his filament to the nation of readers he presupposed, and that remained the common thread of his thinking about his poetry throughout the entirety of his life.

Now, it is one thing to speak of Whitman as the poet of connection; it is quite another to unravel the complexities, at times even the contradictions, surrounding his theory and practice of poetry as communication. I can most vividly explain what I mean by retelling the story of Whitman's relations with Anne Gilchrist, the widow of the Blake biographer Alexander Gilchrist. Upon coming across *Leaves of Grass* for the first time in 1870, Gilchrist was as close an approximation to Whitman's ideal reader as he was ever to have. She read him closely, actively, and enthusiastically – too much so for his comfort. To the pressure of his flesh-become-the-word literary strategy, she applied the counterpressure of her own. When Whitman was foolish enough to send her a ring, she responded by reversing one of his favorite figures: "O the precious letter, bearing to me the living touch of your hand vibrating through and through me as I feel the pressure of the ring that pressed your flesh and now will press mine so long as I draw breath... Perhaps it will yet be given us to see each other, to brave the last stage of this journey side by side, hand in hand."[19]

The shock with which Whitman responded when Gilchrist offered him her hand, as it were, from over the Atlantic is one of the most amusing incidents in the Whitman record; and it is also one of the most revealing, separating as nothing else apparently could the man from the persona. Being the poet of connection was one thing; subjecting himself to the marriage tie was quite another. Her offer of love shocked him to a degree of self-understanding he was not always capable of reaching: the "actual" Walt Whitman, he tried to persuade her, was not the persona of the poems. "Dear friend," he had felt compelled the previous year to write her, "let me warn you somewhat about myself – and yourself also. You must not construct such an unauthorized and imaginary ideal Figure, and call it W. W. and so devotedly invest your loving nature in it. The actual W. W. is a very plain personage, and entirely unworthy such devotion."[20]

Who then was the "real," the "actual" Walt Whitman? If Whitman was ever successful in any of his rhetorical devices, it was surely in this: in confusing the distinction between his life and his art. Years of posing, posturing, and identifying have resulted in obscuring the fact for his time and for ours that there was more distance between author and persona than Whitman, his friends, and his early readers and critics were often able to see. Formulations such as his own "who touches this, touches a man" or Moncure Conway's "he is clearly his Book" were both profoundly true and profoundly untrue. Whitman may have earned the right to use the royal "we" in speaking for "my Book and I," but in truth he was no more interchangeable with his book than he was with his reader. The upsetter of the social conventions in the poetry was the good citizen and loyal family man of real life; the boon companion of mankind, the solitary walker and singer of Brooklyn.

The Whitman drawn for us by the biographical tradition from John Burroughs and Bliss Perry to Gay Wilson Allen and Paul Zweig was a many-sided man of extreme moods and swirling emotions. One of the most convincing portraits of Whitman was that sketched by Edward Carpenter, the fond but critical observer of Whitman in his later years, who was struck by the flagrant contradictions he saw in the man: "Far down too there were clearly enough visible the same strong and contrary moods, the same strange omnivorous egotism, controlled and restrained by that wonderful genius of his for human affection and love." And during a later visit: "I am impressed more than ever with W.'s contradictory, self-willed, tenacious, obstinate character, strong and even extreme moods, united with infinite tenderness, wistful love, and studied tolerance."[21] The riddle which Whitman has presented to his biographers has its additional fascination for also having been one to Whitman himself: "Why even I myself I often think know little or nothing of my real life" ("When I Read the Book").

Out of the attempt to hold together the extremes of his personality came the quality which Whitman was to see as his phrenologically sanctioned "cautiousness." He was a man often on guard, onstage and off.

His comings and goings, entrances and exits, were often carefully planned. He disliked interviews, shunned demonstrative people, and, for all the rhetoric of his poetry, preferred to keep a cautious distance between himself and his actual reader. Ellen O'Connor, the wife of his best friend and herself in love with him, knew in opposition to her own wishes that the handsome, virile man who had the free run of her house was an untouchable: "You could not afford to love other than as the Gods love; that is to love *every body,* but no one enough to be made unhappy, or to lose your balance."[22]

As she well knew, Whitman was too careful in his day-to-day affairs to endanger that precious balance; he fairly bristled with defenses. He kept his own hours. He kept his own room. He kept his thoughts largely to himself. His good friend John Burroughs once commented of Whitman's reticence, "Walt never talked of himself, and we didn't expect it of him. He wasn't given to confiding things, as one woman confides to another. It wouldn't have been in character."[23] On certain subjects, such as his writing, he was notoriously secretive; as his closest confidant, William O'Connor, was to say, "getting information out of him respecting his career or the theory of his poems, that is the eight labor of Hercules."[24] Those who knew him well, knew he was not to be pressed. It was only with Traubel, with the onset of old-age garrulity, that he eased up the tight censorship of his personal life. This tight-lipped, stubbornly private person would not easily have been recognized as the effusive media "personality" into which he made himself for the readers of newspapers and in which guise he was described in the obituary notice of the New York *Times*: "The old poet who for so many years has made the public his confidant during the slow stages of his departure from the world is now at rest."[25]

No doubt, he had his reasons for standing guard over himself; he knew his vulnerability well. The relatively few deep relationships he conducted during his lifetime, mostly with young men of the working class, almost invariably ended in unpleasantness and caused him intense pain. He saw the pattern often enough to have learned to sense its inevitability. The young soldiers, the Peter Doyles and Harry Staffords, even his favorite brother Jeff, passed into and then out of his life, while only a few faces remained constantly near him. Those were primarily the faces of family members, which was one reason for the enduring strength of the family tie in his thinking. But even his family's emotional support could never have been more than a partial source of satisfaction for Whitman, who well knew and suffered from the lack of intersection between his family circle and the circle of his poetry. This hidden spring of resentment was the source of the quick show of anger which seeped into his tough characterization of brother George, the war hero and most "solid" member of the family: "George believes in pipes, not in poems."[26] In fact, the recollection of his family's inability to appreciate his work was to cause one of his most open and unpremeditated shows of emotion in all his multivolume dealings with Traubel.[27]

The kind of family he did not have in New York he came to believe during the war decade he had found in Washington in the home of the O'Connors. They and their friends gave him his first, full-fledged experience of a social circle of intelligent, literate people warmly supportive of him and his work. But even this did not fully satisfy his immense need for contact. If anything could have, it would have been his daily routine of visits in the sprawling, overcrowded army hospitals of the capital. There, as he moved up and down the aisles between beds, bestowing acts of kindness and gestures of affection on the young men, he found the kind of free and easy, no questions asked and no obligations required, reception he had fantasized about since early manhood. For the first time in his life, he stood, as he had always dreamed, at the center of the human circle. That his reception came to him so naturally and spontaneously – he had originally had no intentions of prolonging his trip to Washington beyond determining the condition of his wounded brother – only intensified the experience: "The experience is a profound one, beyond all else, and touches me personally, egotistically, in unprecedented ways... It is delicious to be the object of so much love and reliance."[28] This sentiment was repeated in several letters and must often have been on his mind. Lingering for years in his memory, it was the immediate reason for his habitual old-age overvaluation of the contribution the Civil War had made to the composition of *Leaves of Grass*.

There is an irony to this: Few of his soldier friends knew, nor did Whitman encourage them to know, that their devoted nurse was also a poet.[29] Nor did many of the workingmen with whom Whitman was most at his ease, nor neighbors and other acquaintances. Whitman was always careful about the manner and style of his self-presentation; he had the knack for knowing how to relate to different kinds of people in different ways. Even people who could reasonably have been expected to know better did not always know with whom they were dealing; the reaction of the fiery Polish expatriate Count Adam Gurowski – "My Gott, I did not know that he was such a poet" – expressed the surprise that a fair number of his acquaintances would feel in making a similar discovery.[30]

Whitman liked to speak of the "comrade life" as a higher good than the life of artistic achievement, and doubtless he had his need for thinking so.[31] Formulating the calamus sentiment had been one way, a truly ingenious way, of merging this ideal for human life with his art. But even during the Civil War period of his life, years of intense fraternity in which he came closest to making the ideal of comradely love an integral part of his own existence, the aspirant poet of the people never succeeded in integrating the ideal of his art with the ideal of his life. It was characteristic of Whitman at that time that when he made his daily rounds of the army hospitals, he was given to distributing to the soldiers little tokens of favor – fruits, candies, pocket money, an occasional kiss – but not the "love-buds" of his own poetry. Even during the single most intensive year of his hospital service, it was the making of his poems which he still thought of as "the work of my life."[32]

There would have been nothing especially unusual about this situation – of how many modern writers cannot the same thing be said – had Whitman not spent so much force in asserting that the dichotomy between life and literature need not exist. Seldom has a writer argued the point more insistently and, in the process, invested more of his being in this claim than did the Whitman of the early editions, in which he continually treated the process of making art as analogous to the process of living and figured his persona as passing at will from one to the other. Again and again, here was "Walt" passing through the seams of the book into the arms of the reader: "What the push of reading could not start is started by me personally, is it not?" (1856 version of "Crossing Brooklyn Ferry"). To which the reader's response was to be a rhetorically guaranteed affirmation.

But for all of Whitman's rhetorical skill, this was only one more aspect of his well-cultivated "perfect posturing." Despite the proud assurances and the insistent bravado, Whitman was only one more writer since the beginning of the Romantic era who has needed the fallback of his art to serve him as a compensation for the lack of satisfaction, of completeness, he got from his life. Mrs. O'Connor put this well in writing him, "you have the great out-flow of your pen which saves you from the need of personal love as one feels it who has no such resource."[33] Whitman would have stubbornly denied this claim, but she had her point. The free-flowing personal love he had often theorized about in his poems ran a course increasingly opposite the direction of his personal affairs. His later years could not be said to be happy, convivial ones; his New York-Brooklyn acquaintanceships gradually thinned, his Civil War friendships, on which he had placed his highest hopes, faded away to a few, far-flung correspondences, and finally the circle of his life found its center in a small, isolated house in Camden.

I hope the point is clear: Whitman "coming personally to you" in life and in poetry was two separate, if related, phenomena. We know as much as we are ever likely to know about those to whom the poet came – or did not come – in real life. But to whom did Whitman come in his art? Who was the "you" of Whitman's poems? It is never simple or easy, if it is possible at all, to identify the addressee of a poem; but in the case of Whitman, the question is too fundamental to go unexamined. Was he addressing an audience of men or women, of young or old, of the working or the middle class – to mention some of the categorizations which typically came to his mind? Given Whitman's desire to make his poetry inclusive as poetry had never been before by making it encompass all demographic as well as all geographical sectors of the country, it is not surprising that there are occasional addresses to each of these groups dutifully scattered through his poetry. But in all likelihood, Whitman never paid any of these groups, not even the young men of the working class, with whom he felt a special rapport, anything but an incidental regard when he composed the vast majority of his poems.

A more significant question about the identity of Whitman's "you" is this: Was Whitman addressing an audience which he conceived of as singular or plural? Unlike the previous question, this one can be answered with some assurance that Whitman himself addressed it with clear and serious artistic thought. At times, to be judged by the reflexive pronoun which occasionally followed it, "you," in Whitman's mind, was singular, which was as his thinking about the unqualified individuality of the reading experience would lead one to expect. And this was in harmony with the dynamics of a typical Whitman poem, which works toward a position of increasing intimacy with its audience of a kind one would naturally assume as being possible only with a single reader. But these things notwithstanding, one is more often than not unsure in reading most or all of a Whitman poem whether Whitman is addressing a singular or a plural audience. This was not by chance; it was the result, rather, of careful forethought and strategizing.

As an English-language writer, Whitman faced the dilemma unknown to writers in other European languages of addressing a "you" whose number was normally indeterminate.[34] Whitman was not only aware of this problem but he was also able, as C. Carroll Hollis has pointed out, to turn a potential dead spot in the language deftly into a source of resonance, playing on this indeterminacy in his poems so as to harmonize what would otherwise have been a dissonance between the individual reader and the nation of readers.[35] For a writer as concerned as was Whitman about the loosening of the organic tie between the individual and society, the indeterminacy of the addressee could be turned into an extremely valuable poetic asset, one which Whitman worked with considerable ability, especially in his early editions.[36] In such poems as "Song of Myself," "A Song for Occupations," "To Think of Time," "Crossing Brooklyn Ferry," and "Song of the Open Road," to mention only a few of the many early poems for which the generalization holds, not only can one not easily pin down the addressee as being a singular or a plural figuration but one is under no obligation to do so, since the underlying logic of the audience address of these poems is all for one and one for all. The "you" he was addressing in such poems was typically an absorptive rather than a specified "you," one which, rather like the catalogues, could take into itself any number of individuals or groups.[37] So that when Whitman invites his "you" to partake of the fullness of art and life, he can include simultaneously in this invitation both the individual and the national collective, of which each individual is the potential center. Not every poet would know how to plant a single kiss, as did Whitman, on a thousand brows.

What allowed him to work this strategy as well as he did was the abstract character of his addressee; names, faces, specific details were not only unnecessary but counterproductive. In fact, the single most intriguing hint as to his thinking and imagining about the identity of his "you" is to be found in the apposition he often tacked on afterwards: "you whoever you are." Whitman's "you," in all likelihood, was "whoever you are." The paradox becomes immediately clear: the poet coming personally to "you," the poet saving his kiss especially for "you," the poet inviting "you" to join him on the open road was addressing an unknown, untouchable, hypothesized "you." This was, of course, as the limitations of print and audience, or more exactly, of modern print and modern audience, necessarily dictated. In fact, Whitman, the ex-printer who claimed to "pass so poorly" through the medium of print, was one of the most extreme overreachers of such limitations that the print world has ever seen. Although he had been quick to foresee the revolutionary changes coming with the new printing technology and the changing character of his society and keen to plan his advance upon the American public through the agency of the new technology, there was a contradiction between the personalized poetic relations he was cultivating in his poems and the realities of modern print culture. True, a writer of Whitman's time could reach a larger and more broadly based audience than could writers of previous generations, but he could do so only by communicating across the increasing distance between himself and his readers as their society grew in size and heterogeneity. In these cultural circumstances, Whitman's odd-sounding "you whoever you are" struck just the right note; with its peculiar combination of the intimate and the remote, it captured in a phrase the paradoxical task of Whitman's poetry, one which only a writer of the finest rhetorical skills could have hoped to carry off convincingly: to personalize an impersonal audience. Ironically, none but the most unsuccessful or private author, he most unable or unwilling to reach the broad reading public, could afford to self-publish and orient his writing to a specific "you."

One more time, let the too eager biographical reader of Whitman's poems beware: He who would hunt for a specific lover or personality in or behind Whitman's "you" looks in vain. In evaluating Whitman's manner of address, one should never underestimate the extent of Whitman's own personal caginess and elusiveness. To read the drafts of his poems and letters is to become aware of how manipulated was the degree of intimacy Whitman worked into and out of his literary and epistolary addresses. Judged by the number of times he worked over his address to the reader in his notebooks and trial drafts, it was often a subject for negotiations between Whitman and himself, negotiations which continued into and through the various editions of the printed texts. And even in the finality of print, it is seldom clear what degree of intimacy he wished to establish between himself and his reader. But one thing is certain: People who confused the relations of the poetry for the relations of real life were to be held firmly away at arm's length. In Anne Gilchrist's case, only the distance of the Atlantic Ocean would have sufficed, had Whitman had his choice. And what was her mistake, after all, but doing what one of his most insinuating poems insisted that its reader do: Touch this book and touch a man. Little did she know that Whitman would shrink from such real life contact.

In short, Whitman's "you" is best understood as what, in fact, it could only have been: a hard-worked literary device; I know of no writer who ever worked it any harder than did Whitman. And thus it is, finally, in his poetry and with his pen that Whitman did his speaking and his coming personally to "you." This is another way of stating Harold Bloom's proposition about the meeting of persona and reader in Whitman's poetry: "The poetry of the 'real Me,' intricate and forlorn, is addressed to the 'real Me' of the American reader."[38] Private personalities cast aside, Whitman felt freest to express himself to the reader and did so most ingeniously in his poems. It is here that one is to find Whitman at his greatest; and it is here, in the end, that one must come to evaluate the magnitude and limitations, successes and failures, of his achievement.

In assessing that achievement, I would like to pursue Whitman's own thinking in considering his poems – their ideas, their content, even their conception of the reading process – as inseparable from the context of democracy. In this regard, F. O. Matthiessen's term for describing the literary undertaking of Whitman and his co-workers at a distance as being the creation, in two senses, of a "literature for democracy" seems as appropriate today as it was in Matthiessen's own day.[39] This idea was absolutely central to Whitman's thinking about poetry. For him, "democracy" and "America" were, as he once said, "convertible terms"; and whether taken separately or together, they were key operational terms in his conceptual vocabulary of poetry.[40]

The free convertibility of these terms and the tendency to identify them with his own poetry often led Whitman into a circle of logical reasoning, but before I explain what I mean by this, I would like to juxtapose Whitman's thinking about democracy and literature with that of Alexis de Tocqueville, whose analysis of midnineteenth-century America defined with unusual clarity the territory occupied by Whitman and the writers of his time. In a key chapter of *Democracy in America,* Tocqueville identified the idea of "individualism" as a novel phenomenon accompanying the advent of democracy: "Individualism is a mature and calm feeling, which disposes each member of the community to sever himself from the mass of his fellows and to draw apart with his family and his friends, so that after he has formed a little circle of his own, he willingly leaves society at large to itself." The result, for Tocqueville, was an unhealthy swing of authority from the society to the individual: "Thus not only does democracy make every man forget his ancestors, but it hides his descendants and separates his contemporaries from him; it throws him back forever upon himself alone and threatens in the end to confine him entirely within the solitude of his own heart."[41]

This was a situation which a more self-sufficient writer, such as Emily Dickinson, might have been able to tolerate; for Whitman, however, it was unacceptable.[42] Unwilling to restrict his range to the "centripetal isolation of a human being in himself," he had reached out to the nation through the mediacy of his newspapers in the 1840s and thereafter, once his thinking had matured, through that of his poems. Aloof and elusive as he was by nature, he had devoted his finest artistic thoughts and powers to expressing his individuality in such a way as to write himself – his own name, personality, and ambitions – at large into America. But the script of *Leaves of Grass* was written not exclusively for one but more often for two actors, one a richly fictionalized version of Walt Whitman and the other a no less richly fictionalized personality lacking face or features other than the vague lineaments of modern man or woman. Of that fictional "you whoever you are" he asked and promised no less than he did of "Walt Whitman," stating his proposition perhaps most boldly in "By Blue Ontario's Shore": "The whole theory of the universe is directed to one single individual – namely, to You." Under Whitman's dispensation, the world was his and his readers' simply for the taking.

Such a formulation, put into practice in his poems, placed unavoidably heavy demands upon their presupposed readers, and there are signs that Whitman and his circle were at least intermittently aware of this. John Burroughs, for one, often spoke this view: "Whitman always aimed to make his reader an active partner with him in his poetic enterprise."[43] Or again: "He makes extraordinary demands upon the reader, undoubtedly; he tries him as no other modern poet does or dares."[44] And as Whitman himself was to tell Traubel in one of his numerous remarks of the sort on the subject, "All my poems require to be read again and again – three, four, five, six times – before they enter into the reader, are grasped – filter their way to the undersoil."[45] Whatever the critical insight of these statements, they fail to state the price that such a view would entail for a poet of Whitman's nationalist aspirations: a poetry which was not only difficult but immensely challenging for its readers. No less than Melville with his pose of conviviality, Whitman with his pose of camaraderie was making the most extreme demands upon his readers, asking of them no less than that they rethink their existence with him.

Had he been thinking objectively and dispassionately, of course, he would have known that this was anything but a reliable formula for popularity. But then again, not only did such thinking lie remote from the sources of Whitman's creative imagining but Whitman was far from being able to see the circularity involved in his thinking about his relations with his readers and his country. That thinking went like this: His writing had been called out by the conditions of American democracy, it transformed those conditions into acts of poetry, and those resultant poems, in turn, were to be "absorbed" by the new generation of American readers. This was the logic underlying the concluding statement of his 1855 Preface that "the proof of a poet is that his country absorbs him as affectionately as he has absorbed it." If that statement was also a personal prediction, as I can only suppose it was, it was the most problematic one he made in his career.

The proof should have been before his eyes. A history of scattered sales, few readers, and frequently hostile or obtuse reviews was an indication of how specious his reasoning had been. That reasoning was weakest precisely where it touched upon the relations between writers and readers. Whitman had never scrupulously questioned his assumptions in this regard, which is why he seems never to have appreciated, early or late, how complicated and difficult might be the task of the American writer. Tocqueville had foreseen otherwise, and what he predicted had important implications for Whitman. For if his analysis of the consequences of equality and individuality for democratic culture was correct and the democratic writer was forced to write from a position of a diminishing number of shared themes, concepts, and myths and from a narrowing basis of community, then what was to be the basis of shared assumptions between a democratic writer with nationalist aspirations, such as Whitman, and his reading audience? The young Whitman of the pre–Leaves of Grass years had felt in his bones the force of the cultural situation Tocqueville was talking about and was ready and waiting in 1855 with the poetic answer: "And what I assume you shall assume." But attempts to draw freely on that statement were inevitably to lead him to complications.

In truth, Whitman was far less able to draw on a body of shared assumptions than he commonly believed. To a certain extent, this was simply a matter of personalities; how many Americans of his time were willing to give over their hearts and souls to a man of Whitman's unconventional personality, views, and ideas? If Whitman felt himself unbearably cramped while sitting in the parlors of middle-class homes, how would their residents have felt being yanked out of comfortable circumstances and led out onto Whitman's open road? On a deeper cultural level, though, Whitman was finding himself in the situation that Tocqueville had predicted of a diminishing number of shared symbols and themes available to writers in a decentralized culture. No less than other contemporary writers, Whitman failed badly in his attempts to make direct poetic use of the public realm. His occasional and patriotic poems were as bad as any poems he ever wrote in his maturity; it is a real shock to hear a poet who could sound so like a master of poetic voice in poems such as "Song of Myself" and "Crossing Brooklyn Ferry" sound so like a charlatan in his declaredly public poems. Only the purest self-deception could have led Whitman to believe that he could be the singer of the Civil War, the American Institute, the Centennial Exposition, or any other public gathering or national event.

The public sphere never sat quite as neatly on the private sphere as Whitman, or at least as Whitman the national poet, had theorized. In truth, the inexact fit between the private and the public was always to put Whitman at his unease; but it was also one of the factors which drove him to some of his most inspired creative thinking and imagining about the meeting in his time between the individual and society. Unable to meet his readers on the parade grounds of his society, Whitman plotted to meet them on the more tenable grounds of the public made private (and then remade public) in his audience-address poems. If the reader could not come to it, Whitman would have the public sphere come to the reader:

> The President is up there in the White House for you . . . . it is not
>   you who are here for him,
> The Secretaries act in their bureaus for you . . . . not you here for
>   them,
> The Congress convenes every December for you,
> Laws, courts, the forming of states, the charters of cities, the going
>   and coming of commerce and mails are all for you.
>   ("A Song for Occupations")

For a poet unable to take anything as fixed fact, this was a far more effective and viable way than would have been provided by any more conventional technique for bringing about the merge between the private and the public. But such thinking and strategizing had its price.

The price – the considerable price, I would emphasize – of this view was its devaluation of the objective and the traditional in favor of a radically subjective view of life and culture. In its search for a least common denominator which sacrificed nothing of the dignity or intelligence of "the average man of to-day," Whitman's poetry made that individual, with himself and sometimes through himself, the final arbiter of value and taste. Lest this view degenerate into some form of solipsism, Whitman had insisted on the representativeness of his "I" and "you," the abstractions upon which he balanced his poems. In truth, such thinking made Whitman perform a delicate balancing act in his poems, so slim was their fulcrum and so weighty the burden he placed upon it. But given the cultural circumstances of his society, this was the only way Whitman could make his poetry into the instrumentality he desired for affecting his readers and his society in fundamental ways.

He applied his finest powers to this task; and his achievement, in my opinion, was to have made his poetry into what Harry Levin once called, in a different context, "the richest and most sensitive of human institutions – not a two-dimensional page in a book, but a rounded organism embracing the people by and for whom it was created."[46] *Leaves of Grass* is an American institution in this sense; but it is one which, with its sharply anti-institutional, antinomian edges, could exist only in a complicated relation to its society. There was a frailty of connection inherent in the terms of its conception which reflected Whitman's own tenuous connection to his polity and people. The artist swinging freely through time and space held only by the filament of his art was a figure of the most extreme looseness, as was the conception of the reader free to rethink for himself or herself any and all of the basic conventions of the society.

The most it allowed Whitman to hope for, in a manner of speaking, was to effect a situation for readers parallel to the one he imagined for children in "There Was a Child Went Forth": a myriad of separate instances of readers going forth into the pages of *Leaves of Grass,* each to discover individually his or her separate identity. This was what he meant when he wrote in a self-review of 1860 about the role his poems were meant to perform: "The egotistical outset, 'I celebrate myself,' and which runs in spirit through so much of the volume, speaks for him or her reading it precisely the same as for the author, and is invariably to be so applied. Thus the book is a gospel of self-assertion and self-reliance for every American reader – which is the same as saying it is the gospel of Democracy."[47] But Whitman's gospel of democracy, unlike the only other gospel of which he could have conceived for purposes of comparison, rested on no commonly accepted authority, only on that assumed by its simple separate author. Resting on so narrow a base of support and posed in such highly individualized terms, Whitman's bible could do no more than assert a position for each reader, in Richard Fein's term, of his or her "shared separateness."[48]

We do not readily grant any creative writer entry to the category of gospel, not even gospel made over in Whitman's kind of modern, secularized terms. But what do we grant our writers, and what do we expect their works to *do*? I suppose that the answer to that question is necessarily grounded in the cultural circumstances of the responder. Whitman, living in an age of general literacy when the written word had no cultural rivals for domestic, leisure-time activity, was no doubt justified in answering that question more liberally than would poets and readers in America today. I would not wish to claim that Whitman's poems ever effected national purposes or solved national problems; I do believe, however, that they fulfilled his own ambition "to articulate and faithfully express in literary or poetic form, and uncompromisingly, my own physical, emotional, moral, intellectual, and aesthetic Personality, in the midst of, and tallying, the momentous spirit and facts of its immediate days, and of current America – and to exploit that Personality, identified with place and date, in a far more candid and comprehensive sense than any hitherto poem or book."[49] To have done that much, to have done it with unrivaled artistic vision and power, and to have offered that achievement, printed and bound, to his public was already enough for an American to be considered a national poet.

Notes

1. HOMAGE TO THE TENTH MUSE

1. Whitman told Bucke that he spent that summer, as usual, vacationing on Long Island: "When the book aroused such a tempest of anger and condemnation everywhere, . . . I went off to the east end of Long Island, and spent the late summer and all of the fall – the happiest of my life – around Shelter Island and Peconic Bay. Then came back to New York with the confirmed resolution, from which I never afterwards wavered, to go on with my poetic enterprise in my own way, and finish it as well as I could"; Richard Maurice Bucke, *Walt Whitman* (Philadelphia: David McKay, 1883), p. 26. The story sounds good, but it is probably untrue. In all likelihood, Whitman was too worked up that summer to have left *Leaves of Grass* to its unmediated fate. Besides, various events and incidents place him at home at that time. He was writing and placing self-reviews in New York and Brooklyn journals during August and September, and he was at the Rome brothers' printing house in mid-September when Moncure Conway, Emerson's first delegate, came to see him. And then in early October, he would have had to be in New York to pass Emerson's letter of praise to the New York *Tribune* for publication.
2. William Appleton's and others' speeches were reported the next day in the local press; New York *Tribune,* Sept. 28, 1855.
3. Thirty years after its founder's death, G. P. Putnam's Sons would bring out a handsome edition of the *Complete Writings of Walt Whitman,* and seven years after that D. Appleton and Company would publish Whitman's *Complete Prose Works.*
4. New York *Tribune,* Sept. 28, 1855.
5. *American Publishers' Circular and Trade Gazette* 1 (Sept. 29, 1855): 76.
6. New York *Tribune,* Sept. 28, 1855.
7. *American Publishers' Circular and Trade Gazette* 1 (Sept. 29, 1855): 74.
8. New York *Tribune,* Sept. 28, 1855.
9. Ibid.
10. Whitman clipped several pieces from that issue of *Putnam's,* including the review of his book, which he brought together with other reviews for use as advertisements in the second issue of the 1855 *Leaves of Grass.*

11. In Floyd Stovall, ed., *Prose Works 1892* (New York: New York University Press, 1964), II, pp. 681; Brooklyn *Daily Times,* Oct. 6, 1858; repr. in Emory Holloway and Vernolian Schwarz, eds., *I Sit and Look Out* (New York: Columbia University Press, 1932), p. 147.
12. "Grand Buildings in New York," Brooklyn *Daily Times,* June 4, 1857.
13. "Crystal Palace for the World's Fair, 1853," *American Phrenological Journal* 17 (Jan. 1853): 14.
14. "A Backward Glance O'er Travel'd Roads," in Stovall, *Prose Works 1892,* II, p. 714.
15. Ibid., pp. 717–18.
16. In Horace Traubel, ed., *Camden's Compliment to Walt Whitman* (Philadelphia: David McKay, 1889), pp. 64–65.
17. "Our New Press," Brooklyn *Eagle,* Apr. 19, 1847.
18. "Our Twelfth Volume," Brooklyn *Daily Times,* Feb. 28, 1859.

2. THE EVOLUTION OF AMERICAN LITERARY CULTURE, 1820–1850

1. Andrew J. Eaton, "The American Movement for International Copyright, 1837–60," *Library Quarterly* 15 (Apr. 1945): 95–6.
2. Quoted in Frank Luther Mott, *A History of American Magazines,* I (Cambridge, Mass.: Harvard University Press, 1939), p. 218.
3. Arthur L. Ford, *Joel Barlow* (New York: Twayne, 1971), p. 15.
4. "To a New-England Poet," in *The Last Poems of Philip Freneau,* ed. Lewis Leary (New Brunswick, N.J.: Rutgers University Press, 1945), pp. 112–13.
5. *Edinburgh Review* 33 (Jan. 1820): 79.
6. *Edinburgh Review* 34 (Aug. 1820): 160.
7. James Franklin Beard, ed., *The Letters and Journals of James Fenimore Cooper,* I (Cambridge, Mass.: Harvard University Press, 1960), p. 42.
8. William Charvat, *The Profession of Authorship in America, 1800–1870,* ed. Matthew J. Bruccoli (Columbus, Ohio: Ohio State University Press, 1968), p. 75.
9. Donald Sheehan, *This Was Publishing* (Bloomington, Ind.: Indiana University Press, 1952), p. 79.
10. Washington Irving, *Letters,* ed. Ralph M. Aderman, Herbert L. Kleinfield, and Jenifer S. Banks, II (Boston: Twayne, 1979), p. 779.
11. Ben Harris McClary, ed., *Washington Irving and the House of Murray* (Knoxville, Tenn.: University of Tennessee, 1969), p. 52.
12. Aderman et al., *Letters,* II, p. 659.
13. Ibid., p. 818.
14. Washington Irving, *Letters,* ed. Ralph M. Aderman, Herbert L. Kleinfield, and Jenifer S. Banks, I (Boston: Twayne, 1978), p. 670.
15. Pierre Irving, *The Life and Letters of Washington Irving* (New York: G. P. Putnam, 1864), IV, pp. 237–8.
16. James Franklin Beard, ed., *The Letters and Journals of James Fenimore Cooper,* IV (Cambridge, Mass.: Harvard University Press, 1964), p. 164.
17. James Franklin Beard, ed., *The Letters and Journals of James Fenimore Cooper,* II (Cambridge, Mass.: Harvard University Press, 1960), p. 42.

18. Historical Introduction to Cooper, *The Prairies,* ed. James P. Elliott (Albany, N.Y.: State University of New York Press, 1985), p. xvi.

19. Beard, *Letters and Journals of Cooper,* II, pp. 75, 159.

20. William Dean Howells, "The Man of Letters as a Man of Business," in *Literature and Life* (New York: Harper and Brothers, 1911), pp. 1–35.

21. The story appeared in *Graham's* 22 (Jan.–Apr. 1843): 1–18, 89–102, 158–67, 205–13.

22. Charvat, *The Profession of Authorship in America,* p. 83.

23. Cooper received $500, or slightly more than $10 a page, for it; see J. Albert Robbins, "Fees Paid to Authors by Certain American Periodicals, 1840–1850," *Studies in Bibliography* 2 (1949–50): 99.

24. Whitman, though an ardent reader of Cooper's novels, undoubtedly expressed the irritation of many Americans when he editorialized in 1842 that Cooper was "damning himself utterly in the estimation of all sensible men" in waging a vendetta against his journalistic critics; in Joseph Jay Rubin and Charles H. Brown, eds., *Walt Whitman of the "Aurora"* (State College, Pa.: Bald Eagle Press, 1950), p. 121.

25. James D. Wallace, *Early Cooper and His Audience* (New York: Columbia University Press, 1986), p. 171.

26. Beard, *Letters and Journals of Cooper,* IV, p. 464.

27. Luke White, Jr., *Henry William Herbert and the American Publishing Scene, 1831–1858* (Newark, N.J.: Carteret Book Club, 1943), p. 38.

28. Nicholas Trubner, *Bibliographical Guide to American Literature* (1859, London; repr. Detroit, Mich.: Gale, 1966), p. lxxxvi.

29. I take my statistics from the federal Census Reports of the nineteenth century and from the Census Bureau's compendium, *Historical Statistics of the United States,* Bicentennial Edition, 2 vols. (Washington, D.C., 1975).

30. Whitman himself marveled in print about the phenomenal growth of Brooklyn since the days of his apprenticeship: "Some twenty-five years have passed away since then. Twenty-five years! Brooklyn, from a rural village of a few hundred inhabitants, has grown to be a mighty, rich, and populous city – the third in the United States, and evidently destined to be one of the greatest in the world"; "Henry Murphy," Brooklyn *Daily Times,* June 3, 1857.

31. "Nationality in Literature," *Democratic Review* 20 (Mar. 1847): 264.

32. *Edinburgh Review* 31 (Dec. 1818): 144.

33. Samuel Goodrich, *Recollections of a Lifetime* (New York: Miller, Orton and Mulligan, 1856), II, pp. 379–93.

34. *American Catalogue of Books* (London: Sampson Low, Son and Co., 1856), pp. v–vii.

35. "The Book Trade," *American Publishers' Circular and Literary Gazette* 3 (Oct. 24, 1857): 671.

36. "Publishers and Publishing in New York," New York *Tribune,* Mar. 17, 1854.

37. Brooklyn *Daily Times,* July 31, 1858; repr. in Holloway and Schwarz, *I Sit and Look Out,* p. 39.

38. In Mott, *American Magazines,* I, p. 13.

39. Ibid., p. 341.

40. Robert Bonner quoted in Mary Kelley, *Private Woman, Public Stage* (New York: Oxford University Press, 1984), p. 6. Whitman was very much aware of the Bonner phenomenon and commented on it numerous times during his 1857–9 editorship of the Brooklyn *Daily Times,* in whose pages Bonner occasionally advertised. His feelings toward Bonner and the *Ledger* were deeply and powerfully ambivalent. On the one hand, he admired the magnitude of Bonner's popular success:

> In the entire history of newspaper enterprise there never has been an instance of talent anything akin to that displayed by the immortal Bonner. We look upon Bonner (seriously speaking) as one of the greatest men of the day. When he commenced the paper whose reputation is now so widely extended he was a journeyman printer, earning the usual wages of that craft. At present he would not sell his interest in the New York *Ledger* for a *million dollars.* All this has been accomplished by judicious advertising. With the example of the immortal Bonner before them, how can wide-awake business men in every department of business fail to avail themselves of the benefits of advertising?

He also praised the upwardly educative effect of a mass paper such as the *Ledger* on the general public: "The higher class of literati seem infected with a desire to reach the masses. *Vide* [Edward] Everett and the *Ledger.* We are disposed to differ from those papers which regard Everett as having degraded himself by consenting to write for the *Ledger.* To write in the *Ledger* cannot injure Everett's style or lessen his abilities and learning; while on the other hand, it must tend to elevate and improve the *Ledger* and those who read it." But at other times, Whitman was ready to dismiss the *Ledger* as trash: "The New York *Ledger* is a standing proof of the potency of advertising, and the credulity of human nature. For if many thousands of people can be induced to buy a weak, trashy, high-priced, small-sized paper like that, solely from seeing the monotonous nonsense [Bonner's saturation advertising] with which it covers whole pages of the morning papers, then who can estimate the benefit to the tradesman of an intelligible announcement, recommending a really valuable article?" (Brooklyn *Daily Times,* Dec. 22, 1858; Nov. 24, 1858; and Apr. 10, 1858).

41. Jane Tompkins, *Sensational Designs* (New York: Oxford University Press, 1985), p. 125.

42. A small sampling of this critical literature might include the following: "Authorship," *Arcturus* 1 (1842): 9; Evert Duyckinck, "On Writing for the Magazines," *Democratic Review* 16 (May 1845): 455–60; Edgar Allan Poe, "The Pay for Periodical Writing," *Evening Mirror* 1 (Oct. 1844): 2; "Amateur Authors and Small Critics," *Democratic Review* 17 (July 1845): 62–6; "Author-Bookseller," *Democratic Review* 11 (Oct. 1842): 396–412; "Democracy and Literature," *Democratic Review* 11 (Aug. 1842): 196–200; John Inman, "Magazine Literature," *Columbian Magazine* 1 (Jan. 1844): 1–5; William A. Jones, "Criticism in America," *Democratic Review* 15 (Sept. 1844): 245–9; Caroline Kirkland, "Periodical Reading," *Democratic Review* 16 (Jan. 1845): 59–61; Edgar Allan Poe, "Some Secrets of the Magazine Prison-House," *Broadway Journal* (Feb. 15, 1845); "English and American Literature," *Democratic Review* 22 (Mar. 1848): 207–15.

43. "Works of Alexandre Dumas," *North American Review* 56 (Jan. 1843): 110–11.

44. "The International Copyright Question," *Democratic Review* 12 (Feb. 1843): 118.

45. The writer was George Washington Peck, best known for his Pecksniffian attacks on Melville; quoted in John Stafford, *The Literary Criticism of "Young America"* (1952; repr. New York: Russell and Russell, 1967), p. 121.

46. "It is this peculiar feature in the character of the age, the present position and claims of the people, that has given birth to a new and striking application of poetry to life, which may be expressed in the phrase, Poetry for the People"; "Poetry for the People," *Democratic Review* 13 (Sept. 1843): 266.

47. C. Harvey Gardiner, *Prescott and His Publishers* (Carbondale, Ill.: Southern Illinois University Press, 1959), p. 3.

48. Historical Introduction to Cooper, *The Last of the Mohicans,* ed. James Franklin Beard (Albany, N.Y.: State University of New York Press, 1983), p. xxvi.

49. New York *Tribune,* Sept. 28, 1855.

50. My sketch of Harper and Brothers is based primarily on Eugene Exman's two studies, *The Brothers Harper* (New York: Harper and Row, 1965) and *The House of Harper* (New York: Harper and Row, 1967), as well as on the company archives, now deposited at Butler Library, Columbia University.

51. Quoted in Exman, *The Brothers Harper,* p. 232.

52. "Something like an 'Office,'" Brooklyn *Eagle,* Mar. 25, 1846.

53. Walter Harding and Carl Bode, eds., *The Correspondence of Henry David Thoreau* (New York: New York University Press, 1958), p. 135.

54. "Advertisement," *Harper's Monthly Magazine* 1 (June–Nov. 1850): ii.

55. The quote, but not the conclusion, is from Exman, *The Brothers Harper,* p. 22.

56. The writer, Charles Norton, was editor and proprietor of the semiofficial trade magazine of the publishing industry, which he was at the time transferring to the New York Publishers' Association, which would continue it as the *American Publishers' Circular and Literary Gazette* (the forerunner of *Publishers Weekly*); *Norton's Literary Gazette and Publishers' Circular,* NS 2 (Aug. 1, 1855): 307.

57. Memorandum of Agreement between Harper and Brothers and Sydney Morse and Samuel Breese, Apr. 17, 1844. In Harper and Brothers archive, Butler Library, Columbia University.

58. They were consulting, for instance, a list of western cities categorized in terms of population and of the circulation of their largest newspapers compiled by a western book agent for use by eastern publishers in calculating where to advertise in the West. Memorandum Book, Harper and Brothers archive, Columbia University.

59. Evert Duyckinck, "Introductory," *Literary World* 1 (Feb. 6, 1847): 5.

60. Aderman et al., *Letters,* II, p. 827.

61. There were also many who would have dissented from Duyckinck's optimism about American cultural achievements. One contemporary who did, expressed his reservations in a sarcastic review published in the November

1855 *Putnam's* – the same issue in which there was then appearing before an unappreciative audience the tale "Benito Cereno" by Duyckinck's former protégé – of Duyckinck's own tribute to American letters, the *Cyclopaedia of American Literature*:

> There are many who think that a book about American Literature ought to contain no more than that chapter in the traveler's book, which was entitled "Of the Snakes of Iceland," and which consisted of these words – "There are no snakes in Iceland;" or they would write it as Heine wrote his essay on German editors, in this wise: "German editors, . . . blockheads . . . " Nor would they be much out of the way if the term literature could be used only in its highest sense, as embracing the characteristic and perennial expression of a great national mind; for there is really, as yet, no distinctive and vital literature in this country – a literature destined to reflect and carry down our national life to the latest time – like the literature of the Greeks, for instance. (pp. 549–50)

Incidentally, the only poet named Whitman included in this anthology of American letters or in its updated successor was Sarah Helen.

62. Merrell R. Davis and William H. Gilman, eds., *The Letters of Herman Melville* (New Haven, Conn.: Yale University Press, 1960), p. 80.
63. "Life Without Principle," in *Reform Papers*, ed. Wendell Glick (Princeton, N.J.: Princeton University Press, 1973), p. 158. The title of the essay was a calculated pun; in earlier lecture form it was known as "Getting a Living," "What Shall It Profit?" and "Life Misspent" (Textual Introduction, p. 369).
64. Nathaniel Hawthorne, *Letters of Nathaniel Hawthorne to William D. Ticknor, 1851–1859* (Newark, N.J.: Carteret Book Club, 1910), I, p. 75.
65. In Stovall, *Prose Works 1892*, II, p. 539.

3. GOING FORTH INTO LITERARY AMERICA

1. In Stovall, *Prose Works 1892*, I, p. 15.
2. Ibid., p. 287.
3. In Emory Holloway, ed., *The Uncollected Poetry and Prose of Walt Whitman* (New York: Peter Smith, 1932), II, pp. 247–8.
4. Vivid descriptions of the fires can be found in Philip Hone, *The Diary of Philip Hone*, ed. Allan Nevins (New York: Dodd, Mead and Co., 1936), pp. 169–70; 185–93.
5. Gay Wilson Allen, *The Solitary Singer* (New York: Macmillan, 1955), p. 26.
6. In Stovall, *Prose Works 1892*, I, p. 287.
7. In Holloway, ed., *The Uncollected Poetry and Prose of Walt Whitman*, I, p. 37.
8. "The Editors to the Reader," *New World*, Folio ed., 1 (Oct. 26, 1839).
9. "Cheap Literature," *New World* 4 (Apr. 9, 1842): 242.
10. "To the Gentle Reader," *New World*, Extra Series (Christmas and New Year, 1842–3): 2.
11. One of the most famous reprinting fights of the decade was over Dickens' *American Notes*, which pitted the four major pirates against one another; see Peter S. Bracher, "The Early American Editions of *American Notes*: Their Priority and Circulation," *Papers of the Bibliographical Society of America* 69 (July–Sept. 1975): 365–76.
12. *New World* 5 (Nov. 5, 1842): 305.

13. Horace Traubel, *With Walt Whitman in Camden*, I (Boston: Small, Maynard and Co., 1906), p. 93.

14. Emory Holloway, ed., *Franklin Evans* (New York: Random House, 1929), pp. 5, 249.

15. Allen, *The Solitary Singer*, p. 60.

16. "Boz and Democracy," *Brother Jonathan* 1 (Feb. 26, 1842): 243; repr. in Holloway, ed., *The Uncollected Poetry and Prose of Walt Whitman*, I, p. 69.

17. In Rubin and Brown, *Walt Whitman*, pp. 116–17.

18. Quoted in Allen, *The Solitary Singer*, p. 47.

19. Rubin and Brown, *Walt Whitman*, pp. 44–5.

20. See Gay Wilson Allen, "The Iconography of Walt Whitman," in *The Artistic Legacy of Walt Whitman*, ed. Edwin Haviland Miller (New York: New York University Press, 1970), p. 130.

21. "Daguerreotyping," Brooklyn *Eagle*, Nov. 17, 1847.

22. Traubel, *With Walt Whitman in Camden*, I, p. 367.

23. Joseph Jay Rubin, *The Historic Whitman* (University Park, Pa.: Pennsylvania State University, 1973), p. 83.

24. Whitman offered his services in a letter of June 1, 1842, as a regular contributor to the Boston *Miscellany*, claiming, "My stories, I believe, have been pretty popular, and extracted liberally"; Edwin Haviland Miller, ed., *The Correspondence* (New York: New York University Press, 1961), I, pp. 25–6.

25. Thomas O. Mabbott, "Walt Whitman Edits the *Sunday Times*, July, 1842–June, 1843," *American Literature* 39 (Mar. 1967): p. 99.

26. Rubin, *The Historic Whitman*, p. 85.

27. Edward F. Grier, ed., *Notebooks and Unpublished Prose Manuscripts* (New York: New York University Press, 1984), I, p. 211.

28. The most comprehensive source of information on Whitman's activities during the early and mid–1840s is Rubin, *The Historic Whitman*, whom I follow in most details.

29. "The Editor," *Columbian Magazine* 2 (July 1844): 5.

30. In Mabbott, p. 100.

31. "Some Hints to Apprentices and Youth," Brooklyn *Evening Star*, Oct. 10, 1845; repr. in Florence Bernstein Freedman, *Walt Whitman Looks at the Schools* (New York: Columbia University Press, 1950), p. 69.

32. "Hints to the Young," Brooklyn *Evening Star*, Oct. 23, 1845; repr. in Freedman, *Walt Whitman Looks at the Schools*, p. 72.

33. In Floyd Stovall, *Prose Works 1892* (New York: New York University Press, 1963), I, p. 288.

34. "Ourselves and the 'Eagle,' " Brooklyn *Eagle*, June 1, 1846. Whitman timed his editorial to coincide with the improved appearance of the paper that day in new typeface and celebrated the occasion by beginning the serialization of his novelette, *The Half-Breed*, in the new literary column which appeared daily on the front page.

35. "A Merry Christmas," Brooklyn *Eagle*, Dec. 24, 1847.

36. "The Toils of a Newspaper," Brooklyn *Eagle*, Mar. 16, 1847.

37. "Democracy and Literature," *Democratic Review* 11 (Aug. 1842): 196.

38. "The Stage," Brooklyn *Eagle*, Aug. 17, 1846.

39. In Stovall, *Prose Works 1892*, II, p. 731.

40. "Incidents in the life of a world-famed man," Brooklyn *Eagle*, Nov. 19, 1846.

41. "The Pen," Brooklyn *Eagle*, Sept. 22, 1846.

42. "The World of Books," Brooklyn *Eagle*, Nov. 26, 1847.

43. "A Great American Publishing House," Brooklyn *Evening Star*, Jan. 30, 1846.

44. " 'Home Literature,' " Brooklyn *Eagle*, July 11, 1846.

45. "Vocal Concerts, by Children," Brooklyn *Eagle*, Sept. 19, 1846,

46. "A Poet's Recreation," New York *Tribune*, July 4, 1878.

47. For a similar observation, see Jerome Loving, *Emerson, Whitman, and the American Muse* (Chapel Hill, N.C.: University of North Carolina Press, 1982), p. 56.

4. "I AM A WRITER, FOR THE PRESS AND OTHERWISE"

1. Cleveland Rodgers and John Black, eds., *The Gathering of the Forces* (New York: G. P. Putnam's Sons, 1920), II, pp. xxxii–xxxiii.

2. On Gould and his relations with Whitman, see Rubin, *The Historic Whitman*, pp. 154, 182, 196, 370.

3. Allen, *The Solitary Singer*, p. 100.

4. Rubin, *The Historic Whitman*, p. 220.

5. New York *Sunday Dispatch*, Nov. 25, 1849; repr. in Rubin, *The Historic Whitman*, p. 337.

6. New York *Sunday Dispatch*, Dec. 23, 1849; repr. in Rubin, *The Historic Whitman*, p. 350.

7. On Whitman and the New York *Daily News*, see Rubin, ibid., pp. 244–5.

8. William White, "Whitman's First 'Literary' Letter," *American Literature* 35 (Mar. 1963): 83–5.

9. Miller, ed., *The Correspondence*, I, p. 38.

10. Rubin, *The Historic Whitman*, p. 268.

11. Elizabeth Dunbar, *Talcott Williams* (Brooklyn, 1936), p. 225. In a review of the 1860 *Leaves of Grass*, a local Brooklyn writer commented on this self-conscious change of style: "Years ago we knew him as a New York editor; and for several years later he had been a miscellaneous contributor to the Press; and during all this time his writings were like other men's, no more strikingly marked with individuality of style. And even yet, outside of his 'Leaves,' he writes and talks in most approved conventional style. We make no doubt that the singularity of the 'Leaves' is a matter of principle with their author; the embodiment of a piece of profound sagacity"; Brooklyn *Daily Times*, July 5, 1860.

12. Edward F. Grier, ed., *Notebooks and Unpublished Prose Manuscripts* (New York: New York University Press, 1984), IV, p. 1293.

13. Miller, ed., *The Correspondence*, I, pp. 39–40.

14. Horace L. Traubel, Richard Maurice Bucke, and Thomas B. Harned, eds.,

"Conversations with George W. Whitman," *In Re Walt Whitman* (Philadelphia: David McKay, 1893), pp. 33–4.

15. Horace Traubel, *With Walt Whitman in Camden*, II (New York: Mitchell Kennerley, 1915), p. 503.

16. Traubel et al., *In Re Walt Whitman*, p. 35.

17. "Letters from New York," Washington *National Era*, Nov. 21, 1850; repr. in Rollo G. Silver, "Whitman in 1850: Three Uncollected Articles," *American Literature* 19 (Nov. 1947): 314.

18. Paul Zweig, *Walt Whitman: The Making of the Poet* (New York: Basic Books, 1984), p. 121.

19. Floyd Stovall, *The Foreground of "Leaves of Grass"* (Charlottesville, Va.: University Press of Virginia, 1974), p. 151.

20. This clipping, like most of Whitman's surviving clippings, is in the Trent Collection, Perkins Library, Duke University.

21. Trent Collection, Duke University.

22. Trent Collection, Duke University.

23. This item and those which follow are in the Trent Collection, Duke University.

24. Emerson, "The Poet," in *Essays, Second Series* (Boston: Houghton, Mifflin and Co., 1883), p. 17.

25. The following items are in the Trent Collection, Duke University.

26. Stovall, *Prose Works 1892*, I, p. 233.

27. "A Peep at the Israelites," New York *Aurora*, March 28, 1842; in Rubin and Brown, *Walt Whitman*, p. 32.

28. "The Oratorio of St. Paul," Brooklyn *Evening Star*, Nov. 28, 1845; excerpted in Emory Holloway, "More Light on Whitman," *American Mercury* 1 (Feb. 1924): 186.

29. "Heart-Music and Art-Music," Brooklyn *Evening Star*, Nov. 14, 1845; Whitman also printed this article in Poe's *Broadway Journal* 2 (Nov. 29, 1845) and in modified form as "Music that *is* Music" in the Brooklyn *Eagle*, Dec. 4, 1846; repr. in Holloway, ed., *The Uncollected Poetry and Prose of Walt Whitman*, I, pp. 104–6.

30. "Letters from Paumanok," New York *Evening Post*, Aug. 14, 1851; repr. in Holloway, ed., *The Uncollected Poetry and Prose of Walt Whitman*, I, p. 256.

31. Ibid., p. 256.

32. Grier, ed., *Notebooks*, I, pp. 126–7.

33. John Burroughs, *Notes on Walt Whitman as Poet and Person* (1867; repr. New York: Haskell House, 1971), p. 82.

34. "Letters from New York," Washington *National Era*, Nov. 14, 1851; repr. in Silver, "Whitman in 1850," pp. 311–12.

35. Stovall, *Prose Works 1892*, II, p. 597.

36. Ibid., p. 595.

37. "A Man to Be Proud of," Brooklyn *Evening Star*, Feb. 10, 1853. Whitman would later suggest facetiously that Barnum's talents be put to the test by having him appointed by President Buchanan as governor of the troubled, Mormon-dominated territory of Utah, but he also added a more serious evaluation of Barnum's stature:

Besides, something should be done for Barnum; he has passed middle age, and he is poor. Who says the country owes nothing to Barnum? We contend he is not only an American "representative man," but a great original – just as great in his way as any of the most famous characters in the world are in theirs. Barnum's plans were so vast! even his humbug had sublimity! Nothing of the pistareen about him – but large, like a fifty dollar gold piece.

Ironically, many of these same things would be said in time about Whitman, who was even ridiculed as being the Barnum of poets. "Something for Barnum – Our Own Proposition," Brooklyn *Daily Times,* June 1, 1857.
38. Stovall, *Prose Works 1892,* II, pp. 698–9.
39. Grier, ed., *Notebooks,* I, p. 112.
40. Grier, ed., *Notebooks,* IV, p. 1296.
41. Ibid, p. 1299.
42. Holloway, ed., *The Uncollected Poetry and Prose of Walt Whitman,* I, p. 237.
43. Grier, ed., *Notebooks,* I, p. 112.
44. Details of the printing of the first edition I have culled from Whitman's own comments and from the work of various scholars, especially Rubin, *The Historic Whitman,* pp. 307–10.
45. Edwin Haviland Miller, ed., *The Correspondence* (New York: New York University Press, 1961), II, pp. 99–100.
46. James Brenton, ed., *Voices from the Press* (New York: Charles B. Norton, 1850), p. 306.
47. Ellen B. Ballou, *The Building of the House* (Boston: Houghton, Mifflin, 1970), p. 283.
48. William White, "The First (1855) *Leaves of Grass*: How Many Copies?" *Papers of the Bibliographical Society of America* 57 (Third Quarter, 1963): 353.
49. Nelson Sizer, "I Know Myself 'Like a Book,' " *American Phrenological Journal* 22 (July 1855): 7.
50. *Norton's Literary Gazette and Publishers' Circular,* NS 1 (Apr. 15, 1854): 193.

5. INTENTIONS AND AMBITIONS
1. The best account of the circuitous path through which the 1855 *Leaves* passed before reaching William Michael Rossetti, Whitman's chief champion in England, is in Harold Blodgett, *Walt Whitman in England* (Ithaca, N.Y.: Cornell University Press, 1934), pp. 14–17.
2. *North American Review* 83 (Jan. 1856): 275–7; repr. in Milton Hindus, ed., *Walt Whitman: The Critical Heritage* (New York: Barnes and Noble, 1971), pp. 48–9.
3. Horace Traubel, *With Walt Whitman in Camden,* III (New York: Mitchell Kennerley, 1914), p. 116.
4. Frederick B. Tolles, "A Quaker Reaction to *Leaves of Grass,*" *American Literature* 19 (May 1947): 170–1.
5. Richard L. Herrnstadt, ed., *The Letters of A. Bronson Alcott* (Ames, Iowa: Iowa State University Press, 1969), p. 226.
6. Perry Miller, *The Raven and the Whale* (New York: Harcourt, Brace and Co., 1956), p. 96.
7. There was therefore something particularly appropriate about the greeting

the British man of letters Roden Noel sent to Whitman: "I have often said the chief (if not the only) reason why I want to go to America is to see Niagara, the Yosemite, and Walt Whitman." Letter from Noel to Whitman of May 16, 1886, in Feinberg Collection, Library of Congress.

8. Grier, ed., *Notebooks*, I, p. 144.

9. Norton, *Norton's Literary Gazette and Publishers' Circular*, NS 2 (Aug. 1, 1855): 307.

10. Madeleine Stern, *Heads and Headlines: The Phrenological Fowlers* (Norman, Okla.: University of Oklahoma Press, 1971), p. 54.

11. New York *Tribune*, Mar. 9, 1854.

12. Stern, *Heads and Headlines*, p. 63.

13. See William S. Tryon, *Parnassus Corner* (Boston: Houghton, Mifflin, 1963), pp. 200–4.

14. This review first appeared as "Walt Whitman and his Poems" in the *United States Review* (formerly, the *Democratic Review*) 37 (Sept. 1855): 205–12, and was then reprinted, whether from a text furnished directly or indirectly through Whitman, in Bryant's New York *Evening Post*, Aug. 24, 1855; repr. in Hindus, *Walt Whitman*, pp. 34–41. The Index to volume 37 of the *Review*, as though for old times' sake, misnamed the article as "Walter Whitman and his Poems." In a further irony, a writer in the Aug. 1855 issue of the *Review* said this of James Fields as a poet: "Mr. Fields has exhibited a self-depreciation in the valuation of his own powers which is but seldom evidenced by any poet" (p. 177).

15. "An English and an American Poet," *American Phrenological Journal* 22 (Oct. 1855): 90–1; repr. in Hindus, *Walt Whitman*, pp. 41–5.

16. "Walt Whitman, a Brooklyn Boy," Brooklyn *Daily Times*, Sept. 29, 1855; repr. in Hindus, *Walt Whitman*, pp. 45–8.

17. Ibid., pp. 46–7.

18. Grier, ed., *Notebooks*, I, p. 186.

6. WHITMAN AND THE READER, 1855

1. Jean-Paul Sartre, *What Is Literature*, trans. Bernard Frechtman (New York: Harper and Row, 1965), p. 117.

2. Charvat, *The Profession of Authorship*, pp. 106–10.

3. For a fine description of Melville's professional career, see the Melville chapter in Michael Gilmore, *American Romanticism and the Marketplace* (Chicago: University of Chicago Press, 1985).

4. Charvat, *The Profession of Authorship*, p. 114.

5. Zweig, *Walt Whitman*, p. 12.

6. Grier, ed., *Notebooks*, I, p. 321.

7. Ibid., p. 109.

8. Zweig, *Walt Whitman*, pp. 176–7.

9. Richard Poirier, *The Performing Self* (New York: Oxford University Press, 1971).

10. "You, sir!" Brooklyn *Eagle*, Apr. 13, 1847.

11. Brooklyn *Evening Star*, Oct. 10, 1845; repr. in Freedman, *Walt Whitman Looks at the Schools*, p. 68. As late as the Brooklyniana sketches of 1862,

Whitman was still carrying on his journalistic dialogue "between ourselves and you, gentle reader (we like the old phrase yet)." Holloway, ed., *The Uncollected Poetry and Prose of Walt Whitman*, II, p. 262.

12. M. H. Abrams, *The Mirror and the Lamp* (New York: Norton, 1958), pp. 25–6, 326; cf. C. Carroll Hollis, *Language and Style in "Leaves of Grass"* (Baton Rouge, La.: Louisiana State University Press, 1983), p. 91.

13. Quoted in Henry A. Beers, *Nathaniel Parker Willis* (Boston: Houghton, Mifflin and Co., 1885), p. 82.

14. *The Complete Works of N. P. Willis* (New York: J. S. Redfield, 1846), pp. 668–9.

15. "Topics of the Month," *Holden's Magazine* 1 (Jan. 1848): 57.

16. I take the term from Alvin Kernan, *Printing Technology, Letters and Samuel Johnson* (Princeton, N.J.: Princeton University Press, 1987), p. 94.

17. Brooklyn *Evening Star,* Sept. 15, 1845; repr. in Freedman, *Walt Whitman Looks at the Schools*, p. 66.

18. Brooklyn *Eagle,* Nov. 23, 1846.

19. Letter of Whitman to William D. O'Connor, Dec. 17, 1882; in Miller, ed., *The Correspondence*, III, p. 320.

20. In Stovall, *Prose Works 1892*, II, p. 481.

21. Ibid., p. 216.

22. Ibid., p. 234. Thoreau had used a similar trope in the "Reading" chapter of *Walden* to express his own strong faith in the power of literature to transform its readers: "To read well, that is, to read true books is a noble exercise, and one that will task the reader more than any exercise which the customs of the day esteem. It requires a training such as the athletes underwent, the steady intention almost of the whole life to this object. Books must be read as deliberately and unreservedly as they were written."

23. *Democratic Vistas,* in Stovall, *Prose Works 1892*, II, pp. 424–5.

24. Quoted in Justin Kaplan, *Walt Whitman: A Life* (New York: Simon and Schuster, 1980), pp. 320–1.

25. Grier, ed., *Notebooks*, I, p. 267.

26. Traubel, *With Walt Whitman in Camden*, II, p. 78.

27. Charles Feidelson, arguing from a different perspective, reaches a similar conclusion: "The shift of image from the contemplative eye of 'establish'd poems' to the voyaging ego of Whitman's poetry records a large-scale theoretical shift from the categories of 'substance' to those of 'process.' " *Symbolism and American Literature* (Chicago: University of Chicago Press, 1953), p. 17.

28. Sculley Bradley, "The Fundamental Metrical Principle in Whitman's Poetry," *American Literature* 10 (Jan. 1939): 438–42.

29. First printed in the Brooklyn *Eagle,* June 1, 1846; repr. in Thomas Brasher, ed., *The Early Poems and the Fiction* (New York: New York University Press, 1963), p. 33.

30. Emerson, "The Transcendentalist," in *Nature, Addresses, and Lectures* (New York: AMS Press, 1968), p. 334.

31. John Stuart Mill, "What Is Poetry?" in *Literary Essays*, ed. Edward Alexander (New York: Bobbs-Merrill, 1967), p. 56.

32. For a strong analysis of Whitman as a nontemporal poet, see the chapter on Whitman in John F. Lynen, *The Design of the Present* (New Haven, Conn.: Yale University Press, 1969), pp. 273–339.

33. Basil De Selincourt, *Walt Whitman* (London: Martin Secker, 1914), pp. 74–5.

34. "Essay, Supplementary to the Preface," in *Wordsworth: Poetical Works*, ed. Ernest De Selincourt (London: Oxford, 1966), p. 751.

35. Stovall, *Prose Works 1892*, II, p. 521.

36. Late in life, Whitman remembered Duyckinck and his brother as " 'gentlemenly men' – and by the way I don't know any description that it would have pleased them better to hear." In Traubel, *With Walt Whitman in Camden*, I, p. 139.

37. Grier, ed., *Notebooks*, I, p. 303.

38. Ibid., p. 276.

39. Ibid., p. 335.

7. THE PUBLIC RESPONSE

1. "The New Book Store," Brooklyn *Eagle*, Apr. 14, 1847.

2. William White, "Fanny Fern to Walt Whitman: An Unpublished Letter," *American Book Collector* 11 (May 1961): 9.

3. I make this transcription from the original letter, which is in the Feinberg Collection, Library of Congress. The one characteristic of the poetry which Emerson so appreciated as to underline, its "courage of *treatment*," ironically was the one which would cause him gradually to retreat from his original assessment.

4. New York *Tribune*, July 23, 1855; repr. in Hindus, *Walt Whitman*, pp. 22–3. Hindus gives the most complete collection of early reviews in print, but because he apparently did not work from original sources, his dates are frequently unreliable and his transcriptions occasionally imprecise. I have therefore attempted to verify his work against the original sources wherever possible.

5. When Dana came to collect and publish his anthology of American verse, *The Household Book of Poetry*, with the Appletons in 1858, he omitted Whitman. He did include, however, six Whitman poems, mostly from *Drum-Taps*, in the 1882 edition of the anthology.

6. *Life Illustrated*, July 28, 1855; repr. in James K. Wallace, "Whitman and *Life Illustrated*: A Forgotten 1855 Review of *Leaves*," *Walt Whitman Review* 17 (Dec. 1971): 137.

7. *Putnam's Magazine* 6 (Sept. 1855): 321–3; repr. in Hindus, *Walt Whitman*, pp. 24–7.

8. Kenneth Murdock, ed., *A Leaf of Grass from Shady Hill* (Cambridge, Mass.: Harvard University Press, 1928), p. 19.

9. Ibid., p. 12.

10. Ibid., p. 15.

11. Ibid., pp. 23–4.

12. " 'Leaves of Grass' – An Extraordinary Book," Brooklyn *Eagle*, Sept. 15, 1855; repr. in Hindus, *Walt Whitman*, pp. 84–7.

13. New York *Criterion* 1 (Nov. 10, 1855): 24; repr. in Hindus, *Walt Whitman,* pp. 31–3.

14. Boston *Intelligencer,* May 3, 1856; repr. in Hindus, *Walt Whitman,* p. 61.

15. *North American Review* 82 (Jan. 1856): 275–7; repr. in Hindus, *Walt Whitman,* pp. 48–9. The truthfulness to nature for which Hale praised *Leaves of Grass* had an interesting parallel in the immediately preceding review of Longfellow's *Hiawatha,* which praised it as "the first poem which savors of the prairie or the mountain hunting trail" (p. 274). One person's truthfulness to nature was apparently another's artificiality.

16. Repr. in Hindus, *Walt Whitman,* pp. 80–4.

17. "Studies Among the Leaves," *Crayon* 3 (Jan. 1856): 30–2; repr. in Hindus, *Walt Whitman,* pp. 52–4.

18. Frank Luther Mott, *A History of American Magazines,* II (Cambridge, Mass.: Harvard University Press, 1938), p. 159. The review was reprinted by Whitman in the collection of reviews he had sent out in 1860 to advertise the third edition, *Leaves of Grass Imprints* (Boston: Thayer and Eldridge, 1860), p. 51.

19. Her remarks on Whitman and on *Leaves of Grass* appeared in the New York *Ledger* of Apr. 19 and May 10, 1856, respectively; the second piece is reprinted in Emory Holloway and Ralph Adimari, eds., *New York Dissected* (New York: Rufus Rockwell Wilson, 1936), pp. 162–5.

20. There is no thorough study of midnineteenth-century reviewers and reviews of poetry similar to that which Nina Baym (*Novels, Readers, and Reviewers: Responses to Fiction in Antebellum America*) has done of fiction. To know more broadly about the cultural preconceptions of midcentury Americans about the genre of poetry and to have a better-rounded picture of poetry reviews and reviewing would enable one to discuss various literary-cultural issues, such as author-reader relations, on a more systematic basis.

21. "Something That Shakespeare Lost," *American Publishers' Circular and Literary Gazette* 3 (Jan. 31, 1857): 65–7. This article was reprinted from Dickens' *Household Words,* but despite its authorship by the English writer and academic Henry Morley, I take its premises to be equally applicable to the conditions of midcentury journalistic criticism in America.

8. WHITMAN AND THE READER, 1856

1. Moncure Daniel Conway, *Autobiography* (Boston: Houghton, Mifflin and Co., 1904), I, p. 215.

2. These pieces are collected in Holloway and Adimari, *New York Dissected.*

3. Ibid., p. 48.

4. Ibid., p. 52.

5. "Publishers: Their Past, Present, and Future in the U.S. – The Present," *American Publishers' Circular and Literary Gazette* 1 (Nov. 17, 1855): 165.

6. "Publishers: Their Past, Present, and Future in the U.S. – The Future," *American Publishers' Circular and Literary Gazette* 1 (Dec. 29, 1855): 263.

7. Miller, ed., *The Correspondence,* I, pp. 41–2; see also the editor's note, p. 41.

8. William White, ed., *Daybooks and Notebooks* (New York: New York University Press, 1978), III, p. 735.

9. Ibid., p. 743.
10. Ibid., p. 737.
11. Ibid., p. 742.
12. Ibid., p. 732.
13. Ibid., p. 729n.
14. This notebook, in the Feinberg Collection of the Library of Congress, has been published by Harold W. Blodgett, ed., *An 1855–56 Notebook Toward the Second Edition of Leaves of Grass* (Carbondale, Ill.: Southern Illinois University Press, 1959); but I have used the more rigorously established scholarly text given by Grier; Grier, ed., *Notebooks*, I, pp. 226–43.
15. Grier, ed., *Notebooks*, I, pp. 227, 234, 239, 242.
16. Stern, *Heads and Headlines*, pp. 117–18.
17. This contract of Feb. 16, 1854, is in the Sophia Smith Collection, Smith College.
18. Advertisement in *American Publishers' Circular and Literary Gazette* 3 (Sept. 19, 1857): 606.
19. Repr. in Holloway and Adimari, *New York Dissected*, p. 171.
20. Lewis M. Stark and John D. Gordon, eds., *Whitman's "Leaves of Grass"* (New York: New York Public Library, 1955), p. 9.
21. The letters have been widely reprinted and can be found together in Walt Whitman, *Complete Poetry and Collected Prose*, ed. Justin Kaplan (New York: Library of America, 1982), pp. 1326–37.
22. Ibid., pp. 1329–30.
23. Edward F. Grier, ed., *Notebooks and Unpublished Prose Manuscripts* (New York: New York University Press, 1984), VI, pp. 2134–5.
24. D. H. Lawrence, *Studies in Classic American Literature* (1923; repr. London: Mercury, 1965), p. 157.
25. In preparing the first English edition of Whitman's poems, William Michael Rossetti took the liberty of retitling this poem, "Fit Audience"; William Michael Rossetti, ed., *Poems by Walt Whitman* (London: John Camden Hotten, 1868).
26. Lawrence, *Studies in Classic American Literature*, p. 168.
27. The term comes from his old-age autobiography, *Specimen Days*; in Stovall, *Prose Works, 1892*, I, p. 16.
28. Grier, ed., *Notebooks*, I, p. 145.
29. In "One's-Self I Sing," the programmatic poem destined to become the lead poem of later editions of *Leaves of Grass*, whose thought and phrasing Whitman worked on for years.
30. In an unusually fine analysis of Whitman's sensibility, Richard Fein describes this phenomenon in terms of a general tension in Whitman between the "Self-Sustaining Ego" and the "Communal Ego": "Implicit in Whitman's role of the liberated ego is the experience of loneliness – the procreant urge to merge with others side by side with the procreant urge to assume one's separate uniqueness or the inability to merge with others." "Whitman and the Emancipated Self," *Centennial Review* 20 (Winter 1976): 41–2.
31. "Song of Myself" and "As I Ebb'd with the Ocean of Life," 1855 and 1860 poems, respectively.

32. Sharon Cameron, *Lyric Time* (Baltimore, Md.: Johns Hopkins University Press, 1979), p. 225.

33. I take the term from *Democratic Vistas*; in Stovall, *Prose Works 1892*, II, p. 419. The entirety of the passage in which the phrase is found, even if stated in Whitman's most impenetrable prose manner, is relevant:

> The [artistic] process, so far, is indirect and peculiar, and though it may be suggested, cannot be defined. Observing, rapport, and with intuition, the shows and forms presented by Nature, the sensuous luxuriance, the beautiful in living men and women, the actual play of passions, in history and life – and, above all, from those developments either in Nature or human personality in which power, (dearest of all to the sense of the artist,) transacts itself – out of these, and seizing what is in them, the poet, the esthetic worker in any field, by the divine magic of his genius, projects them, their analogies, by curious removes, indirections, in literature and art. (No useless attempt to repeat the material creation, by daguerreotyping the exact likeness by mortal mental means.) This is the image-making faculty, coping with material creation, and rivaling, almost triumphing over it. This alone, when all the other parts of a specimen of literature or art are ready and waiting, can breathe into it the breath of life, and endow it with identity.

34. Emerson, "Experience," in *Essays, Second Series*, p. 81.

35. In his projected new dictionary of the American language, Whitman performed the following verbal exercise with the issue of the subject-object relationship:

a good innovation

employer	– employee
offender	– offendee thing offended
server	– servee
lover	– lovee
	– thing loved
hater	– hatee
	– thing hated
suspecter	– suspectee
receiver	– receivee
	receiver
	(thing received)

In White, ed., *Daybooks and Notebooks*, III, pp. 675–6.

36. Emerson, "The Poet," *Essays, Second Series*, p. 37.

37. *Specimen Days*, in Stovall, *Prose Works 1892*, I, p. 16.

38. An exception to this statement was Thoreau, who met Whitman in the fall of 1856 and hand received a copy of the second edition, in which he took particular interest in "Song of Myself" and "Crossing Brooklyn Ferry." A second response was that of his English friend Thomas Cholmondeley, whom Thoreau had introduced to Whitman's writing. Cholmondeley wrote back on May 26, 1857, to express his strong, contradictory feelings about the poetry:

> Here are "Leaves" indeed which I can no more understand than the book of Enoch or the inedited Poems of Daniel! I cannot believe that such a man lives unless I actually touch him. He is further ahead of me in yonder west than

Buddha is behind me in the Orient. I find reality and beauty mixed with not a little violence and coarseness both of which are to me *effeminate*. I am amused at his views of sexual energy – which however are absurdly false. I believe that rudeness and excitement in the act of generation are injurious to the issue. The man appears to me not to know how to behave himself. I find the gentleman altogether left out of the book! Altogether these leaves completely puzzle me. Is there actually such a man as Whitman? Has anyone seen or handled him? His is a tongue "not understood" of the English people. It is the first book I have ever seen which I should call "a *new* book" and thus I would sum up the impression it makes upon me.

In Harding and Bode, eds., *The Correspondence of Henry David Thoreau,* p. 481.

9. "PUBLISH YOURSELF OF YOUR OWN PERSONALITY"

1. Miller, ed., *The Correspondence,* I, p. 44.
2. Grier, ed., *Notebooks,* I, p. 353.
3. In Fredson Bowers, ed., *Whitman's Manuscripts, Leaves of Grass, 1860* (Chicago: University of Chicago Press, 1955), p. 189.
4. Brooklyn *Daily Times,* Oct. 24, 1857.
5. She wrote him on June 24 in response to his letter of June 20: "You say that Fowler and Wells are not the right men to publish Leaves of Grass. I am sure they are not. I can tell you more of their malpractice about it, when you come. You say also that they are *willing* to give up the plates. Now it occurred to me that it was quite possible that some trifling money consideration prevented you from obtaining them." She then offered, and he apparently accepted in a return letter, fifty dollars toward the purchase of the plates. Feinberg Collection, Library of Congress.
6. "To a Pupil," in Bowers, ed., *Whitman's Manuscripts,* p. 188.
7. I closely follow Bowers in the dating and ordering of Whitman's manuscript poems of the late 1850s.
8. Bowers, ed., *Whitman's Manuscripts,* p. 122.
9. Ibid., p. 124.
10. Ibid., pp. 96, 98.
11. Miller, ed., *The Correspondence,* I, p. 45.
12. "Amusements," Brooklyn *Daily Times,* May 17, 1858.
13. "Poem of Joys," in Bowers, ed., *Whitman's Manuscripts,* p. 214.
14. Carl Bode, *The American Lyceum* (New York: Oxford University Press, 1956), p. 235.
15. Grier, ed., *Notebooks,* IV, p. 1437.
16. Grier, ed., *Notebooks,* VI, p. 2242.
17. Ibid., p. 2234.
18. Ibid., p. 2230.
19. Ibid., p. 2236.
20. Grier, ed., *Notebooks,* IV, p. 1437.
21. In Emory Holloway, "Whitman as His Own Press-Agent," *American Mercury* 18 (1929): 486.
22. The question of dating is complicated by the fact that the editor's name was

never carried on the masthead of the paper, but Whitman's unmistakable mark was on the paper through the spring of the year. The campaign begun in February and continued through the spring for Sunday public transportation has the clear sound of Whitman; and the editorials attributing "the best blood in Brooklyn" to the Dutch (March 14), mentioning "Fowler and Wells' excellent paper" *Life Illustrated* (Apr. 10), and attacking in a rather nasty fashion his former boss at the New York *Aurora* Anson Herrick (Apr. 18), taken together could only have come from Whitman.

23. In fact, he even editorialized about the necessity of the impersonal in journalism:

> No reason that we can imagine can be given for preferring the personal in journalism, except that it flatters the egotism of some and advances the personal or political importance of other editors . . . To intrude the writer's personality into his argument, cannot enhance the weight of his opinion, or increase the cogency of his logic; it only calls the reader's attention off into extraneous reflections as to the probable motive of the writer . . .
> If a man publishes a sheet for the edification of a small select circle of his friends, it may be well enough for him to avow the authorship of the articles, in order that his name may have its due weight among those with whom he is intimate; but if he sets up as a guide and instructor of the public he should sink his individuality in the cause he advocates, and send his arguments forth to obtain credence by their intrinsic force, and not by any adventitious recommendation his signature may or may not communicate to them. ("The Personality of the Press," Mar. 7, 1859)

24. "Rowdyism Rampant," Brooklyn *Daily Times,* July 26, 1858.
25. "What They Want," Brooklyn *Daily Times,* Nov. 12, 1857.
26. "Is There Room for a New Daily Paper in New York?" Brooklyn *Daily Times,* Aug. 20, 1857.
27. "The Press and Its Power," Brooklyn *Daily Times,* Aug. 26, 1857.
28. "The public for whom these tales are written require strong contrasts, broad effects and the fiercest kind of 'intense' writing generally"; "The Sunday Papers," Brooklyn *Daily Times,* Dec. 13, 1858.
29. "Spice," Brooklyn *Daily Times,* Apr. 14, 1857.
30. "City Young Men – The Masses," Brooklyn *Daily Times,* Apr. 19, 1858.
31. Brooklyn *Daily Times,* Nov. 17, 1857.

10. 1860: "YEAR OF METEORS"

1. "All About a Mocking-Bird," New York *Saturday Press,* 3 (Jan. 7, 1860): p. 3; repr. in Allen, *The Solitary Singer,* p. 232.
2. Miller, ed., *The Correspondence,* I, p. 46.
3. The kind of national poetry they would publish by Whitman was typified by his brassy, patriotic Civil War poem, "Beat! Beat! Drums!" which appeared in the Sept. 28, 1861, issue of *Harper's Weekly.*
4. William W. Thayer, "Notes from an Autobiography," *The Conservator* 25 (June 1914): 55.
5. In Kaplan, *Walt Whitman,* p. 247.
6. Their enthusiasm for Whitman was part of their generally aggressive, upbeat style of publishing following the success of their Redpath biography of John

Brown. Several days before writing Whitman, they had solicited "an *American* novel, capable of creating a sensation in the literary world" from William Douglas O'Connor, until then published only as an occasional story writer for the magazines; and in a follow-up letter, they tried to overcome his resistance by forecasting that this hypothetical first novel – *Harrington*, as it would be called – would sell twenty-five thousand copies. Letters of Feb. 6 and Feb. 23, 1860, from Thayer and Eldridge to O'Connor, in the Bliss Perry Collection, Harvard University.

7. Miller, ed., *The Correspondence*, I, p. 49.
8. Ibid., p. 53.
9. Whitman once told Traubel, "My theory is that the author might be the maker even of the body of his book – set the type, print the book on a press, put a cover on it, all with his own hands"; Traubel, *With Walt Whitman in Camden*, II, p. 480.
10. Davis and Gilman, eds., *The Letters of Herman Melville*, pp. 198–9.
11. Grier, ed., *Notebooks*, I, p. 410.
12. Stovall, *Prose Works 1892*, II, pp. 414–15n.
13. Bowers, ed., *Whitman's Manuscripts*, p. 12.
14. It would become more common still in the editorial revisions he made of this edition for the fourth *Leaves of Grass*, as even a cursory reading of the "blue book" will reveal. See the facsimile volume of Arthur Golden, ed., *Walt Whitman's Blue Book* (New York: New York Public Library, 1968).
15. Bowers, ed., *Whitman's Manuscripts*, p. 112.
16. Ibid., pp. 86, 88.
17. Kaplan, *Walt Whitman*, p. 236.
18. Bowers, ed., *Whitman's Manuscripts*, p. 100.
19. Ibid., pp. 90, 92.
20. Ibid., pp. 74, 76, 78.
21. Stovall, *Prose Works 1892*, I, p. 138.
22. Other instances of Whitman's rhyming off of the "me" include the "sea-me" rhyme in "Ethiopia Saluting the Colors" and "Yet, Yet, Ye Downcast Hours"; the "thee-me" rhyme in "My Canary Bird," "Passage to India," and "Thou Orb Aloft Full-Dazzling"; and the "me-identity" rhyme in "Song of the Redwood-Tree."
23. Roy Harvey Pearce, introduction to facsimile edition of *Leaves of Grass, 1860* (Ithaca, N.Y.: Cornell University Press, 1961), pp. xlvi–xlvii.
24. Whitman was a less fallacious self-critic than is often noted. He knew well at the time of their composition the importance of what we now see as his major poems – "Song of Myself," "Crossing Brooklyn Ferry," "Out of the Cradle Endlessly Rocking," and "As I Ebb'd with the Ocean of Life." The confusion lies in the fact that, as his intentions changed during and after the 1860s, so did his standards of judgment, which led him to revise not only the texts of these poems but also his evaluation of his work past and present.
25. He was to describe most explicitly the power the beach exercised over his imagination in *Specimen Days*:

> There is a dream, a picture, that for years at intervals, (sometimes quite long ones, but surely again, in time,) has come noiselessly up before me, and I really

believe, fiction as it is, has enter'd largely into my practical life – certainly into my writings, and shaped and color'd them. It is nothing more or less than a stretch of interminable white-brown sand, hard and smooth and broad, with the ocean perpetually, grandly, rolling in upon it, with slow-measured sweep, with rustle and hiss and foam, and many a thump as of low bass drums. This scene, this picture, I say, has risen before me at times for years. Sometimes I wake at night and can hear and see it plainly.

Stovall, *Prose Works 1892*, I, p. 139.

26. Horace Traubel, *With Walt Whitman in Camden*, ed. Sculley Bradley, IV (Philadelphia, Pa.: University of Pennsylvania Press, 1953), p. 196.
27. Letter from Thayer and Eldridge to Whitman, Aug. 17, 1860, in Feinberg Collection, Library of Congress.
28. Letter from Thayer and Eldridge to Whitman, June 11, 1860, in Feinberg Collection, Library of Congress.
29. Thayer, "Notes from an Autobiography," p. 55.
30. George S. Phillips, quoted in Charles Glicksberg, "Walt Whitman Parodies: Provoked by the Third Edition of 'Leaves of Grass,' " *American Notes and Queries* 7 (Mar. 1948): 168.
31. New York *Saturday Press* 3 (May 19, 1860): p. 2.
32. Thayer and Eldridge, he wrote his brother from Boston on May 5, "expect it [*Leaves of Grass*] to be a valuable investment, increasing by months and years – not going off in a rocket way, (like 'Uncle Tom's Cabin.')"; Miller, ed., *The Correspondence*, I, p. 52.

11. WHITMAN AND HIS READERS THROUGH THE CENTURY

1. Edward Carpenter, *Days with Walt Whitman* (London: George Allen and Unwin, 1906), p. 47.
2. This was a part of the letter Whitman, writing in O'Connor's name, sent overseas to his literary agent for use in preparation of the first English volume of his selected poems; in Miller, ed., *The Correspondence*, I, p. 348.
3. Traubel, *With Walt Whitman in Camden*, I, p. 271.
4. Quoted in *The Conservator* 9 (July 1898): 70. Fields, the successful publisher of many of midcentury America's leading writers, sent Whitman a hundred dollars anonymously through John Burroughs during a low point in Whitman's fortunes in the winter of 1879–80. That gesture, however, did not satisfy Burroughs:

> When Fields gave me this one hundred dollars to send him it struck him at just the right time. Fields gave Aldrich $10,000, and other authors $10,000. But every one enlarges on the help given Walt. They gave Aldrich and Howells and Sarah Orne Jewett purses of $5,000, and more, and *they* didn't need it.

Quoted in Clara Barrus, *Whitman and Burroughs, Comrades* (Boston: Houghton Mifflin Company, 1931), p. 189.
5. Letter from Melville to Duyckinck, Apr. 5, 1849; in Davis and Gilman, *Letters of Herman Melville*, p. 83.
6. San Francisco *Chronicle*, May 19, 1878. A clipping of this review is in the Harned Collection, Library of Congress.

7. New York *Tribune,* Nov. 19, 1881. A clipping of this review is in the Trent Collection, Duke University.

8. New York *Tribune,* Apr. 22, 1876. A clipping of this article is in the Trent Collection, Duke University.

9. Letter from Howells to Stedman, Dec. 5, 1866; *Selected Letters,* ed. George Arms et al., I (Boston: Twayne, 1979), p. 271.

10. A case in point was the opinion of Whitman's former acquaintance from the *Saturday Press,* Thomas Bailey Aldrich, who referred to Whitman's ambition to be "a poet for the *People*" only to conclude, "There never was a poet so calculated to please a very few." Letter of Aldrich to Edmund Stedman, Nov. 20, 1880; in Ferris Greenslet, *The Life of Thomas Bailey Aldrich* (Boston: Houghton, Mifflin, 1908), p. 138.

11. Miller, ed., *The Correspondence,* IV, p. 386.

12. Horace Greeley, "Literature as a Vocation," in *Recollections of a Busy Life* (New York: J. B. Ford and Co., 1868), pp. 450–1.

13. From the "The Custom-House" introduction to *The Scarlet Letter,* ed. Harry Levin (Boston: Houghton Mifflin Company, 1960), p. 6.

14. The phrase comes from "For Us Two, Reader Dear," a poem published in *Good-Bye My Fancy* (1891) but excluded from the final edition of *Leaves of Grass* (1891–2).

15. New York *World,* May 21, 1876. A clipping of this interview is in the Harned Collection, Library of Congress.

16. Stovall, *Prose Works 1892,* II, p. 725.

17. Ibid., p. 368.

18. Ibid., p. 391.

19. Letter from Gilchrist to Whitman, Sept. 4, 1873; in Harned Collection, Library of Congress.

20. Miller, ed., *The Correspondence,* II, p. 170.

21. Carpenter, *Days with Walt Whitman,* pp. 32, 38.

22. Letter from O'Connor to Whitman, Nov. 20, 1870; in Feinberg Collection, Library of Congress.

23. Barrus, *Whitman and Burroughs, Comrades,* p. 339.

24. Florence Bernstein Freedman, *William Douglas O'Connor* (Athens, Ohio: Ohio University Press, 1985), p. 221.

25. New York *Times,* Mar. 27, 1892; a clipping of the obituary is in the Harned Collection, Library of Congress.

26. Traubel, *With Walt Whitman in Camden,* I, p. 227.

27. Traubel, *With Walt Whitman in Camden,* III, pp. 525–6.

28. Miller, ed., *The Correspondence,* I, p. 142.

29. One of the most fascinating instances of such a failure of recognition was that of Benton Wilson, a young soldier befriended by Whitman in Armory Square Hospital in 1863. Wilson was to write Whitman after the war, "A few days ago I picked up a paper through my Friend Hamilton containing an article regarding Walt Whitman the poet which was the first indication I had of your being an author." The subsequent on-again, off-again correspondence of the next several years between Whitman and Wilson, one of perhaps a dozen admiring young men who named their sons after Whitman,

revealed how difficult it could be for Whitman to define the proper distance between himself and his "dear" (toned down from "dearest") addressee. Letter of Wilson to Whitman, Dec. 16, 1866; in the Feinberg Collection, Library of Congress. For Whitman's letters to Wilson, see Miller, ed., *The Correspondence,* I, pp. 323–4; II, pp. 95–6.

30. Quoted in letter of Ellen O'Connor to Whitman, Nov. 24, 1863; in Feinberg Collection, Library of Congress.

31. Traubel, *With Walt Whitman in Camden,* II, pp. 242, 370–1.

32. Miller, ed., *The Correspondence,* I, p. 185.

33. O'Connor to Whitman, letter of Nov. 20, 1870; in the Feinberg Collection, Library of Congress.

34. Although his audience-address manner was far from his mind when Whitman had his persona boast in "Song of Myself," "I too an untranslatable," the task of capturing the ambiguity of his addressee presents one of the greatest difficulties to the translator of *Leaves of Grass.* Is Whitman's "you" to be rendered as singular or plural, and in languages in which the singular also connotes intimacy, how can the translator control with subtlety the degree of distance between persona and reader?

35. Hollis, *Language and Style in "Leaves of Grass,"* pp. 94–5.

36. Whitman did not use this strategy uniformly or consistently during his career. As Hollis has noted, Whitman used it freely in the first two editions, less freely in the third edition, and then less frequently thereafter. In poems such as Calamus, where he was interested in addressing a narrower audience than the nation, or conversely, in public performance poems, in which he tried to reach the collective more directly, such a strategy simply was not appropriate; ibid., pp. 120–1.

37. Perhaps the best example is the catalogue elaboration of "You whoever you are" in section 11 of "Salut au Monde!"

38. Harold Bloom, ed., *Walt Whitman* (New York: Chelsea House, 1985), p. 9.

39. F. O. Matthiessen, *American Renaissance* (New York: Oxford University Press, 1941), p. xv.

40. In *Democratic Vistas*; Stovall, *Prose Works 1892,* II, p. 363.

41. Alexis de Tocqueville, *Democracy in America,* ed. Phillips Bradley (New York: Vintage Books, 1954), II, pp. 104, 106.

42. In her service to selfhood, as described here by Roy Harvey Pearce, Dickinson clearly outflanked Whitman: "She is the extreme American Protestant self which, when it comes fully alive in its greatest poems, is in effect able to set its institutional and religious commitments aside and be radically and unflinchingly itself, radically and unflinchingly free. In that freedom there is at once loss, denial, pain, release, certainty, and victory." Roy Harvey Pearce, *The Continuity of American Poetry* (Princeton, N.J.: Princeton University Press, 1961), pp. 180–1.

43. In *The Conservator* 6 (Aug. 1895): 1.

44. In *The Conservator* 6 (Sept. 1895): 2.

45. Traubel, *With Walt Whitman in Camden,* VI, p. 408.

46. Harry Levin, *Grounds for Comparison* (Cambridge, Mass.: Harvard University Press, 1972), p. 143.

47. Brooklyn *City News,* Oct. 10, 1860; repr. in *Walt Whitman's Autograph Revision of the Analysis of Leaves of Grass* (New York: New York University Press, 1974), p. 143.
48. Fein, "Whitman and the Emancipated Self," p. 40.
49. Stovall, *Prose Works 1892,* II, p. 714.

Index

Cambridge Studies in American Literature and Culture

Editor

Albert Gelpi, Stanford University

Charles Altieri, *Painterly Abstraction in Modernist American Poetry: Infinite Incantations of Ourselves*

Douglas Anderson, *A House Undivided: Domesticity and Community in American Literature*

Steven Axelrod and Helen Deese (eds.), *Robert Lowell: Essays on the Poetry*

Sacvan Bercovitch and Myra Jehlen (eds.), *Ideology and Classic American Literature*

Mitchell Breitweiser, *Cotton Mather and Benjamin Franklin: The Price of Representative Personality*

Lawrence Buell, *New England Literary Culture: From the Revolution to the Renaissance*

Patricia Caldwell, *The Puritan Conversion Narrative: The Beginnings of American Expression*

Peter Conn, *The Divided Mind: Ideology and Imagination in America, 1898–1917*

Michael Davidson, *The San Francisco Renaissance: Poetics and Community at Mid-Century*

George Dekker, *The American Historical Romance*

Stephen Fredman, *Poet's Prose: The Crisis in American Verse*

Albert Gelpi (ed.), *Wallace Stevens: The Poetics of Modernism*

Paul Giles, *Hart Crane: The Contexts of* The Bridge

Richard Gray, *Writing the South: Ideas of an American Region*

Alfred Habegger, *Henry James and the "Woman Business"*

David Halliburton, *The Color of the Sky: A Study of Stephen Crane*

Susan K. Harris, *19th-Century American Women's Novels: Interpretive Strategies*

Margaret Holley, *The Poetry of Marianne Moore: A Study in Voice and Value*

Lothar Hönnighausen, *William Faulkner: The Art of Stylization*

Lynn Keller, *Re-making It New: Contemporary American Poetry and the Modernist Tradition*

Anne Kibbey, *The Interpretation of Material Shapes in Puritanism: A Study of Rhetoric, Prejudice, and Violence*

Robert Lawson-Peebles, *Landscape and Written Expression in Revolutionary America: The World Turned Upside Down*

Robert S. Levine, *Conspiracy and Romance: Studies in Brockden Brown, Cooper, Hawthorne, and Melville*
John Limon, *The Place of Fiction in the Time of Science: A Disciplinary History of American Writing*
Jerome Loving, *Emily Dickinson: The Poet on the Second Story*
Elizabeth McKinsey, *Niagara Falls: Icon of the American Sublime*
John McWilliams, *The American Epic: Transformations of a Genre, 1770–1860*
David Miller, *Dark Eden: The Swamp in Nineteenth-Century American Culture*
Warren Motley, *The American Abraham: James Fenimore Cooper and the Frontier Patriarch*
Brenda Murphy, *American Realism and American Drama, 1800–1940*
Marjorie Perloff, *The Dance of the Intellect: Studies in Poetry in the Pound Tradition*
Karen Rowe, *Saint and Singer: Edward Taylor's Typology and the Poetics of Mediation*
Barton St. Armand, *Emily Dickinson and Her Culture: The Soul's Society*
Eric Sigg, *The American T. S. Eliot: A Study of the Early Writings*
Tony Tanner, *Scenes of Nature, Signs of Man: Essays in 19th and 20th Century American Literature*
Brook Thomas, *Cross-Examinations of Law and Literature: Cooper, Hawthorne, Stowe, and Melville*
Albert von Frank, *The Sacred Game: Provincialism and Frontier Consciousness in American Literature, 1630–1860*
David Wyatt, *The Fall into Eden: Landscape and Imagination in California*
Lois Zamora, *Writing the Apocalypse: Ends and Endings in Contemporary U.S. and Latin American Fiction*